Rosie's Daughters

The "First Woman To" Generation Tells Its Story

*Born during WWII, shaped by the `60s,
they didn't take "no" for an answer.*

Matilda Butler
and Kendra Bonnett

Iaso Books
A Division of Two Bridges Press
Berkeley, California

ROSIE'S DAUGHTERS: THE "FIRST WOMAN TO" GENERATION TELLS ITS STORY

Publisher's Cataloging-in-Publication Data

Butler, Matilda.
    Rosie's daughters : the first woman to generation tells its story / Matilda Butler and Kendra Bonnett.
    p. cm.
    Includes bibliographical references and index.
    ISBN: 987-0-9793061-9-8   ISBN: 0-9793061-9-1
1. Women—Biography. 2. Women—United States—History—20th century. 3. Women's rights—United States—History. 4. World War, 1939-1945—Women. 5. Women—Employment—United States—History. I. Title.

HQ1426 .B86 2007
305.420973—dc22   2007938295

Printed in the United States of America
10 09 08 07   1 2 3 4 5 6 7 8 9

BOOK AND COVER DESIGNS BY REES MAXWELL

To all of Rosie's Rosebuds.

Contents

Prologue: A Tale of Generations

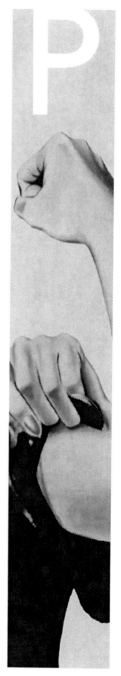

Rosie's Daughters is the story of women born between 1940 and 1945. Their stories were shaped by the 1960s and are told from the perspective of their 60s. I was born in 1942 and am in the middle of this story, this collective memoir of a generation.

As I compare my life with the lives of women in other generations, I am aware of important differences in our experiences and worldview. To understand these differences, I interviewed women born during World War II (we were the only "ration-stamp babies" in U.S. history with our own coveted books from birth). In the carefully considered responses of these women, I heard resonances of key events and social changes that define generational influence in our lives. Collectively, we are Rosie's daughters, and this is an account of our lives told in narratives, quotes, events, and pictures.

We are not Rosie's *only* daughters. We have older and younger sisters, but I limited my interviews to women born during the war. My wartime generation arrived in the 1960s still in its teens. We experienced the Sexual Revolution together; we started jobs just as sex discrimination at work was prohibited by the Civil Rights Act of 1964; etc. Like Forrest Gump, we had an uncanny ability to participate in history—in our case, social history. As the oldest among us were getting married, oral contraceptives—always known just as The Pill—became available. Historical changes in divorce laws (1969) and abortion laws (1973) affected us dramatically as young wives and mothers.

Our lives are shaped by the times in which we live, but they are also shaped by the long line of women in each family who shaped the family itself. Let me suggest an analogy: perhaps you know about the mitochondrial DNA throughout our cells that, unlike DNA in our chromosomes, comes exclusively from our mothers because all cells in our bodies are descendants of our mothers' eggs and *their* mothers' … mothers' eggs, in an unbroken line to the oldest female human ancestor. This decisive example of female influence is paired in my mind with "kitchen table DNA." Some of the things we say because our mothers said them were probably favorite sayings of our maternal grandmothers and great-grandmothers as well. Female beliefs, values, sayings, and strengths have been passed from mother to children around the kitchen table or campfire since the beginning of humanity.

Of course, I am thinking of my stalwart Arkansas and Oklahoma foremothers, whom I will introduce to you briefly. But I hope you have been lucky enough to inherit the mitochondrial DNA of similar foremothers.

My Maternal Tree

William Strauss and Neil Howe, in their book *Generations*, developed a widely adopted naming scheme for 14 generations of (European-)American life since 1584. My cohort belongs to the 11th generation. According to the actual birth years of *my* foremothers, our foremothers belong to the following generations:

- Our great-grandmothers, 11 million women: *Progressive Generation (born 1843-1859)*
- Our grandmothers, 22 million women: *Lost Generation (born 1883-1900)*

- Our mothers, 31 million women: *G.I. Generation (born 1901-1924)*
- Our generation, 24 million women: *Silent Generation (born 1925-1945)* – subdivided in this book into prewar and wartime (Rosie's Daughters) cohorts

Great-Grandmothers' Generation

All generations are distinctive. The events of their times create a national character and sensibility that becomes embodied in each generation's knowledge, attitudes, and behaviors. My great-grandmother, Mary Jane Grogan Sparks, was born in 1858 when America had just 32 states.

Great-grandmother's birth date makes her part of the Progressive Generation (1843-1859). By the time I knew her, she was famous in our family for wearing seven petticoats under her long skirt and wanting to change them between photographs in order to look different in each picture.

A few of her famous contemporaries are Ida Tarbell (author of *The History of the Standard Oil Company* exposé), Alice Stone Blackwell (activist, daughter of feminist Lucy Stone), and Fannie Farmer (cookbook author and developer of standard cooking measurements).

The Progressives lived through the Civil War and Reconstruction in their youth. As young adults they witnessed technological inventions such as the telephone and light bulb that would change lives worldwide. They lived through an era of increasing fervor for social reform, including "women's issues" such as economic rights, child labor, universal education, suffrage, and prohibition.

Great-grandmother Sparks walked from Georgia to Arkansas shortly after the Civil War. She and her family made the three-month journey on foot because the wagons were overloaded with household goods. Her story about how many shoes she wore out along the trail was told so many times that none of us can swear to the actual number.

Great-grandmother Sparks didn't have electricity until after World War II. She always cooked on a wood-burning stove, and kept food cool in a nearby spring. When she finally got an electric refrigerator in the late 1940s, her great treat was to savor a vanilla ice cream bar in the afternoon. Great-grandmother Sparks had a sixth-grade education, but raising 11 children left little time for reading anyway.

Her husband owned the general store in a small town near the Buffalo River in rural Arkansas. When he died, she lived with one of her daughters in Ozark, Arkansas. Her savings were her only income. Each month, she paid her daughter $5 for her food and housing. Living with a son or daughter was the norm at the time.

Grandmothers' Generation

Maternal grandmother Lou Lavona Sparks Calderhead was the fifth of Great-grandmother's 11 children. Born in 1885 when America had grown to 38 states, she belongs to the Lost Generation (1883-1900). Her age-mates include Alice Paul (author of the Equal Rights Amendment), Eleanor Roosevelt (First Lady, social-cause champion), and Edna Ferber (author of *Show Boat* and *Giant*).

Social class dictated just how "lost" members of The Lost Generation were. Upper-class children and those in the growing middle class attended elementary and some secondary school. Childhood in the innocent 1900s did not prepare them for the horrors of World War I, which was fought with 19th-century tactics against 20th-century technology. When author

Gertrude Stein told Ernest Hemingway, "You are all a lost generation," a generation was named.

Children of the lower class were more likely to work in factories or on farms than at any time before or since. They had correspondingly less school attendance in their "adolescence," a term coined at the time to describe the years from puberty to adulthood.

Casual drug use (including cocaine in Coca-Cola), high homicide rates, the Great War, the influenza epidemic of 1918, and Prohibition marked the young adulthoods of the Lost Generation, while the Great Depression and World War II shaped their midlife. They witnessed America's entrance onto the world stage as a superpower. They were young when the Wright brothers flew for 12 seconds at Kitty Hawk in 1903, but many lived until 1969 to watch Neil Armstrong become the first person to walk on the moon.

Grandmother was raised in a rural community in Arkansas and attended school until the fifth grade. After marriage, she and her husband cultivated 160 acres adjacent to his parents' land just outside Jasper, Arkansas. Under the Homestead Act of 1862, they received title to the land after living there for five years. They built a small home and started their family. Although they later moved to Oklahoma in search of employment, our family still owns the land and has the transfer deed signed by President Taft.

Influenza came into her Oklahoma home in 1918. My mother and two of her brothers became ill as did she, but no one in our family died. Influenza killed 250,000

Americans—twice the number who died in World War I. Praying for his family's recovery, my grandfather promised God that, if his wife and children were spared, he would not leave for work each day until he helped with the chores. My mother remembered him hanging wet laundry on the clothesline each morning.

My grandmother was a teetotaler, but Prohibition (enacted in Oklahoma 13 years before the United States) affected her life every day. Her husband was the sheriff of Payne County during that time. His often-dangerous job was to find stills in the backcountry and catch bootleggers bringing whiskey back from Kansas.

The Depression hit my grandmother especially hard. By then, my grandfather owned a car dealership in Stillwater, Oklahoma, and went bankrupt when no one could afford a new car. They would have lost their home except for Grandmother's ingenuity. She walked over to Stillwater A&M (now Oklahoma State) and asked if there might be a visiting professor who would like to rent a home. As a result, she had income from their home while she rented a less expensive house on the south side of town. Her two older sons were working; they helped out whenever they could. My grandmother planted a "Depression Garden" that fed her family all summer, and she canned everything else to get them through the winter. The family was sustained during that period mainly by my grandmother's cleverness and determination.

Grandmother always saved much, spent little. Later in life she lived with a brother for a few years, helping him on his chicken and egg farm, and then with a son and daughter-in-law in California. The last four years of her life she lived with my parents. Like her mother before her, she expected to live out her days in the home of one of her children.

Mothers' Generation

My mother, Flossie Jewel Calderhead Butler, who was born in Arkansas in 1909 when there were 46 states, is a member of the G.I. Generation (1900-1924). Oklahoma, her home for more than 90 years, was just two years old at the time of her birth. Her sisters-in-time include Jessica Tandy (actor), Virginia Apgar (physician, developer of the Apgar Score for the needs of newborn infants), and Eudora Welty (Pulitzer Prize winner, "First Lady of Southern Literature").

My mother was born before the passage of the Nineteenth Amendment that granted her the right to vote. The first White House Conference on Children, held in her birth year, led to child labor laws that protected her generation. The G.I. Generation was affected by World War I and prohibition in their early years, but it was the Depression and World War II, just as we were being born, that had the greatest impact on their lives.

World War II brought people together and made them civic-minded. That spirit endured: women went to work as Rosies and then yielded their wartime jobs to returning G.I.s and moved their young families into new suburban tract homes. An era of unparalleled middle-class prosperity followed. In their elder years, this generation of senior citizens (a term first coined for them) has been fairly secure financially because of Social Security and Depression-induced savings.

Mother was the eldest child and only daughter in a family of six. Seeing her father go bankrupt was a life lesson that my mother spoke of even in her 90s. She left college in order to work. When she married in 1933, with the Depression still in progress, her groceries included canned goods that had lost their labels in shipment. She never knew what was inside but bought them because they were cheaper than labeled ones. When she opened a can (with an opener she continued to use until she died), all too often she found plums. After the Depression and the war, of course, she lived out her life in a period of prosperity and technological change that enabled her to do things and see places that her parents could not have imagined. She refused to ever buy canned plums again.

As was typical for most women of her generation, my mother quit working when she married. She knew she would need to save, even from meager earnings in those early years, so that they could build a good life and have money for the future. Clothes were mended. My sister's hand-me downs were part of my "new" wardrobe each season. When fashions changed, my mother and grandmother restyled last year's clothes in a semblance of the new fashion. Everything was reused in our household long before the concept of recycling became popular. Mother took fabric from a pretty, but outgrown, skirt and made a pillow she stuffed with old plastic bags. She saved the covers of Christmas cards and used them the following year to decorate the tops of packages, eliminating the need for ribbon. The Depression always whispered financial caution in my mother's ear.

When women of my mother's generation reached their retirement years, they could no longer count on moving to the home of one of their children. G.I. Generation women had fewer children; rural families had moved to cities; children had taken work farther from home and relocated often by their own preference or their company's command. Moreover, the retirement years became much longer. Although women in my family have always lived long lives, the average lifespan of an American woman has increased by about three decades in the past century. Women in my mother's generation needed more money to take care of themselves as they aged.

The Depression made the American government and citizens aware of the devastating problems that occur when people lack economic security. When the Social Security Act was passed in 1935, only half of those over 65 had enough money to meet their economic needs. Fortunately for Mother's generation and those to follow, the Social Security Act was first amended in 1939 to provide survivor benefits to spouses and was amended again in 1965 to include health care through Medicare.

Because she had applied the three lessons of the Depression (save, save, save) even in a time of prosperity, and because the government underwrote minimum levels of economic security and health care in retirement, my mother did not need to move in with her children nor require them to take care of her financially. In contrast with her mother and grandmother, my mother lived in her own home until she died. But she, like others in her generation, did expect children to help in a care-giving role. Throughout the later years my sister checked on my mother several times a day, bringing her meals, taking over routine shopping and services, making appointments and driving her to them, and so on. Many women in my generation have moved back to the towns where their mothers live or, if living locally, have taken early retirement in order to be their mothers' caregivers.

My Generation

I will round out this tale with a brief mention of my own generation and the generations of our daughters and granddaughters. As I mentioned, I was born in 1942, in the middle of what I call the "First Woman To" (FW2) Cohort of the Silent Generation. Mercifully, I shorten this label to FW2 Generation women or just FW2 women in later pages. There were 48 states when I was born. The Silent Generation was smaller than our mothers' G.I. Generation, a fact attributed to the Depression, deferred marriage, and increased use of birth control.

My sisters-in-time include Joan Baez (folksinger, political activist), Doris Kearns Goodwin (presidential historian, author), Nancy Pelosi (Speaker of the House), Billie Jean King (professional tennis player and tireless crusader for women's parity in tournament sports), Aretha Franklin (singer, *You Make Me Feel Like a Natural Woman*), and Wonder Woman (first female superhero, debuted in All Star Comics in 1941).

Strauss and Howe say the Silents are "stable, thorough, loyal, private, and hard-working." That sounds like us. They also say that the "story of [the Silents] will read ... like the middle pages of a book written mainly about somebody else." Again we agree. We didn't experience the life-shaping events of the Great Depression or World War II as our G.I. parents did, and we were vastly outnumbered by the Baby Boomers. But we instigated the cultural revolution of the 1960s (think Janis, Joan, and Joni). From the late 1960s onward we used our better educations and the new anti-discrimination laws to combine work and family in new lifestyles, and over and over again we found ourselves the right age at the right time to become the First Women To push against previously closed doors of opportunity. Enough said: the rest of this book is about us.

Most of our children belong to the generation known popularly as Generation X, born between 1961 and 1981. Gen Xers, at least based on my personal knowledge of them, do not deserve their slacker reputa-

tion in the mass media. Since I have three sons and an honorary fourth son, all in this generation, I was concerned for some time that the Gen X reputation might become self-fulfilling. Just the opposite is true: no one cares for other people or the future of the planet more than they do.

Our grandchildren belong to the Millennial Generation. This chrysalis generation will emerge as something extraordinary—millions of extraordinary somethings. Our hope is that their bright futures will not be eclipsed by stupid things that older generations do—just as loving adults hoped on our behalf in the dark days of World War II.

My generation's tale continues...

Rosie the Riveter: Origins of the FW2 Generation

9:27 AM Wednesday, August 12, 1942

"Ed, you can't go. Not now."

"Flo, I know you don't want me to. But when Ed Mac left for training camp, when he stood there next to the train holding our baby, I realized I have just as much to fight for as he does. Even more. We have a family and he doesn't."

"But your cousin was in ROTC. He enlisted as an officer. You'll be a private."

"Lots of men are signing up as privates. Honey, what's really the matter?"

"How will I manage? Matilda Lou's six months old. Barbara Ann's four and a half—"

"I've got that figured out. I called your mother yesterday. She'll come stay with you until I get back. Honey, please drive me downtown. I've got to do this."

4:18 PM Wednesday, August 12, 1942

Ring. Ring. "Hello Flo. Can you come get me?"

"Ed, what happened? You sound strange."

1st peacetime draft in US begins • Roosevelt elected to 3rd term • Avg. income: $1,725 • Nylon stockings first sold

"I failed the physical, can you believe it? As soon as the doctor saw my flat feet, he stamped me 4F. Maybe I can grow arches. Anyway, I'll be waiting outside."

And that's my family's war story. Cousin Ed Mac rose to the rank of colonel and served in France. My father never grew arches and didn't make it into the Army. Instead, he worked for a war-related machinery company. He made his own contribution to the war effort, as did so many other 4Fs.

However, it wasn't just men who helped the nation during World War II...

Rosie Made the Difference

Women took physically demanding jobs in defense factories, shipyards, steel mills, foundries, lumber mills and munitions plants. In addition, many white-collar positions opened up to women for the first time. They became bank tellers, cashiers and bookkeepers. Their ability to excel in a man's world not only challenged stereotypes but also elevated this new woman to iconic stature— Rosie the Riveter. She was

Longing won't bring him back sooner...
GET A WAR JOB!
SEE YOUR U. S. EMPLOYMENT SERVICE
WAR MANPOWER COMMISSION

a woman portrayed in overalls and polka-dot bandana welding, riveting, and setting records for the speed she could produce ships and planes.

Norman Rockwell in his *Saturday Evening Post* cover for May 29, 1943, depicted Rosie as the female Paul Bunyan. His Rosie was modeled on a poster entitled *We Can Do It* that J. Howard Miller at Westinghouse created for the War Production Coordinating Committee. After the 1943 song *Rosie the Riveter* became popular, Miller's poster was given the same name.

When a six-million-strong army of Rosie the Riveters answered the call to work in factories and offices across the country, they overcame many expectations about women's roles and capabilities, but age-old barriers didn't come crashing down, nor did opportunities for women open up overnight. The attack on Pearl Harbor brought out 750,000 women to apply for work at war plants in the first few months of our entry into war, but only 80,000 were hired. As more men were needed on the battlefields, the government urged women to join the workforce and they did. The number of women employed increased from 12 million to 18 million. By the end of the war, one quarter of all women were working. One-third of the female defense workers had previously been full-time homemakers. In addition to these large numbers, an additional 400,000 women had joined the military.

What were the experiences of these women as they entered the male world of work?

- Inez Sauer, a Boeing tool clerk, remembers her male supervisor saying, "The happiest duty of my life will be when I say goodbye to each of you women as I usher you out the front door."

- Alison Ely Campbell recalls her early days at the Kaiser Shipyard. "The all-male crew met us with cold, stony stares.

Office of War Information, 1943

"Among the single women, the picture is one of almost complete employment. But only one of five of the married women have gone to work. Moreover, the wives … represent the most abundant supply of workers. Since our ability to keep the production machine running in high gear depends largely on the enlistment of women workers, the public attitude toward this issue—and especially the attitude of wives—is of paramount interest."

Media campaign persuades millions of women to go to work • Women's Auxiliary Army Corps (WAAC) signed into law

The foreman, whose job was to train us, took us around and showed us each our 'territory', told us briefly what to do, and gave us each a huge book filled with drawings of every section that went on the ship. Period. ... The guys obviously had made a pact not to talk to us—to freeze us out. But we were friendly, doing the job. After a couple of weeks, they not only thawed out but actually enjoyed us and we enjoyed them."

The changes went beyond the specific experiences at work. Inez Sauer continues her story: "My mother warned me when I took the job that I would never be the same. Mother said, 'You will never want to go back to being a housewife.' At that time I didn't think it would change a thing. But she was right, it definitely did. . . . at Boeing I found a freedom and an independence that I had never known. After the war I could never go back to playing bridge again, being a club woman ... when I knew there were things I could use my mind for. The war changed my life completely. I guess you could say I finally grew up."

Similarly, Lockheed riveter Sybil Lewis recalls: "You came out to California, put on your pants, and took your lunch pail to a man's job. This

was the beginning of women feeling that they could do something more."

The number of women who helped with the war effort is even larger than the story told by the swollen employment figures. Millions more women volunteered through the Red Cross and other service organizations. With Eleanor Roosevelt their role model, volunteers learned new skills, both organizational and technical.

Internment of Japanese-Americans begins • Movie: *Casablanca* • Battle of Midway • Aaron Copland's *Rodeo*

Although the work was exhilarating, most employed women made way for the returning soldiers and left the workforce after the war. Rosie Delana Jensen Close remembers, "V-E Day, on May 8, 1945, was a day of celebration, but one of mixed emotions for us. We lost our jobs. The Yuba plant would no longer make guns. We said our good-byes, and when the foreman of my section shook my hand and said good-bye, he added, 'You were the best man I had.'"

These women never forgot their experiences or what they accomplished. Tessie Hickam Wilson, another Rosie, had moved with her husband from Albuquerque to San Diego and found work at Consolidated Vultee Aircraft Corporation making parts for the B-24. She says, "We women who worked during the war opened the door for other women later—we proved women could do it."

Is There Anything Women *Can't* Do?

Suddenly, in the crisis of World War II, old assumptions were forgotten. New questions were asked: Is there anything women *can't* do? Can they make steel, guns, jeeps, trucks, tanks, artillery shells, bombs, airplanes, ships? Can they drive 10-ton trucks loaded with war supplies? Can they ferry new fighters and bombers? Can they tow aerial targets for gunnery practice?

This army of Rosies, forged in labor and service, played a critical role in the war effort, but their great gift to future generations was an entirely new paradigm for thinking about women's working roles. The belief that "women can't do men's work" prevailed for two centuries of the Industrial Revolution. Rare bastions of male employment were opened to women after long debate about the physical and moral impact of work outside the home on "the weaker sex." Always they could, and they did. Knowing the contribution women made during the war, Rosie generation mothers conveyed an implicit message to their daughters: "If you ever need to, you can do it."

Rosie's Daughters

In the domestic sphere, most women in Rosie's generation raised their daughters with the same expectations of marriage, homemaking, and child rearing they'd had, but fresh memories of economic hardship and social disruption during the Depression and World War II made them wary of what the future would hold. Rosies encouraged their daughters to attend college and acquire employment skills. Their daughters obtained—though it was woven through marriage, child-bearing, and divorce—much more education than women in Rosie's generation had received.

In preparing their daughters for an uncertain future, women in Rosie's generation passed along legacies of adaptability and self-assurance that have helped to make their daughters' lives rich in economic and social contributions as well as self-discovery.

Kay Bailey Hutchison,
First female Senator
from Texas

"I have often said, we will know we have succeeded when there are no more stories about the first woman anything, when the stories are about the great performance of a company whose chief executive officer just happens to be a woman, not about the fact that she is CEO."

The "First Woman To" Generation

Those of us born in the war years, between 1940 and 1945, would quickly acknowledge the wind at our backs. Even the oldest among us was scarcely in kindergarten before the war was over, families were reunited, and life ... did *not* return to normal. The post-war boom and a national sense of well-being carried us through our elementary- and high- school years—launching us into adulthood. Most of the world was America's *de facto* dominion. Housing, goods, and services flowed from the American cornucopia. America could indulge itself and rebuild war-shattered countries at the same time. Our self-interested idealism overseas was complemented by the civil

(May 8) Victory in Europe (V-E) Day • Atomic bomb dropped • Japan surrenders & WWII ends • 6,500 TV sets

rights movement at home. Yes, it was true that black Americans were getting the short end of the stick. In our high-school and college years, we wanted to be part of the solution, not the problem. No generation of women could write a better scenario of good fortune and adversity in which to test its mettle.

Looking back after several decades, we can better understand why Rosie's Daughters, members of a small wartime generation, have played an outsize role throughout their adult lives. We designate Rosie's Daughters as the "First Woman To" or FW2 Generation because they can claim more *firsts* in personal change, educational attainment, and career achievements than any previous generation of women of comparable size. (In sheer numbers, our younger sisters of the Baby Boom generation will always overshadow us.)

While the wind at our backs helped thrust us forward, every achievement from the 1960s onward was arduous and usually off the map of adult life drawn for us by our mothers. All our gains were the culmination of determined individual efforts. When acknowledging these efforts, newspapers in the 1970s used the acronym "FW2" as a tagline for women—most from our generation—who became the first to achieve prominence in a male-dominated field. Each FW2 story cheered us on then, as it does now.

What Does "First" Mean?

For as long as people have sought opportunity, fought injustices, explored uncharted territory, and striven to accomplish more, a few men and women have always earned the position of being The First: First Man on the Moon, First Woman Nobel Laureate, First Female Senator and First African-American President of a Major University. But it takes more than one individual's achievement to change perceptions at the societal level.

Since the country's founding, women have achieved firsts, but they achieved them primarily as isolated distinctions. That is, when a woman achieved "firstness" of a particular kind, other women did not immediately follow. When Elizabeth Blackwell became the first woman physician in 1849, she was not followed by a large number of female physicians. Belva Ann Lockwood's achievement in 1872 of becoming the first woman admitted to practice law before the U.S. Supreme Court did not spur numerous female lawyers to follow. When Jeannette Rankin was elected to the U.S. House of Representatives in 1916, women across the country did not follow her into Congress. As important as their achievements were, these individuals did not break down barriers or change societal perceptions.

Women's "firsts" result in real change when they achieve two milestones. First, they involve a *critical mass* of women. Second, they occur under *ordinary circumstances*. Rosie's generation achieved the first milestone but not the second. Millions of Rosies flourished in male roles. They changed societal perceptions of women's abilities, but only in the extraordinary circumstances of wartime. Rosie's daughters have been able to achieve both milestones.

The Great Discontinuity

Certain moments or periods of history are regarded as discontinuities— sometimes even as they happen—because assumptions, rules, or possibilities are so altered by events that the future, whatever it proves to be, cannot be the same as the past. Within the life spans of the oldest FW2 women, for example, the split-second events in which "everything changed" began with Japan's attack on the United States in 1941. Looking across the first six decades of these women's lives, and the events that created this continuing discontinuity in our lives at significant points in our maturation, we find:

1945 The explosion of the U.S. atomic bomb over Hiroshima;

1949 The explosion of a Soviet atomic bomb, which generated talk of possible nuclear holocaust that filtered down even into our elementary schools;

1963 John F. Kennedy's assassination;

1968 (the *annus horribilis*) The assassinations of Martin Luther
King Jr. and Robert Kennedy; the Tet Offensive in Vietnam,
war riots, political convention turmoil;

1989 The fall of the Berlin Wall;

1991 The dissolution of the Soviet Union;

2001 The 9/11 attacks on New York's World Trade Center and the
Pentagon, and the downed Flight 93.

These singular events changed our world, almost within a moment. However, the *social* changes that transformed American life did not happen as singular events. Yet they changed our lives even more significantly.

Long waves of social discontinuity roll through a population and gain strength as more and more people experience the epiphany, the psychological "click," that something about the past and present is unacceptable and must be rejected. The great discontinuity in women's rights in our lifetime took that form: women rejected their unequal and unchosen status in society. (In women's studies classes, the famous "click" is quoted from Ibsen's *A Doll's House*—TORVALD: "Before all else, you are a wife and a mother." NORA: "I don't believe that any longer. I believe that before all else I am a reasonable human being.")

The period of great social discontinuity in women's rights extended from the publication of *The Feminine Mystique* in 1963 to the *Roe v. Wade* decision in 1973. Of course, new laws and rulings affecting women's rights are added to the record each year, but they extend or sometimes qualify the rights secured during the 1963-1973 decade rather than reverse them.

Laws and decisions were only the backdrop for what was happening in our lives at that time. From matriarchs of the women's movement like

**Sherry Lansing,
First female president of
20th Century Fox**

"I got promoted [at MGM] to senior vice president, and I went to the head of the studio and I asked for a raise, to be equal to the guy who had the same job. I was told…'Look, we have to pay him more because he has a family to support.' I have to say, at the time, I accepted that. Why? I was raised at a time when a woman wasn't supposed to have a career. She was supposed to get married and have two children."

Alice Paul (who went to jail for women's suffrage in 1907, authored the Equal Rights Amendment in 1921, and instigated the sexual discrimination clause in the Civil Rights Act of 1964) to the young FW2 women (we ranged in age from 18 to 23 in 1963), a sense of sisterhood and unbounded possibilities pervaded our thoughts and actions. Whether it was 20,000 women marching down Fifth Avenue to "Strike for Equality" on the 50th anniversary of women's suffrage (August 26, 1970), a dozen women working to collectively raise their consciousness, or a single woman speaking up for equality at home or at work, social change was afoot.

"What do women want?" The same observers who understood the underlying causes of black protest were at a loss to explain women's dissatisfaction. Women's lives were certainly not more difficult than before. The impetus for change came not from oppression but from liberation. Large families and household drudgery no longer occupied a woman's entire life. Liberation movements around the world made any thoughtful news reader and television viewer aware that unwarranted restrictions, however benevolent their intentions, seem like oppression to the restricted group. The founding documents of our nation had never protected American women in the same measure as American men. The disparity finally became unacceptable.

The American story is that each man has the right within the law to fulfill his own destiny. The great discontinuity of the 1960s amended that story to include each woman's right to fulfill her own destiny within the same law that applied to men. Once Rosie and her singular predecessors like Marie Curie and Amelia Earhart had proved that women can perform well in all fields, it eventually became a matter of identifying and scrapping the discriminatory laws and "gentlemen's agreements."

Often FW2 women stumbled individually on laws and work rules that others had not thought to question. Every door had to be tested to see if it would open as it was supposed to, and often the woman at the door was very committed to walking through it. She asserted her right to major in math or engineering, to be admitted to graduate school, to become a management trainee, to receive the same pay as a man in a similar position. Each step along the way, FW2 women met resistance and unfavorable attitudes much as the Rosies had. They had to change their own hearts and minds first and then those of parents, friends, professors, husbands, neighbors, and employers. Changes occurred one person at a time.

The FW2 Generation women embarked on journeys of personal growth and set daring goals. They sorted out the strengths and limitations of the traditional values with which they had been raised. They pushed through educational and employment barriers. They outgrew unrealistic dreams of a Prince Charming who would make life perfect for them. They did become wives, mothers, and homemakers, but they also joined the Peace Corps, experimented with alternative lifestyles, earned professional degrees, and entered scores of occupations in which women had been virtually unknown. They were also the first generation to divorce in record numbers, raise children as single moms, struggle with addictions, come out as gay, and rebel and adapt as only rare women had done before.

Extraordinary Accomplishments

Who are these FW2 women? You'll find them everywhere. They may be your mother, your sister, your best friend, your boss or co-worker, your doctor, your lawyer. Some have well-known names and faces. When large numbers of FW2 women entered high-profile fields and showed what they could do, many of them became famous. We acknowledge the stamina, perseverance, and well-deserved fame of FW2 women like:

Nancy Pelosi,
First female Speaker of the House, 2007

"This is an historic moment – for the Congress, and for the women of this country. It is a moment for which we have waited more than 200 years. Never losing faith, we waited through the many years of struggle to achieve our rights. But women weren't just waiting; women were working. Never losing faith, we worked to redeem the promise of America, that all men and women are created equal. For our daughters and granddaughters, today we have broken the marble ceiling. To our daughters and granddaughters now, the sky is the limit. Anything is possible for them."

- Martha Stewart, Anita Roddick, Sherry Lansing, and Diane von Furstenberg in business;
- Diane Sawyer, Molly Ivins, Nina Totenberg, Leslie Stahl, Charlayne Hunter-Gault, and Jane Bryant Quinn in journalism;
- Nancy Pelosi, Kay Bailey Hutchison, Barbara Boxer, and Pat Schroeder in politics;
- Billie Jean King, Virginia Wade, Wilma Rudolph, and Margaret Smith Court in sports;
- Alice Waters in American cuisine;
- Activists Sarah Brady, Angela Davis, and Patricia Ireland;
- Authors Erica Jong, Robin Morgan, Maxine Hong Kingston, Rita Mae Brown, Sue Grafton, Janet Evanovich, Susan Wittig Albert, Annie Dillard, Anne Rice and Arlie Russell Hochschild;
- Singers Joni Mitchell, Joan Baez, Diana Ross, Aretha Franklin, Helen Reddy, Vikki Carr, Martha Reeves, Gladys Knight, K. T. Oslin, Mama Cass and Brenda Lee;
- Actors Jill Clayburgh, Mia Farrow, Bette Midler, Marsha Mason, Stockard Channing, Barbra Streisand and Madeline Kahn;
- Producer/director Penny Marshall and scriptwriter/director Nora Ephron;
- Choreographers Twyla Tharp and Judith Jamison;
- TV talk show host Sally Jessy Raphael and TV personality Judge Judy;
- And the list goes on both in depth and breadth.

Many more FW2 Generation women are not as well-known for their accomplishments across an amazing range of fields as they deserve to be. To name a few:

- Wilma Mankiller, first female chief of a large Native American tribe (Cherokee);
- Shirley Muldowney, known as the "First Lady of Drag Racing," the first woman licensed as a top fuel dragster, won the Top Fuel Championship three times;

- Astronaut Shannon Lucid, record holder for most flight hours in orbit (223 days) of *any* non-Russian and for any woman in the world;
- Marguerite Ross Barnett, first African-American woman to become president of a major university (University of Houston);
- Catherine D. DeAngelis, first female editor of *The Journal of the American Medical Association*, (perhaps the most widely cited source of medical information);
- April Glaspie, first U.S. female ambassador to an Arab country (Iraq);
- Penny Harrington, first female police chief of a major city (Portland, OR);
- Shirley Peterson, first female commissioner of the IRS;
- Roberta Ramo, first female president of the American Bar Association;
- Judy Rankin, first woman to win more than $100,000 in a season in professional golf;
- Judith Rodin, first female president of an Ivy League university (University of Pennsylvania);
- Nannerl O. Keohane, first woman to head a major women's college (Wellesley) and a major research university (Duke);
- Jane Friedman, first (and currently only) female CEO of a large, global publishing house, HarperCollins;
- Antonia Novello, first female Surgeon General of the US;
- Donna Shalala, Secretary of Health & Human Services; President, Hunter College of CUNY; Chancellor, University of Wisconsin; President, University of Miami;
- Olivia Cole, first African American actor to win an Emmy as Outstanding Supporting Actress in a television movie (*Roots*);
- Julia Phillips, first woman producer to win an Oscar for Best Picture (*The Sting*);

- Julia Chang Bloch, first Asian-American ambassador (US ambassador to Nepal);
- And this list goes on as well.

What Made FW2 Women Succeed?

Why did these women, a whole generation of FW2 women, want to open so many closed doors? And what enabled them to succeed?

The simple answer is: timing and precedent. It's no accident that FW2 women's achievements have coincided with four decades of dramatic social, economic and cultural upheaval. When these women found themselves facing new opportunities and challenges, they sought new solutions that their mothers would not have considered because of legal and social barriers that existed until the 1960s.

Seeking to balance themselves on the cusp, Rosie's daughters also had to interpret mixed messages: While women *could* succeed in a man's world, they *should* set their sights on marriage and family. Education was a good thing—serving as an important resource in the event they ever *had* to work—but careers should not replace their jobs as wives and mothers. This is the generational story of FW2 women—the novel dilemmas they faced (and continue to face) are undeniable, but mixed messages from the past create "approach-avoidance" conflicts (if you will permit me some psychologizing) that did not trouble older and younger women who saw either no "approach" or no "avoidance" in the same situation. Rosie's daughters had to improvise at every turn, and they did so with great energy, creativity and accomplishment.

Since a generation is more than a collection of individuals and their experiences, we must further acknowledge the place and time in which the important shared events of generational experience occurred. The place is the home of the Declaration of Independence, the Constitution, and the Bill of Rights. It is also the home of New England's town-meeting philosophy of fairness and the westerner's belief in endless frontiers. Women in my birth year were 18 when John F. Kennedy accepted the

Democratic Presidential Nomination with these words: "We stand at the edge of a New Frontier—the frontier of unfulfilled hopes and dreams..." Eighteen-year-old women have many unfulfilled hopes and dreams.

Contributing Factors of the 1960s. In the right place, timing is everything. When they say that the 1960s were the decade of sex, drugs, and rock and roll, you'll notice which major distraction of youth is mentioned first. FW2 women came of age in the 1960s, at the beginning of the sexual revolution just as The Pill was becoming available (introduced in 1960, but not available in all states or always to unmarried women). Helen Gurley Brown's *Sex and the Single Girl*, a best seller in 1962, taught us more about sex than we ever learned from mother. In 1963 Betty Friedan published *The Feminine Mystique*, which launched debates about sex, marriage, and power.

In that same year some FW2 women traveled to Washington, DC, to join in the March for Jobs and Freedom and on a hot, humid August day stood transfixed as Martin Luther King delivered his "I have a dream ..." speech. Three months later, President Kennedy was shot in Dallas, and television brought images of the assassination and funeral directly into their living rooms. They'll always remember those events as stark sequences of black and white images that branded their young adult lives.

**Anna Eshoo,
Congresswoman**

"You can see why it's so important that women be everywhere and be part of everything. ...because we're shaped by different life experiences and our world views are a little different, and it's important to have all those views at the table."

The Civil Rights Act became law in 1964 when President Johnson called on Congress and America to pass the bill as a monument to Kennedy. With the 11th-hour addition of the word "sex" to Title VII of that bill, the Act prohibited the practice of an employer "to discriminate against any individual with respect to his [*sic*] compensation, terms, conditions or privileges of employment, because of such individual's race, color, religion, sex, or national origin." Even as the darkness of the Vietnam War descended on America, women and black Americans had a new reason to be hopeful for the future.

Contributing Factors of the 1970s. In the 1970s, some women bought their first copies of *Ms. Magazine*. Others only looked at it on the newsstand, believing that their husbands would never permit such a magazine in the house. The Equal Rights Amendment (ERA) had been introduced in every Congress since 1923. It finally passed both the Senate and the House and, in 1972, was sent to state legislatures for the 38 needed ratifications. Early the next year, *Roe v. Wade,* successfully argued by FW2 Sarah Weddington, began a new and unfailingly contentious chapter in the story of reproductive choice.

Contributing Factors of the 1980s. FW2 Generation women in education and business in the 1980s had decoded the alphabet soup of EEOC, OCR, Title VII and Title IX regulations and began to benefit from them. The Equal Employment Opportunity Commission (EEOC), born of the Civil Rights Act, issued regulations that made sexual harassment of women illegal in the workplace. The ERA passed in 35 states but failed to become law because it fell short of ratification by three states. Title IX, the legislation that prohibited discrimination on the basis of sex in federally funded education programs, meant that many of these women's daughters participated in sports programs previously closed to women.

As FW2 women entered middle age, the divorce rate spiked. Often couples just outgrew one another—many women had gone back to school in the `70s and wanted to pursue careers, while some husbands just wanted younger wives.

Contributing Factors of the 1990s. By the 1990s, hormone-replacement therapy became the mantra of the physicians of FW2 Generation women. The economy was booming; their net worth was rising. They, their partners and their children grew accustomed to numerous job opportunities and higher salaries in what can best be described as a New Economic Order that seemed to defy conventional wisdom. New economic sectors such as e-commerce appeared virtually overnight on computer screens. FW2 women felt a growing optimism about the future of the globe as well. The main geopolitical premise of their lives, eternal conflict between capitalism and communism, was suddenly stamped "expired" when the Soviet Union collapsed and democracy overtook Eastern Europe.

Contributing Factors in the new millennium. As FW2 women were turning 60 in the 2000s, hormone therapy proved not to be a fountain of youth after all. In fact, it had menacing side effects—increasing the risks of breast cancer, heart attack, and stroke—that cause apprehension to this day. In 2006, researchers at M.D. Anderson Cancer Center announced that 2003 marked the first drop in breast cancer rates since a steady yearly increase began in 1990. The 12 percent drop among women ages 50-69 occurred in the first year that millions of women, cautioned about risks by the Public Health Service in 2002, stopped taking HRT.

Early in the new millennium the 9-11 tragedies, close to home, shook their lives. Future terror attacks were a menacing possibility in major cities. The war in Iraq made world peace seem like a distant dream. In different ways, FW2 women sought serenity and security in the activities of daily life.

In the new millennium, moreover, FW2 Generation women became aware that the new economic order was subject to the same boom and bust cycle as the old economic order. Many of them saw their investment portfolios plummet faster than they had risen. Future retirement security was also threatened by defaults and new policies of both private and public pension systems. The economic downturn affected many of their children as well. Empty nests refilled as children returned home to regain their financial footing. Many FW2 women began talking about postponing their much anticipated retirement plans. For years to come, it seemed, life might continue to be a juggling act for this generation of jugglers.

Rosa Parks refuses to give up seat to white rider; year-long Montgomery bus boycott begins • *Lolita* published

Origin and Method of *Rosie's Daughters*

Every book has a story of how it came to be. The major ideas for a book about the FW2 Generation began to come together in my mind when I attended the 40th reunion of my class at National Cathedral School for Girls, a private Washington, DC, high school. In one joint session, we were seated around tables in the cavernous room where four decades earlier I had studied English Lit, American History, French, and Algebra every afternoon and evening. Representatives of each quinquennial class reunion spoke about their experiences, telling stories that were alternatively humorous and serious because of the momentous times in which we all have lived. I was struck by how the stories of my class differed from those of women who graduated even five years earlier or later.

Once back in my California home, my thoughts returned many times to that session. For the most part, despite good educations, women who graduated earlier than my class did not seek careers but found fulfillment as wives, mothers, and homemakers. Women who graduated some years after my class took their careers and the juggling act of work and family for granted. They were fulfilling a pattern they had observed and planned for.

My class had a much more complicated and even confused story to tell. When we were in high school, we expected to spend our lives in traditional roles. (Our high school even taught us how to entertain, including the protocol of tea service.) Some time after that—in fact, at different times for different reasons—unprecedented numbers of us switched tracks and pursued careers. None of us remember thinking, "Well, of course that's what I'll do." Instead, we opened doors and moved in what seemed to be the right direction until the next doors appeared, then repeated the process. By trial and error, we became proficient in careers that we never imagined when we were the well-chaperoned charges of our alma mater in Washington. Combining careers and children presented novel challenges, but we were young and

Elvis has TV debut • John Foster Dulles introduces word "brinkmanship" • Grace Kelly marries Prince Rainier III

energetic. I assume we were among the role models that the younger alumnae observed, inspiring them to think, "Well, of course that's what I'll do."

As a psychologist, my curiosity led me to a formal study of many Rosie's Daughters to better understand whether "war babies" truly belonged to a generation of women on the cusp of change or whether I was listening to an isolated set of women's experiences. I interviewed more than 100 women across the United States—north, south, east, west, and central. Multi-hour interviews, some conducted in person but the majority by telephone, were tape-recorded, transcribed, and computer-indexed.

The result of my research is this collective memoir of a unique generation of women. I hope their stories will speak to you as they did to me, from whatever generational perspective you read this account. I hope that some of the intergenerational differences revealed in their stories will help you to better understand how your own story has been influenced by the times in which you have lived. As I continue my research on the FW2 Generation in its multigenerational context, I welcome hearing from you. You can contact me through my website: www.RosiesDaughters.com. If you'd like to document your story using the questions I asked, you'll find the full interview schedule on the book's website.

Experiences of the FW2 Generation were extracted in the women's own words and organized with respect to the lifecycle events of education, marriage, children, work, divorce, and spiritual discovery, which became the themes of chapters two through seven. In addition to the interviews, I assembled statistics and compiled a biographical database of prominent FW2 women to clarify and amplify these themes. A surprising number of these women, the famous face of our generation, had written memoirs, which I read and categorized according to the lifecycle events listed above. Interviews and autobiographical accounts proved to be very complementary in identifying commonalities among FW2 women.

The final chapter brings the stories of this collective memoir into a new conceptual perspective on the imbalances and "insufficient funds" in women's lives. I believe that women of all ages, but particularly women who have experienced that psychological "click" of a new or renewed mindfulness for how the rest of their lives will unfold, will benefit from Chapter 8's "holistic balance sheet" of the Seven Life Capitals.

I discuss how our individual portfolios of Emotional, Physical, Cognitive, Spiritual, Social, Financial, and Temporal capital are essentially all the assets that we carry forward from the past and present into the future. Day by day we make withdrawals from them to accomplish life's work and enjoy life's pleasures. That is as it should be: spending from these accounts and replenishing them. However, as one FW2 interview after another made clear—and always with different specific circumstances—women feel they are obligated to spend (give) on behalf of others. They do not feel similarly obligated to replenish the accounts on their own behalf.

As a social scientist I view *balanced and replenished accounts of the Seven Life Capitals* as an innovation in living that will appeal to many women and help them make more forward-looking choices. A Seven Life Capitals mindfulness about everyday decisions can be learned and practiced by anyone.

I asked my colleague Kendra Bonnett to join forces to produce a book from this rich information. Our challenge was to preserve the life stories so generously given by the women I interviewed, to analyze the themes and extract life lessons, to juxtapose comments from some of the more famous FW2 Generation women with Everywoman, and to remind ourselves and our readers about the times in which these stories took place.

A Few Final Words of Explanation

First, I recognize how small a cross-section of FW2 Generation women I was able to study directly. But I have learned a great deal about the breadth and depth of Rosie's Daughters in the course of my research, and I hope that Kendra and I are able to pass that knowledge on to you.

Second, I'm both an observer *and* a participant in this story. Each of these roles influences the other. You'll read some of my stories along with those of the women I interviewed. They began when I was born a pioneer, a proud and grateful product of Oklahoma. My middle-class childhood was secure and uneventful, in the happiest sense of that term. From high school onward, I sampled schools two years at a time: an OKC public high school, a private high school in Washington, the University of Oklahoma, Boston University for the BA, Stanford University for the MA, and finally Northwestern University for the PhD. You might think the law was after me, but in fact the last three schools were chosen in coordination with my first husband.

After Northwestern I was a postdoctoral research associate at U.C. Berkeley's School of Public Policy, a researcher and lecturer in the Stanford Communication Department, and then an executive at the Far West Laboratory for Educational Research and Development in San Francisco. During those years, I was active in the women's movement—chairing Committees on the Status of Women for two professional associations; writing a book (*Women and the Mass Media: A Sourcebook for Research and Action*); directing the national Women's Educational Equity Communication Network; publishing regularly about other women's issues; marching for the passage of ERA; and much more that memory of those hectic years cannot reclaim. As I often heard in the interviews of *Rosie's Daughters*, women's careers are not mapped out in advance, at least not to the same extent as men's careers. Each of my positions led of its own accord to the next opportunity, even leading me into business.

Entrepreneurship seemed to be in the water where we lived in Silicon Valley. My second husband and I founded an electronic publishing and software company, Knowledge Access. I was president and he was chief technologist. My five-year foray into business stretched into ten years and then fifteen, each of them a postgraduate education in business, technology, or the future of publishing.

Eventually we sold the company, looked around and realized that Palo Alto was no longer the sleepy little town where we raised the children, and moved to the open country on the road to Monterey. The lessons of land, orchards, and animals now occupy us, along with teaching, research, and writing. Like other FW2 women, I echo Tennyson's *Ulysses* with heartfelt conviction: "I am part of all I have met."

Now let's see what FW2 Generation women want to tell us...

School Days, Dear Old Golden Rule Days: The Education of the FW2 Generation Women

College Bound

I checked my watch again. I had become an afternoon mail watcher. The acceptance letters foretold the future in their crisp, typed pages. One by one they appeared, but the decision had to be deferred until they all arrived. What would the decision be?

Although I was planning for graduate school, the decision wasn't mine. I waited for my husband to decide which offer he would accept. When he chose Stanford's Graduate School of Business, it was my turn. I submitted my application to Stanford's Communication Department. Fortunately, I was accepted; otherwise I wouldn't have attended graduate school during that first California sojourn. But later I'll...

Later has always been an important concept for women, since we put our wishes behind those of others. My mother made it through the Hard Times with thoughts of *later* when she could spend some of the scarce household money for things that *she* had been doing without. Her mother in turn had rented the family home in Stillwater and moved into humbler quarters so that *later* when the family had more money they could reoccupy their own home.

Gage Worth, educational goals replace "wife of" dream

The whole limiting role of what women could do was stultifying. My mother was adamant about me being a nurse or a teacher or a secretary. She thought it was very forward-looking to consider the possibility that I might someday be on my own and would have to have the ability to work. There was never any discussion of advanced degrees. My father said, "She's not going to secretarial school; she's going to the university."

They expected I would get married by 19, 20 or 21. If you didn't get married by 24, you were an old maid. I think their expectations of me were always that I would be the "wife of." I remember thinking in my early college years that the person I aspired to be like was Jackie Kennedy—never doing anything in my own regard but just being married to the right person. I think that kept me from doing a lot of things that I otherwise would have done. I still had it in my subconscious that I had to be a little bit on the

Bernadine Healy
President of the American Heart Association and the American Red Cross and director of the National Institutes of Health where she created the Women's Health Initiative

"You never get more than you dream for, so you better have big dreams both for yourself and for those that you are leading."

My generation on the cusp did not think much about *later* during our college years. We were full of energy and enthusiasm for events that lay immediately before us. Each of us would attend college and be a good or acceptable student. We would date; we would be pinned; we would be engaged; we would have a memorable wedding; we would set up cute little households within our budgets; we would become pregnant and raise a nice family; we would be active in our community. We might finish college or not; it was more important to have attended college than to finish.

Given the seriousness with which we pursued our education and careers or other endeavors in the decades to follow, I wish I could say that we were torn between two scenarios for our lives: our own nebulous dreams of individual accomplishment and the fully written script of a traditional life that our parents, teachers, and boyfriends all seemed to take for granted. Did we defer our own dreams for *later*? No, that wasn't true of me or the FW2 women I interviewed. At that age, our own expectations for womanly milestones and satisfactions were the same as everyone else's.

Gestapo Chief Adolf Eichmann is captured • FDA approves the Pill • Soda pop first sold in aluminum cans

straight and narrow because I was going to be "wife of," which is funny because I never was.

Because I was going to be a medical technologist, I had been in a pre-med program as an undergraduate. As soon as I finished college, I took off, practically the next day, on a freighter to Spain. I focused entirely on third-world politics and dependency and the link between media and politics. That's what prompted me to go back to school to study political science and then communication. If I could have found a program in political communication specifically I would have chosen that, but I had to piece it together by myself. I got a master's in political science and a Ph.D. in communication. It seems I've always worked, but never as a medical technologist.

I married between my sophomore and junior years. Being married meant that I transferred from the University of Oklahoma to Boston University to be in a college near my husband's school. Husbands never moved to be near their wives' colleges in those days.

I didn't have a strong sense of what my major should be. I was intrigued with geology (Oklahoma has a lot of it), but my geology professor assured me that "girls" don't work at geological sites. I chose communication arts because my sister's boyfriend suggested it. I took radio and television courses and did well. I enjoyed working at the campus radio station. Communication research at Stanford was the closest match I could find to my undergraduate field. Like many FW2 Generation women, I have to admit that each decision worked out well for me. But they weren't really my decisions.

My story sounds odd in the 21st century, but it illustrates two contradictions in the education of FW2 Generation women. First, while we went to college, we allowed others to shape our experience; we rarely pursued our own dreams. Our parents were the first shapers; they insisted that we continue on to college. Although the Depression had denied many of them a degree, they had seen the G.I. Bill open education

Katherine Campbell, years before she realized her dream

I wanted to change to pre-med. I was told women couldn't go into medicine; the professors would give me a hard time. Meanwhile, the chemistry professors were all saying I should go into chemistry because that's what I was good at. Who would guess? Girls were not supposed to be good at those things. It was a big surprise to me, but I changed majors and did very well. I was near the top of my class.

When I graduated I planned to get a job and an apartment, find out who I was and start living. But the head of the chemistry department said I should apply for a National Science Foundation Scholarship. I got the fellowship, married and went to graduate school. I never seemed to make decisions; they just seemed to get made. Somehow things found me. I didn't find them. I got my MA, but I already knew I didn't want to be a chemist.

In 1975 a friend said she was taking aptitude tests and asked me to do it too. The counselor told me I should go to medical school. I said, "I'm too old. They don't take anybody older than 29." The counselor said, "There are five medical schools here. Why don't you just apply?"

to millions. They found ways to be successful without a degree, but they recognized education as key to their daughters' futures as well as their sons' – educated men and educated women were a natural match for each other.

The second contradiction was that our parents wanted us to be employable through our college education but not necessarily to practice the specialties we had studied. Culturally rich majors were favored by women who did not expect to work. If a woman needed to work, she would be constrained by locally available jobs anyway.

"Luckily, my parents made me go to college," explains Charlyne Tucker. "Mom had given up college so her father would be able to send

I did and got into two. One of the schools had only started taking women in 1971.

It was easy to go to school after having worked. It was a little harder when I had to go to the hospital and stay up all night, but my husband took the brunt of that. When you're the one doing what you think is fun, you don't mind being tired or deprived. I was the oldest in my class and in my late 30s by my residency. People said, "You're going to be 41 when you start your practice." I said, "I am going to be 41 anyway so I might as well be doing something I want to do."

her younger brothers to school during and after the Depression. My Dad had gone to junior college and knew the value of an education. He especially wanted his daughters to go because he wanted us to be able to make a living on our own, in case we had to. As it happened, all three of us have been on our own much of our adult life."

While we had more educational opportunity than our parents, our options were limited in where we went to school, for how long, and in what courses, majors and extracurricular activities we would pursue. "I went to a junior college," says Helen Young. "My father was of the old school." He said, 'Two years of college is probably enough because you're just going to get married anyway.' He also advised me to take business-secretarial courses because that would probably be the only kind of job I could get without four years of college."

Diminished Dreams

With high-school diploma in hand, we walked out into the world with three options—get married, attend college, or go to work. If it was to be a career, there were also only three conventional choices. We could teach, type or take temperatures. These stereotypes of women's careers

Emily Post—U.S.'s *grande dame* of etiquette—dies at age 86 • *To Kill a Mockingbird* wins Pulitzer Prize

Natalie Tannenbaum, finally finding a career

My father said, "There are two nice professions for a woman—teaching or nursing. Pick one, and I'll pay for it." I said, "All right, I'll pick teaching." I got my credential, and it was crap. It was almost impossible to make it through those Ed courses at that point in my life but I did.

I taught for many years and quit for three years when my son was born. Then I went back half time. I saw once again how incongruent teaching was with me. I'd always wanted to be a therapist. I applied for a graduate program and got in. I went one term and just hated it. It was hokey. It was really a counselor program. So I stopped that, and one day in my exercise class a good friend mentioned a fabulous master's program in social work. I applied and got in. I loved it.

I commuted for a whole year. This was 1989. I took our son to his school, drove to Portland, attended class and spent the night. The gates were opened and my juices flowed. These wonderful professors were informing me, and I got an exposure to feminist thought and healing.

were in the air around our young lives, not only at school but also in homes where fathers worked and mothers stayed home or, in cases of necessity, worked in traditional women's jobs. The stereotypes were in the airwaves of television. *Father Knows Best, Ozzie and Harriet* and *Leave it to Beaver* showed wives baking cookies and vacuuming in high heels and pearls. Early television almost never portrayed a woman in a powerful career, such as the attorney Amanda Bonner played by Katherine Hepburn in the 1949 movie *Adam's Rib*.

The sex-typing of occupations was so thoroughly ingrained in our culture that anyone asked to draw a teacher, a secretary or a nurse would produce a picture of a female. In a school experiment a while later, students were shown pictures of "Doctor Jane" and "Nurse David," both in white uniforms. When the students were later asked to sketch and label what they had seen, they invariably produced "Doctor David" and "Nurse Jane."

Women graduating from high school in the late 1950s and early 1960s understood that there were few options open to them after college other than marriage. Office work, teaching, and nursing were considered the safest bets. It's hard to imagine today that young women's dreams of be-

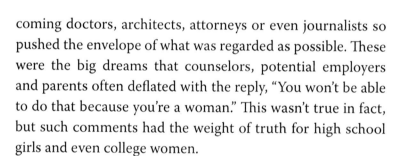

The second year I received a National Institute of Mental Health stipend that paid for my education. I had to do my placement at the state hospital so my husband and son moved up with me. They had this fabulous urban experience.

That same year, my mom lay dying of cancer in my parents' apartment in the same city where I was working. Dad was taking care of her. I got to get my master's degree and be with my mom while she was dying. That was incredible timing. In 1991 I received my Masters of Social Work. I got it all in my forties—marriage, a child, and an education in my chosen field.

coming doctors, architects, attorneys or even journalists so pushed the envelope of what was regarded as possible. These were the big dreams that counselors, potential employers and parents often deflated with the reply, "You won't be able to do that because you're a woman." This wasn't true in fact, but such comments had the weight of truth for high school girls and even college women.

"My parents told me I should be a teacher," recalls Angela Harlan. "They remembered that teachers got paid even during the Depression ....There was a career day at our high school. A friend told me he was going to be a pharmacist. I decided that I wanted to go to the pharmacy part of the career day. My father said, 'You can't do chemistry. That would be way too hard for you.' I told him they also have one on orthodontia. My father said, 'Oh, no, you would have to know a lot of math for that. You couldn't do that.' I told him there is one on being a nurse. He said, 'Ah, you know what nurses do. They have to clean bed pans.' This guy was not helpful."

Sarah Weddington, Attorney who argued and won *Roe v. Wade*

"At McMurry College, a small Methodist liberal arts school in Abilene, I ... followed a traditional route, graduating with secondary-education teaching credentials for English and speech, but I harbored the dream of going to law school. During my senior year, I went to talk about this with the dean, who told me I should not even think of it; his son was in law school and was finding it very difficult. No woman from McMurry had ever gone to law school; it would be too strenuous for me. That was when I decided I was going."

JFK establishes the Commission on the Status of Women with Eleanor Roosevelt as its head

Madeline Lefkowitz, career goals dating from high school

As a teenager I worked on Capitol Hill. One day I told Ted Sorenson, "I'm going to be a labor lawyer." He said, 'Sure. I've heard of women becoming lawyers and I've heard of women going into labor. But, I've never heard of a woman who was a labor lawyer." He thought that was a pretty good joke.

During the 60s, I didn't do much self-actualizing academically and only went to college for a year. Then in the early 1970s, with my kids in school, I went back to the university and got my bachelor's degree. Because I wanted a marketable bachelor's degree, I took library science with a concentration in languages. I was studying Hebrew, Spanish and Russian at the same time.

In 1976 I finally graduated. I found a job as a librarian but I was the lowliest of all librarians because I just had a bachelor's degree. I could be a circulation librarian. I couldn't be a reference librarian or cataloger. I certainly wasn't going to be director of the library. My career was a real dead end without an MLS. I realized it would take as much time to get a master's in

Lucy Ewing translated her experiences at an international high school into thoughts of going into the Foreign Service. But a field trip to Washington, DC, at the end of her junior year changed everything: "We went to the State Department, and I thought this is the career for me. I asked about overseas employment and what kind of education and degrees were needed. This very patronizing man looked at me and said, 'Look, honey, if you want to go overseas you might as well just come on board as a secretary. That's your best shot at getting an overseas tour. We don't hire professionals except men.' That was 1959. I was disappointed and knew I didn't want to be a secretary in the Foreign Service. So, of course, I tell the story that I ended up marrying a Foreign Service officer."

The story of our education is about the way we were advised and constrained and how we came out the other side. Some women followed the path charted for us, but others changed schools and majors along the way. Many rekindled their early dreams a decade or more later or established new goals as their needs and interests became more defined by time and life's myriad experiences.

The greatest transformation of FW2 Generation women is that over time we stopped taking "no" or "you can't" for an answer. We often re-library science as to get the law degree I had wanted since I was a teenager. After two years of being a librarian I took the LSAT and did well. I had kids and a husband, so I chose a local law school. I also decided I had to go full time or not at all.

My husband was tremendously supportive. Not just in the sense of earning a living but when he saw I was really busy, really studying intensively, he would make dinner. He would take the kids here and there and he would take every burden he could off of my shoulders. It was great.

People would say "Why are you back in school again?" I would just say, "Look, I'm going to turn 40 soon and whether I do anything with my life or I don't, I'm still going to be 40. Why shouldn't I do what I always wanted to do?" I got my degree in 1981 when I was 39, pushing 40.

turned to college after our children were born to finish degrees or receive advanced training. And finally, perhaps decades later, we ignored the restrictions on fields we could enter and listened to our own counsel.

As we matured, FW2 women struggled to find identities that were authentically our own, not the identities wished upon us by others. Sometimes it took years of marriage, children and even divorce before we figured it out and went back to school. For many of us, our educational experience was divided into two phases. The first phase, directly out of high school, was more or less dictated to us. In the second phase, which so many FW2 women came around to, we found our own paths.

Education often changed our social status in a way that our mothers and even our fathers never anticipated. America was a more stratified society in the first decades after World War II than it is today. Apart from race, the common rules of precedence were fivefold:

1. Women were subordinate to men;
2. Children were subordinate to parents;
3. Uneducated were subordinate to the educated;
4. Employees were subordinate to employers;
5. Poor were subordinate to the rich.

Margaret Thompson, education lets her move forward

My husband thought that [finishing my undergraduate degree] was the dumbest thing to do. Why did I need a degree when I already had three children? He thought I was just going to stay home and take care of those babies. I did get my degree while caring for our three small children, and then I did stay home. I was a stay-at-home mom for 20 years until he decided he wanted a 40-year-old wife and a 20-year-old girlfriend.

[Margaret saw an ad to become a travel agent and took the training in the period before her divorce became final. She was a travel agent for almost 10 years. Then after a second marriage and divorce 18 months later, when her new husband reverted to his alcoholic drinking, she was ready to do something different.]

I decided I would go back to school. I was trying to figure out what it was I wanted to do so I applied to graduate school to get a master's in social work. I figured it was a pretty eclectic degree. I took the GRE, scored high in math and was accepted. I thought, "Well I guess I'm going to have to go to school now." I was a full-time student for 2 years, received my master's

It was a common experience of FW2 women, in either the first or second phase of their education, to secure a career that paid well and perhaps promoted them to management. Parents were unprepared for the transformation of a daughter into a well-educated, well-paid manager. In working class and lower middle class families, a successful daughter was a status anomaly. She had progressed from the lowest rank in the family to perhaps the highest, especially if she had become a doctor or a lawyer. The parents' quandary was simply that successful sons could be bragged on, while successful daughters had to be explained.

Following the Plan

Going to college usually meant living away from home for the first time, which made college a period for personal growth and increased independence. "I went to Berkeley," says Claire Whitney, "and that was a major change. I had thought about going to San Jose and living at home. Half the benefit of college is to get away from home and to find yourself, meet new people and really expose yourself to life….I did the kind of socialization you need to get in a new group of people and learn to live with other kinds of people…the whole experience of being away from the family, the self-actualization."

1940 1950 1961 1970 1980 1990 2000
Two black students admitted to the University of Georgia, and one is FW2 Charlayne Hunter-Gault

in social work and have worked as a medical social worker ever since. In 1999, my hospital started an MBA program in conjunction with the university. The hospital agreed to pay my tuition. I thought, "I have no life, I might as well do this." I finished that in 2001. Now I have two master's degrees. Everybody keeps asking, "What are you going to get your Ph.D. in?" They all think I should have one.

In the 1940s and 50s, parents rather than peers defined a child's actions. Parental authority was accepted. This was before Madison Avenue discovered teens as a lucrative market and began flattering their attractiveness and maturity. In general, as teenagers we didn't choose our own clothes, didn't spend hours at the mall with friends, and had little economic or social power. Living restricted lives in high school meant that going away to college was a big deal. "I was an only child and I had never been away from home or had roommates," recalls Hannah Prescott. "It was my first experience of being on my own."

For many of us, college was our first exposure to a wide range of personalities, cultures and backgrounds. Even if one's own family had its dysfunctional aspects, they were our own experiences and we considered them "normal." As inexperienced young women living away from home for the first time, every problem that arose was a test. For the most part our transitions from high school to college were easy, if limited. "I began to see myself as being academically successful," says Angela Harlan, "but only in terms of what others thought I should pursue." Carol Lampton really blossomed: "I loved the college experience. Those were happy, exciting years. They were an opportunity to get some validation. In fact, in my junior year

The Bay of Pigs invasion ends in disaster • FW2 Wilma Rudolph sets women's record for 100-meter dash

Statistics of our Educational Journey:
Then and Now

Education opens doors to self-esteem, personal growth, employment opportunities, and economic security. It has taken women a long time to overcome societal and even personal obstacles that prevented FW2 generation women from equal access to this important avenue. How far have we come?

The data on the facing page and the photographs on the following two pages show the extent to which fields of study were sex-segregated in 1964, a year chosen as the mid-point of the years when many FW2 women were graduating from college.

In that year, for example, women were 98% of those receiving bachelor's degrees in Home Economics and just 0.5% of those receiving degrees in Engineering, 88% of the Health Professions (nursing is a large component) degrees and only 1% of Communications degrees.

To show the considerable progress over the decades, I've included comparable data for 2000. For example, while women still dominate Home Economics (88%), they now receive 20% of the Engineering degrees and 61% of the Communications degrees. All the fields once dominated by men now graduate large numbers of women, significantly changing the face of opportunity.

Photograph p. 46: Student National Education Association
Photograph p. 47: Student Engineers Club

Bachelor's Degrees Conferred in 1964 & 2000:
Percent Female within Fields of Study

	1964	2000
Home Economics	98%	88%
Health Professions	88	84
Education	77	76
Foreign Language & Literature	70	71
English Language & Literature	65	68
Visual and Performing Arts	58	59
Psychology	41	76
Public Administration	37	81
Social Sciences and History	33	51
Mathematics	32	47
Biological/Life Sciences	28	58
Multi/Interdisciplinary Studies	26	67
Philosophy & Religion	21	38
Physical Sciences	14	40
Business	8	50
Architecture	4	39
Agriculture	2	43
Communications	1	61
Engineering	0.5	20
Number of Bachelor's Degrees Conferred	195,917 (42%)	707,508 (57%)

I told my parents that I thought I might like to go to graduate school, and they kind of blinked. I enjoyed college so much that I wanted to perpetuate it. At the time, I didn't see any marriage prospects on the horizon." And as JoEllen Brown puts it: "It was very exciting. I had a wonderful time." This was "a time of finding out I could thrive and enjoy college, a lot of self-discovery, finding out what my true interests in life were."

For some FW2 Generation women the experience was marked by considerable difficulty. Problems not necessarily of their own making marred the college years and even caused women to drop out of school. "I lived in the dorm," says Jean Woods. "That was horrible because I had a manic-depressive as a roommate, although then I had no idea what that was. She was just nuts and made my life miserable."

We often didn't know how to access either academic or family resources to get out of a bad situation. "College was a very tough time for me," recalls Frances Judson. "I struggled with my college choice. My father told me, 'You have to make that decision because you're the one who has to live with it.' During my junior year I ran away to a friend's house in New York where I stayed for a while. My parents came back—they'd been off on a trip somewhere—and rescued me, took me

home. They were always understanding about these crises in my life, which was very comforting. They were my safety net. I went to work as a nanny and then went back to the college and finished a year behind my classmates."

Mary Jackson, however, didn't have the love and understanding of parents to see her through: "I was the only child of a divorced mother who had cancer while I was in high school. She was also extremely neurotic and had mental problems. I had wanted to go east and had applied to several women's colleges, but my mother was so ill that I hastily applied to a local coed, private university and turned the others down. The doctors said she could live six months or up to two years. She actually died very quickly.

"So there I was going to a college I didn't want to attend in a town where I didn't want to be. I had terribly mixed feelings about it. I was in a state of shock, and the first year I was very depressed. Those were still the days when cancer was a bad word, and you didn't even talk about breast cancer. Death was still in the closet. I did tell my roommates what had happened to me. They were sympathetic, but then it was like 'okay, get on with it.'"

Annalee Draper, rebels after a year at a woman's college of her mother's choosing

Eventually I rebelled and transferred without telling my parents until two weeks before the new semester. They were against me going to a large coed university. I sprung it on them as a *fait accompli*. I had done all the paperwork because I was afraid of opposition. That was my big rebellion.

After graduating, I took a trip to Jamaica. Life seemed real; totally stimulating. I sat at a beach bar and said to the beach boy and bartender, "I love this place. I want to come and work here. What can I do?" They consulted each other and said, "You can do two things. You can be a nurse or you can teach." I had never considered either. I figured I couldn't be a nurse because I didn't think I would like emptying bedpans. I decided I could be a teacher. I went back to college for a fifth year and got my certification. Then I returned to Jamaica and got a job teaching.

[*After Jamaica, Annalee spent many years in Europe teaching English to European business people while pursuing her art career. Almost 30 years after her initial rebellion, she came home to take care of her mother.*]

Financing College According to the Plan

In the late 1950s and early 1960s, colleges and universities had limited scholarships for women. Legislation for Federal and state loans and grants as well as educational savings plans had yet to be written and passed, with the earliest of these becoming law in 1965. Most of the prestigious scholarships for advanced degrees were open only to men. This meant that the majority of women in this time period were dependent on their families for college tuition. When their families could not afford the expense, they left school or accepted a less expensive alternative. "My younger brother was going to Harvard," explains Suzanne Fielding, "and [my parents said that] it made more sense financially for me to go to a less expensive school. I never questioned what was, I think, more of a financial decision [on the part of my parents] than anything else. I didn't protest it."

Perhaps we would have been more creative in looking for scholarship funds or in figuring out how to combine work and school if marriage hadn't been such a respected alternative. "I was in college for a year after high school," recalls Amelia VanWyck. "But my father came down with tuberculosis and he couldn't afford to continue to send me to college.

I wasn't sure whether I wanted to continue in art or teaching. I called the university with an idea to upgrade my skills for going back to Europe. When I called to get information about a course, I ended up being passed around from one department to another for a whole morning. Finally, I found myself talking on the telephone to a very nice Hispanic woman, and she was dangling this scholarship. She said, "Why don't you apply for this scholarship? I've just gotten a grant." I said, "Who me? I think I'm too old." She said, "How old are you?" I responded, "I'm 51." She said, "So am I, don't let that stop you." She really encouraged me so I went ahead and applied. As it turned out, half the women on scholarship in that program were over 45. I got my degree in 1995.

I worked for a while then married when I was 19. We had been dating since I was 16. I probably always knew we would marry, but we wouldn't have married that early if it hadn't been for my having to drop out of college."

Shaping the Plan

Although parents were the primary influence for most women going to college, high-school boyfriends were also critical factors. "My choice of college was based on the fact that my boyfriend went to the Naval Academy," says Nancy Scott. "I hated that nearby college but I had chosen it because I wanted to be close to him. A lot of my choices were made because I was interested in one man or another."

Soviet Valentina Tereshkova is first woman in space • Travel to Cuba made illegal • Stamps: 5 cents

Ruth Spiro, more education gives her self-esteem

It was a turning point for me, [her brother committed suicide; her father died exactly one year later; several close friends died; two children of close friends died of brain tumors; her marriage was unraveling] and I went to school after that. I happened to get a fabulous professor, and one course turned into four years and a degree in landscape drawing. In the meantime things weren't great between my husband and me. He had been through all this stuff with my commuting to be with my father as he was dying and to help my mother. It was just an angry, angry time; school gave me a place to hide away from the house.

School also gave me some intellectual stimulation when I still had relatively young kids. It touched a creative bone that I didn't know I had. It was an excellent transition. I was still compulsive enough to want to do well, which required time. I was probably pulling away, but I also began to gain some self-esteem. Going to school at night with kids is never easy, but it gave me what I needed at that time. However, not one soul acknowledged my graduation. That's when I really began to stand up and take notice. I graduated in 1981.

As boyfriends turned into husbands, their influence grew. As Roberta Katz explains, "I went to a women's college. When I left I had a boyfriend at home. He gave me a very hard time when I was at school. He didn't want me to go away to school. We had an awful lot of conversations and nasty letters back and forth....I switched back to a university near home, married him at the end of my third year and finished college."

Some women changed their majors after marriage, believing they didn't have to think about a career. "I went to the university, pledged a sorority and was president of the pledge class," explains Virginia Garfield. "Then I met my future husband, and we married after our sophomore year. I would not have married had I not been able to continue school and graduate. When I met him I was going to major in languages and go to the UN to be an interpreter. I was taking Russian and thought it was so cool. Then after I met him I thought, I'll never work so I'll just major in what I like. I changed to political science, history and government."

From the perspective of the 21st century, it's hard to realize how influential men were in the lives of women in college in the early 1960s. We had not been encouraged to think of ourselves as independent beings and so looked to the men in our lives for clues about what to do next.

Martin Luther King, Jr. Civil Rights March, Washington, DC

"I had wanted to be a psychiatrist," recalls Cynthia Fletcher. "I was moderately serious about it but as soon as I met my first husband, I switched to English because he was in English. I would do this several times in my life: have a gentleman, get wildly interested in whatever he was interested in and change my major."

Dropping Out of the Plan

Women dropped out of college for many reasons. When they did, it was considered acceptable by their peers, their parents and society in general. The rule that "You have to be twice as good as a man to get the same job" was daunting. With few professional opportunities open to them, many women concluded that marriage and staying home with children was about as good as it was going to get. If the marriage took place before the college degree was earned, there was little pressure to continue. A common joke was that you had an MRS degree. For those who worked to put their husbands through undergraduate or graduate education, the joke became that you had a PHT degree. As Lois Cameron tells us: "I went to the university for a year and a half to get a secretarial degree. I planned to

Martin Luther King arrested in Birmingham protest march • Congress passes the Equal Pay Act

Deanna Greenlaw, a greater sense of service

A series of events woke me up—the Bay of Pigs, the Kennedy assassination, the Cold War. It seemed that the whole world was going crazy. I was frightened. I thought we were going to have a nuclear war off the coast of Florida. It seemed like in the next heartbeat Kennedy was shot. TV gives great tragedy, and that event was our collective first experience of seeing something so fearful and so awful over and over again. It profoundly affected me. It woke me up to the larger world.

I took English in college and I was not happy. After Kennedy was shot I said, "I don't want to do this anymore. There is something out there to which I know I can contribute." I became involved in the student peace union. That's when I decided I could go into a joint major of sociology and psychology. I ended up graduating without knowing exactly what I wanted to do, but I was imbued with some greater sense of service that I had to give if I wanted to remake America in the way that I believed it should be or that I remembered my childhood as being.

finish the second year, but my boyfriend and I decided we were going to get married. My father basically said, 'I can either pay for college or for a wedding but I can't do both.' That was very hard for me. I was sad to leave school. I didn't let on to my parents that it hurt, but it did."

Lyndon B. Johnson, swearing in as President, Air Force One

Rekindling our Dreams

As the years passed, the dream to finish the degree grew stronger for many women. We didn't have many role models for going back to school. Our mothers had stayed home even after the children went off to college. Yet many FW2 Generation women did go back to school, some not graduating until the 1980s and 1990s. "In 1982, with the boys both in college," says Lucy Ewing, "I decided to enroll in college and finally finish

The Kennedy assassination was a clarion call that America was not living up to its dream. I don't mean that just in the Jeffersonian sense, although the call of Jeffersonian democracy has always been very much a part of my makeup. I mean the myth of the nuclear family, the

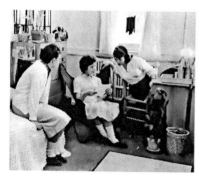

good life, the 1950s dream that we were all raised on. I felt if we don't as individuals make a difference and are not willing to stand up for what we believe in, then we deserve the worst. For me it was a wake up call, and it's guided my life ever since. It wasn't that I was trying to dismantle America or that it was evil. It was more that I was trying to remake it, at least in those early days, into some kind of idealized dream. I felt a vision, a hope and belief in something greater than ourselves.

the degree that I'd started 20 years earlier. I finished in 1984 with a degree in political science. I love politics and history as well as philosophy. I liked studying the political philosophers so it ended up being fun. I did very well and got into the honor society."

Although Amelia VanWyck had quit college when her father became ill, she went back while her children were young. "I went to school, in part, because I wanted to talk to an adult. I was always afraid my mind was going to stagnate if I was here with the kids all the time. My husband was gone a lot so school gave me balance. Over the years I had taken a lot of whatever I found interesting. We finally moved to a town that had a four-year college. I pulled all of my hours together and had a major in business and a minor in economics and accounting. I got my degree just before I was 40."

While some women just wanted to finish the degree, others dreamed of advanced degrees, professions, new careers, better

Kennedy family leaves Capitol after funeral ceremony

Governor George Wallace says, "Segregation now, segregation tomorrow, segregation forever"

Vickie Baker, reminds us what we were required to overcome

I remember talking with my English history professor about a Marshall Fellowship and being told, "Don't you realize that the Marshall Fellowships, just like the Rhodes Scholarships, are for men only?"

I got into law school, but unbeknownst to me it had a quota of three women a year. We used to meet in the only women's restroom in the building. It had a tiny lounge, and of us could meet at the same time. Being a woman in law school at the time was a lonely and isolated experience.

In 1968 after student deferments were pulled, we thought more women would find a place in the incoming class. But again there were only three women. All of this experience was leading up to me having my eyes swept back and realizing what the world was doing to women and what a bum deal we were getting all the way around. It didn't take very long for me to become a pretty staunch feminist.

At my law school women received 25 percent less scholarship money than our male counterparts. Even with a straight 4.0 GPA, a male student received 100 percent scholarship,

skills and personal change. The road to these goals was often bumpy, circuitous and complicated. Responsibilities to husbands and children often meant that we were multitasking before anyone even used the term. Although some husbands were supportive, many women pursued their education with no help from their husbands and sometimes in spite of active opposition. We had no expectations of equality in those marriages so even small amounts of assistance from husbands were appreciated.

Joan Baez, Civil Rights March, Washington, DC

While some women knew what they wanted to do and were eventually able to get the requisite education, other women moved beyond their early goals. These women found new passions or new needs in their lives and used education as a way to reach these goals.

37 neighbors in Queens, NY witness Kitty Genovese's murder from their apartments and fail to help

but a woman only got 75 percent. A classmate who couldn't come up with the 25 percent tuition she owed at the end of her last year went to the assistant dean and threatened to cry and throw herself on the floor if he didn't forgive what she owed. She was a 4.0 student and on the law review. "Oh, my God," he said, "don't do that! I'll tell the registrar to take care of it." She suggested I try the same tactic, but I told her I was too proud to resort to "feminine wiles." I ended up paying, even though I was Order of the Coif, 6th in my class, pregnant and desperately in need of financial assistance since my husband was only making $85 a week. At the time I thought I was lucky to be among the chosen few and accepted the idea that a woman was worth only 75 percent of a man! Wow, where were our heads?

Shaped by the Times

During the interviews, I asked each woman to tell about her life, not about what was going on in the outside world. However, the early 1960s had been a time of so much political and social upheaval that most women felt they could not tell their own stories without at least mentioning the times that helped shape their lives.

Among the many changes stands one event—the assassination of John F. Kennedy—that is so singular as to be forever etched in our minds. We can never forget the details of where we were (I was in my apartment in Cambridge, Massachusetts), what we were doing (I was preparing parmesan fried chicken for a picnic before the Harvard-Yale football game the next day), how we heard about it (I turned on television several hours after the shooting), who we first talked with about it (I walked across the hall to ask my neighbor if she had heard the news, which of course she had), how we spent the rest of that day (in front of the television) and the following day (had the picnic at a nearby park with friends while we discussed how only the day before we had been so excited about Kennedy's scheduled appearance at the football game and now the sadness at his death), how we saw Jack Ruby shoot Lee Harvey Oswald as he was

Congress passes Civil Rights Act • National Conference of State Commissions on the Status of Women

Marjorie Appleby, always responsible for her younger sisters during the long years of her mother's illness

I was living in New York City and was excited to have been accepted to continue my education in a college there. Then my father called about one more move in a lifetime of moves. This time to Missouri. He said, "I really need you with us. I'll pay your way if you will come." This meant I had to apply to a university near our new home. My father said, "You need to be a teacher. You had better enroll in education." But on my way to the post office to mail my application, I thought to myself, "I don't want to be a teacher." That's not what interested me when I was in school. I went back to my apartment, opened up the envelope and changed my major to biology. I had had only one biology course but I liked it. I ended up taking 36 hours of biology and 18 hours of chemistry and physics, which surprised my dad. That was my major independent move.

[Years later, Marjorie and her family hosted an American Field Service high-school student. He became like a family member, and they were sad when he left. Marjorie told him they would visit the following summer.]

being transferred to a more secure prison (eating lunch in front of the television set, which most of us watched continuously for many days).

The political and social upheaval of the times changed many "sweet young things" into knowledgeable, politically active adults who cared about their country, wanted to make it a better place and were deeply shocked by the assassinations and civil-rights abuses. "I went to Mississippi for civil rights," says Jessica Kleinman. "I was in Mississippi in the summer of `63 helping put together a civil-rights newsletter. I arrived about three days after Medgar Evers was shot. I went there because I wanted to be involved but I don't think I appreciated the danger I was in. I was also in the march on Washington. I was pretty actively involved."

While political and social events were changing the lives of many women, the accepted conventions of the early 1960s had an equally important impact on many women of the FW2 Generation, including Valerie Bradford: "I went to junior college one year," she says, "and did not have anything specifically in mind except being a nurse. Then I went to surgical training at a nearby hospital. After that I worked a few months in surgery before starting LPN training. I thought about becoming an RN but, at that time, you could not get married during your RN training.

In preparation I decided to take some Spanish so that at least I could do a few things with his mother. When we went to Costa Rica, I could get along crudely. I also got hooked. By 1988 I was going to school full time. Finally the department decided I had taken all the courses necessary for a Spanish major so they admitted me to a master's degree program.

I got my master's in 1990 and was pulled into teaching. That's when I discovered what I really am—a teacher. I started teaching college classes. In 1992 I got my education specialist certification. I wanted to get a Ph.D., but I couldn't get it locally so I began commuting to a school 4½ hours from home. In 1995 I got my Ph.D. In ten years, I went from zero Spanish to my Ph.D. in Spanish language acquisition.

I certainly wanted to get married and have a family. So I went into LPN training, did very well, met and married my husband."

That's just the way it was. Restrictive rules had to be accepted or challenged. When we chose to challenge them, we usually won but at a high personal cost. In fact, a woman's personal cost in braving the higher education system was always higher than a man's. In addition to put-downs that were all the more disconcerting because they seemed gratuitous (why bother to demean another human being?), we had to ex-pect personal questions from educators and employers that could not be asked today. "When I applied to medical school," explains Katherine Campbell, "the surgeon who interviewed me said, 'Are you going to have children?' I said,

President Lyndon B. Johnson meets with Martin Luther King, Jr., Whitney Young and James Farmer.

'No, I'm not planning to.' He said, 'Well, what are you going to do about it?' I had just had a tubal ligation and I told him that. They would never ask a question like that now."

Slowly we came to reexamine the laws, rules and traditions that we had grown up with. We quietly rejected many of them, each of us in her own time. Each person has her own breaking point or moment of revelation. We started college accepting a world of contradictions and limitations. By the time we collectively finished, more than just our minds had changed. Our immediate worlds had changed us, and henceforth we would be changing them.

Someday My Prince Will Come:
The FW2 Generation Marries

Sounds of Wedding Bells Rang in Our Heads

In the late 1950s and early 1960s, FW2 Generation women imagined almost exclusively a future in which they would marry, have children and live happily ever after. While this seems like an oversimplification, it is the scenario mentioned by virtually every woman I interviewed. When asked to reflect on their goals and dreams at the time they graduated from high school, typical responses included:

- "Of course, I knew I'd go to college. But I didn't see getting a college degree as a way of helping my career. I didn't imagine I would ever have one. I wanted to get married."
- "I wanted to go to college, have a pretty wedding and have babies."
- After college, I wanted to get married. No woman in my family had ever worked."
- "I think I was like everyone else. I planned to go to college, marry, raise a family, do community work and have dinner ready when my husband came home."
- "I thought I'd work for a while after college, fall in love, get married, have children and live happily ever after."

Cynthia Fletcher, looking for Mr. Right

After two and a half years of college, I married a man I had met my freshman year. He was five years older and had a Ph.D. in history. We had a fancy wedding and I got pregnant right away. I had two children by the time I was 21. When I started college, I wanted to be a lawyer. As soon as I met my husband, I switched to History, his field. When I married, I quit school but went back once my children were in nursery school.

The '70s were a tumultuous decade. Since my husband was a professor, we were able to take several graduate students on a wonderful field trip to Europe. One of the students was getting his Ph.D. in journalism. He was eight years older than I. We fell in love and I took the two children and ran off to be with him. When I ran off, it was the first time I had ever driven by myself anywhere. It was just wild. It was the middle of winter and I didn't stop for a hotel because I had never checked into a hotel by myself. I just kept going in my little Beetle. To be brief, I got a divorce and married Thomas. I started taking some journalism classes and completed my degree.

"Love and marriage / Go together like a horse and carriage"

The FW2 Generation listened to Dinah Shore and Frank Sinatra sing these lyrics in the mid-1950s. It all seemed so simple. We married younger than women do today. Census data shows that in 1960, on the average, women first married when they were 20. By 2000, the age at which women first married had increased to 25. As a result, we were more naïve at each stage of courtship and marriage than women are today. Many of us had dated little so we didn't have much basis of experience from which to make a good marriage decision. Mostly we were virgins. We certainly had not lived with a man before marriage; to do so would have created a scandal. We married before we had become our own persons.

I was one of those with a long list of life goals, and I got started on many of the items right after high school. I began college and continued that experience after marrying my high-school sweetheart between my sophomore and junior years. Then I had my first child and still went to college, even getting my master's degree without taking any time off. I remember one October morning walking from the Kenmore "T" station, along Commonwealth Avenue, to the Boston University campus. The air

Actually I can't be too brief because I need to add that I divorced Thomas, and then remarried him again. He was my second and third husband. I married him again because I didn't like being on my own. Thomas really was very sweet and probably knew it was a bad idea but went along with it anyway.

About that time, I started working part-time in the public library. They pay practically nothing. But working in a public library in a college town is probably the nicest thing going. [*continued*]

was as crisp and sweet as the bite of a fresh-picked apple; the first red and yellow leaves of fall were strewn on the sidewalk and crunched beneath my feet. I rejoiced, thinking, "I'm so lucky. I'm married; I have a beautiful baby; I'm in this exciting and challenging communication program." I was only 20 years old when I married but thought I was a discerning and sage individual. What did I know? In the `60s, we all thought that we wouldn't change much once we were adults. We had no idea how much we would grow or in what directions.

Father Knows Best

The FW2 Generation had a shared vision of our adult selves based partly on our parents' lives and partly on images from books, movies, and television that influenced us in the 1940s and 1950s. In grade school, most of us learned to read with the Dick and Jane textbook series where we also learned that mothers stay home and bake cookies while fathers go off to work. By the time we tuned in to television, we watched *The Adventures of Ozzie and Harriet* that premiered in 1952, *Father Knows Best* that began in 1954 and *Leave It to Beaver* that started

Loni Anderson,
Actor

When Loni was young and talking about her dream to be an actress with a big home, her mother said, "When you grow up, you'll probably live like Bea [their neighbor]. You'll have a nice little house like this one, and you'll be lucky if you have a really nice husband like hers, or a nice man like Daddy."

Cynthia Fletcher's story concludes, finding Mr. Right and herself

"I met Arthur, my fourth husband, in the library. At the time, I was married to Thomas and Arthur was married. The beginning of the 1980s was marked by turmoil. Arthur is 14 years older and is a lawyer. I divorced Thomas again and Arthur divorced his wife. A lot of what happened I've repressed because there were bad scenes. I don't want to sound flippant about this but there was a lot of pain and grief all the way around. But you get through it. To get through it, I became a legal aide. I went back to school because that's what I always do. I go to school very well. I found it fascinating to study a field I was interested in when I first went to college. After we got married, I worked in Arthur's office, ever so briefly. Mostly I was a receptionist, so I never used my legal aide degree. But schooling gave me the vocabulary.

Arthur is even more strong-minded than I am so it's working out very well. He gives me the opportunity and the great encouragement to do things that I have never done before. We even ski and play tennis. These are things that I had never thought I could do or would do.

in 1957. These shows all presented an idealized sameness in which mothers stayed home, fathers worked and children were clean-cut and well-mannered.

Harriet Nelson, Margaret Anderson and June Cleaver were traditional homemakers. Episodes that took them away from that environment usually portrayed them as incompetent and ill-equipped for the larger world, but completely comfortable cleaning the house in dresses, high heels and a string of pearls. Only now can I see why I didn't think it unusual to do the same thing. Only I vacuumed after a day at work, hence my dress, high heels and pearls.

In one episode of *The Honeymooners*, another show from the 1950s, Ralph Kramden had been notified that he was losing his job as a driver for the Gotham Bus Company. When his wife Alice suggests that she could go to work, he says: "I've got my pride. Before I'd let you go to work, I'd rather see you starve." That's a funny line, but it isn't hard to see why so many FW2 Generation women assumed their future was as a wife and mother.

David Halberstam wrote in his book *The Fifties* that "family sitcoms reflected—and reinforced—much of the social conformity of the period.

First American astronaut walks in space • President Johnson outlines his plan for the "Great Society"

My children and marrying Arthur are definitely the two best things in my life. When I was married to husbands in the university, they were always wrapped up in their careers. University life and university politics took all their time. I don't have that with Arthur because he was already established in his career."

Joan Baez,
Folk singer, non-violence activist

After her wedding ceremony, Joan says, "I drank champagne, glued myself to David's side between chatting with relatives, and twisted the new gold band around the third finger of my left hand thinking what fun it was to have a new name. The concept of keeping one's name, not to mention identity, was not yet born in me. But the idea of becoming a wife, and, hopefully, a mother, was thrilling. I was going to be Joan Harris, and David and I were going to have bushels of babies and save the world at the same time."

There was no divorce. There was no serious sickness...Families *liked* each other, and they tolerated each other's idiosyncrasies.... Ward Cleaver once asked June, 'What type of girl would you have Wally marry?' 'Oh,' answered June. 'Some very sensible girl from a nice family...one with both feet on the ground, who's a good cook, and can keep a nice house, and see that he's happy.'" June Cleaver's response sounds like the starting point for the marriages of FW2 Generation women. But because of historical forces and our unwillingness to tolerate a variety of unsatisfactory marriages that our mothers had endured, we were actually in the vanguard of the redefinition of marriage from the mid-1960s onward.

The Watts riot leads to 34 deaths, 1,000 injuries and 4,000 arrests • Nat "King" Cole dies • Lava lamps first sold

Natalie Tannenbaum, still haunted

I went off to San Francisco the summer between my junior and senior year to connect with the culture of my times. There was a group of us and I smoked dope for the first time. I got a ride back to college with a guy who was going through the LSD experiment at Stanford. I didn't know him very well, but he was part of the group of people that I knew. He was tired and wanted to spend the night on the way. I was totally innocent, totally stupid, went ahead, got into a motel, and curled up on my side of the bed. He raped me. I was a virgin. I had really been holding on to my virginity. That was just the worst thing that ever happened.

We got up in the morning and finished the drive to college. Girlfriends supported me but there was a lot of shame and confusion. I tried to bury that experience but it has haunted me.

Years later, I met my future husband at the child welfare office where I was working. Jim was getting his master's degree and was supporting himself and his family as a caseworker. He was going through a divorce with his childhood sweetheart. They had a shotgun marriage

The Marriage Road

Naïve Drivers. When it was time to get on the marriage road, the FW2 Generation didn't have a license and didn't have an accurate map of where we were going. Charlyne Tucker says, "I struggled in college and did not have much self-confidence when trying to plan my life. Dating did not take much of my time. When I moved to an apartment in 1965, I met many singles, mostly with a whole lot more experience than I had. One guy invited me to dinner and, before we left the restaurant, asked if I would move in with him. Needless to say I was shocked. I made up some excuse, and he took me home right away. Naïve does not come close to describing me."

We may have been naïve, but that didn't stop us from getting married. Ann Baxter recalls those early years: "My marriage just wasn't right from the start. Both of us were way too naïve to have gotten married at the time we did. We just didn't have a clue. I feel that my upbringing was very sheltered and promoted naïveté. I was never encouraged to develop myself, to ask questions about things or to understand the world. When I left high school, and even college, I was just going forward totally blind. I had no idea what I was doing." In so many interviews, these words came spilling out: *We married too young. We were both immature and naïve*

Rolling Stones hit *I Can't Get No Satisfaction* changes pop lyrics toward overt sexual references

and had unsuccessfully tried to make it work. Jim was too raw from his divorce and I was too needy and unresolved in my own self. So I left. Jim and I stayed in touch but I needed to become more grounded. I went into therapy and came together as a woman, as a person. I took a job and was good at it.

Years later, Jim and I reconnected and married. One horrible piece still haunts me. I think the combination of my parents' Viennese morality giving me the impression that sex is a terrible thing and that rape has, to this day, kept me out of touch with my own pleasure, my own sexuality.

and would have made a better brother and sister than husband and wife. We were just kids. We weren't old enough. I didn't know how to be married and I didn't know how to have a family.

Unexpected Hazards on the Road. Naïveté may have contributed to the difficult transition from dating to finding the right marriage partner. But sometimes males created impossible situations that left women traumatized.

Several women mentioned date rape, a term that didn't exist at the time and wouldn't be used until 1981. Back in the 1960s, we blamed ourselves for whatever went wrong. We thought that if everything went right it was because the man was a gentleman. If something went wrong, it was our fault. "For years I blamed myself for the date rape," Diane Boxwood explains. "That was my first

Canda Mitans, life shaped by an early decision

I discovered I was pregnant when I returned to college in the fall. We had met that summer and dated for about three months. I called Larry and he told my parents the news. I was rushed back very quickly, met at the airport by my parents and my husband-to-be, and whisked off to be married. It was all very hush-hush. I had to tell everyone that we were secretly married during the summer. For years and years I adhered to that. I never told anyone. I look back now and think that never grew from me. It was what my parents wanted. I've realized in later years that I was never given a choice and it never occurred to me to ask for a choice. The decision was "you'll get married and you'll have this child," and that's what I did. It might not have been the best thing all the way around, but it wasn't ever considered that there were other options. I moved straight from my parents' home to my husband's home. I had no chance to become my own person.

My husband was an alcoholic. Towards the end, he even became physically abusive. It was hard living with an alcoholic, with a person who considered me an idiot and just missed no

Cokie Roberts,
Senior news analysis for NPR and political commentator for ABC News

I decided I was wasting the best years of my life. I was 22 and I was about to be an old maid! Steven began to get a sense of how fed up I was one day when we stopped at a rest stop on the Jersey Turnpike and decided to share a Danish pastry. I was raised to believe a woman always gave a man the best piece of everything, and Steven was raised to expect that. That day, when I ate the center out of the Danish and left him the crust, he knew I was truly ticked.

experience with sex. It hurt like hell. I didn't tell anyone, not a single soul. For years I thought that it was my fault. My parents would have been absolutely devastated had I told them. I wasn't dating much at all. I was very shy."

On-Ramps to the Marriage Highway. "If you didn't get married by the time you were 24, you were an old maid." No one wanted that outcome and FW2 women married for at least six key reasons:

- We fell in love;
- We wanted to please our parents;
- We wanted to get away from a dysfunctional birth family;
- We thought it was the right time;
- We didn't know what else we could do; or, in some cases,
- We were pregnant.

Most of us went directly from our parents' home to our husband's home. It was rare that we lived on our own. It was as if we were born with a sell-by date. If we stayed on the shelf

opportunity to pound that in. Even though we saw my parents quite a bit, I was really guarded with them about the problems that I had in my marriage. I always felt that I had gotten myself into this scrape and I really didn't want to involve anyone else.

I didn't have many resources as far as gathering strength or getting any kind of good input from anyone so I really had no positive feelings about myself. I certainly stayed in that relationship a lot longer than I should have because I just didn't have any confidence about leaving. Towards the end of those nine years, I told him I was leaving. At that point, he agreed to go to a marriage counselor, which was something I had asked him to do for years. After twelve months of counseling, I finally had the strength to know myself well enough to know that I could go. I also realized that I could manage on my own. I wasn't sure how but it was the beginning of my getting to know who I was. [*continued*]

too long, we might never be bought. The sooner we married the better. If we didn't marry by the end of college, we had to figure out how to support ourselves while accomplishing the "Get Married" item at the top of our to-do list.

Falling in love. Dating problems did not deter most women from the goal of marriage. Once we found love, we happily married. JoEllen Brown, like many women, dated little, fell in love and quickly married. "In college," she recalls, "I met and ultimately married the only person that I had actually dated. He was my first love." Many of us thought that was the way love and marriage worked.

Pleasing our parents. Of course, it wasn't always as simple as falling in love. Marriage might have been the result of finding one's soul mate. However, it sometimes involved finding the person who would meet with your parents' approval. Dee Johnson found herself in a situation that other women echoed: "In 1965 I met my husband through my aunt. We went out a couple times before I went to Europe and then dated again when I got back. I married him even though I don't think I was in love with him. My mother and stepfather thought he was wonderful."

Cokie Roberts

To succeed as a young woman meant finding the right guy. Marriage became very, very important because that was pretty much it. That was your goal in life. The man you married not only determined your well-being and sense of happiness, he also determined your status.

Birth-control activist Margaret Sanger dies • "Credibility gap" is a new phrase • Nat'l debt: $329 billion

Canda Mitans' story concludes, finds light at the end of the dark tunnel

Then I did it again. In the nine years that I was single I made such great strides. I was proud of the life that I had made, proud of myself. I was really becoming a person I liked. Then I met this guy and we ended up getting married. He was an alcoholic and abusive. I lost all the ground I had gained. I went all the way back to being under someone's thumb again and not able to think for myself. I still don't really understand how that could happen to me, but it did. That went on for five years until I divorced him.

I've been in a loving and mutually supportive relationship for 15 years now. I was hesitant to remarry and so lived with him for seven years before making the commitment. I kept thinking, "A third marriage? Why would I want to do that?" We were both going to a counselor who kept asking why we didn't marry. Finally, she told us to make two lists, one with all the reasons *to* marry and the other with all the reasons *to not* marry. We realized we had some old ideas that weren't valid and we married. You see, he is 12 years younger than I am. We're a really good fit. We work through our problems. He's willing to look at his problems, my problems, our

Priscilla Presley, Actor and business executive

Presley recalls one afternoon in February of 1967 when she and Elvis were engaged. They drove by a beautiful ranch that was for sale. She says, "This was my perfect dream house. I fell in love with it and began to picture Elvis and me living there alone. It was small enough for me to handle myself. I could clean it and take care of Elvis, bringing him his breakfast in bed."

Escaping from home. Even now, we maintain the myth that everyone in the `40s and `50s had wonderful childhoods. After all television showed happy families. Most of us had stay-at-home moms, so we should have been well cared for and well loved. But there were many dysfunctional families, just as now, and they had a big impact on our lives. Marriage was often the most feasible escape. Sandra Ray married even before finishing high school: "I married my childhood sweetheart six weeks before I graduated. He had graduated three years earlier. My family life was terrible. My alcoholic stepfather was the major reason."

Rosemarie Brack got pregnant and then married to remove herself from a difficult family. Forty years later, she looks back and recalls: "My mother was bi-polar, and my father was an alcoholic. My mother was driving me nuts. I believe the primary reason I got pregnant was to get out from under her. I just thought that would be the easy way out. You're not smart enough at that age."

problems. And I'm willing to do the same. We're not afraid to talk about them and examine them. We work really well together."

Robert F. Kennedy & President Lyndon B. Johnson

Timing is right. The fourth reason women married was because it was time. Martha Corelli made up her mind to get married even before she was dating anyone simply because she wanted to marry at the same age her mother married. "I told everybody that I was going to get married in June of 1965," she says. "This was before I had even met my future husband. There was someone at work, and I just decided I was going to marry him. One day I kind of kidnapped him and that was the beginning of our courtship....my dream since I was a little girl was to get married and live happily ever after like some fairy tale." Dee Johnson, on the other hand, was tired of always being the bridesmaid and never the bride. "Why did I get married? It was just time. I was 23 and had been a bridesmaid many times."

Lacking alternatives. While marriage was a positive goal for many women, some married because they didn't know what else to do. With mothers who stayed home, few role models of working women, limited career opportunities and professors who discouraged women from graduate study, it is hardly surprising that some women married not so much from the desire to wed but from the lack of an alternative vision. Jessica Kleinman recalls that period well: "At the end of my senior year,

Cheryl Norton, a parallel life

My husband had the mindset that the man went out and worked and did what he had to do. It was two parallel worlds - very much "woman's work" and "man's work." I did all the family stuff on my own. I marvel today at the families where men are changing diapers and washing babies. That never happened in my life. In fact, the funniest picture we have is when my mother was visiting and we went out shopping and left the baby with my husband. We came back and my husband is sound asleep. The baby was just a couple of months old. My husband is sound asleep on the sofa and the baby is just lying on his stomach.

I met my husband at the job where I was working the summer between my junior and senior year of college.

I got engaged and actually did get married. I was still quite a teenager because I would want to break up with him, and he wouldn't want to break up. Then he would want to break up, and I wouldn't. Honestly, I got married at the end of that fourth year of college because I didn't know what else to do. I didn't have a clue."

Necessitating reason. Pregnancy was the reason to marry that trumped all others. We might otherwise have waited for the right man to come along. We might have postponed a wedding. We might have broken an engagement. In fact, a close college friend confided to me her decision to not marry just as guests were arriving for her fifth wedding shower. She was a drama major and carried out the role of the day, oohing and aahing over each present. Then 24 hours later, she returned the gifts.

For most of us married in the pre-*Roe v. Wade* days, if we got pregnant and an illegal abortion was not possible or even considered, we immediately married. Raising a child born "out of wedlock" (as we used to say) was not considered acceptable. We knew such an act would disgrace both our parents and ourselves, and we assumed that our child would be disgraced as well. In truth, raising a child on our own would have been

We married that September and then I finished my degree the following year. For the rest of the '60s, I was like most newlyweds, trying to make a marriage work and learning how to live with somebody else. I worked to provide the secondary income in the family until I got pregnant. I did everything very much on schedule according to the acceptable standards for that time.

The only thing that was different was that two years after we married, when I was pregnant, we moved to Evanston, away from our families. Even then I realized I was the first person in our family, of all my siblings and cousins, everyone, that ever left the family group. It was pretty hard. I was lucky that it was only a two-hour car ride, but it was hard moving to a city where you didn't know anybody. I quit work when I had the first baby. Then I had another baby two years later. By the end of that decade, I had acclimated to living in a new city and had met people, other women with babies, who lived around me. [*continued*]

difficult in the early 1960s when there were few job opportunities for women and limited childcare options.

Wealthy families might send a pregnant daughter to a second home or even to Europe. While that seems extreme, there were many middle-class families who wanted to protect their social standing in the community and were willing to spend money to send a daughter to a home for unwed mothers where she would give birth and then put the infant up for adoption. The story line was that the daughter was away at school or helping to take care of a sick aunt or grandmother.

When I gave birth to my second child, my hospital roommate was "an unwed mother." The baby was never brought to her, which was my first clue. I quickly figured out that I could talk with her about a lot of things, but I wouldn't mention my baby or her baby. Evanston, Illinois, where I was living at the time, had a well-known home for unwed mothers called The Cradle. My roommate's parents were from out of state. When they visited her, they also never mentioned the baby. At one point, a woman came by with the adoption papers for her to sign. They pulled the drape around her bed, and I was glad she had privacy at a moment that would alter her life in a major way. Yet young women at that time were told to "forget it."

Jacqueline Suzann's *Valley of the Dolls* becomes a bestseller • National Organization for Women organized

Cheryl Norton's story continues, the expected life

My husband said he was 100 percent for me going back to school in the 1970s. But he would not give me any help as far as childcare or anything. I had to get babysitters. I had to plan my schedule around how I could arrange things. I even did a project rather than a thesis because the thesis required a lot of library work but I could do a project from my house. But I did it and I loved it. I got my master's degree in library science. I did that completely on my own with no help from my husband whatsoever.

I never used that degree, but I did it. I did some part-time work every once in a while and some volunteer work. I was active in the community. Much of the volunteer work I did involved writing newsletters for organization and eventually I was offered a paying job doing the newsletter for the Jewish Community Center. That was really neat.

Then it seems that all of a sudden we're retired and living in Florida. My husband bought my parents a condo down here a few years ago. Then we started looking around and bought a home for ourselves. My husband is semi-retired, still working a little bit. I've been living the

Of course, you can't. Or you can't forget forever. Thanks to the Internet, many of these women are now reconnecting with a daughter or son, and a surprising number are reconnecting with the women they knew during their months at "the home." Although the experience in many homes was as good as was possible, in others the young women were not allowed to use their own names or were only allowed out of their rooms at night.

Ann-Margret entertains troops in Vietnam

Back to Love and Marriage

Stephanie Coontz, an FW2 Generation woman, is the director of research and public education at the Council on Contemporary Families as well as a history and family studies professor at Evergreen State College in Olympia, Washington. In her recent book, *Marriage, A History: From*

Miranda Rights become law as a result of Supreme Court decision in Miranda v. Arizona

life of an active retiree.

Looking back, my husband has never really objected to whatever I wanted to do. For example, when my Mother was alive, I might decide to go spend the day with her and then stay on for dinner. He never objected. Later I moved her closer to us. He never ever objected to anything I wanted to do. But did he ever help or do anything? No. I see men who help a lot and I also see men who object a lot, so I guess I was lucky.

Deep down inside I really wanted something more fulfilling. Deep down inside I always thought it would be great to be an attorney or to be in international politics. I was never able to fulfill that. I never had the opportunity. I just followed the life that was expected of me. Not that I'm unhappy about it, but if I had been born ten years later I probably would have done something else. [*continued*]

Obedience to Intimacy, or How Love Conquered Marriage, she discusses the historical reasons for marriage and describes how women who didn't work had no real option other than to marry and to stay married. "Marriage," she writes, "was a lot more stable when women had to give in to everything their husbands wanted. But it was also less satisfying, not just for women but for many men who never quite understood why their wives were so unhappy or withdrawn."

She continues, "As late as the 1970s, many American states retained 'head and master' laws, giving the husband final say over where the family lived and other household decisions. According to the legal definition of marriage, the man was required to support the family, while the woman was obligated to keep house, nurture children, and provide sex."

Coontz's examination of marriage in the past, along with Cathleen Rountree's research on successful marriages in the present, provides insight about the world in which the FW2 Generation began their first marriages and the evolution of intimate relationships. In *The Heart of Marriage*, Rountree seeks to understand what makes some marriages not only work but flourish with the result that both partners are enhanced rather than diminished. During Rountree's interview

Mao's *Little Red Book* is translated into English • Popular words: Swinger, jumbo jet and body count

Cheryl Norton's story concludes, surviving a marriage is an accomplishment

In the beginning when I was thinking about your questions I thought I really didn't accomplish anything in my life but after really, really thinking about it I decided I did. I raised two great kids. The other thing is that we survived a marriage, which I think is pretty damn good too. Obviously we've had our ups and downs just like anybody else but we stuck through it. A funny thing happened recently. Not long after my son married, he and his wife had a big fight. She called me and said they're having this fight and that my son told her that he never heard his mother and father raise their voices to each other. I cracked up. I don't know what house he was living in. But obviously that's how our kids see us. So I guess we did a good job of convincing them everything was wonderful.

There were six of us that hung out together starting in college. I'm the only one that's married to the same person after 40 years, which I think is very interesting. They all have been through divorces and some have been married two or more times. Two have never remarried. So staying together is an accomplishment.

with one young couple, Janmarie describes her view of the changing landscape of love within her marriage when she recalls thinking, "Now this is love; this is it. Now I finally know what love is. What was I feeling before? That was just puppy love; it was fun but this is the real thing." She's right. In many marriages love does mature and get better. Some couples find this to be true in their first and only marriage. For others, it becomes the joy of a later marriage. My partner and I talk about this. Often on this plateau of happy marriage, challenging work, and time with family and friends we suddenly realize that our love has grown again in some way. The sixth sense of a long-married couple. We look in each other's eyes, smile, and nod hello to the new relationship.

Janmarie, later in the same interview says, "People marry so that someone else will take care of them. That's dangerous. There's a me and there's a him and there's something higher, which is us, that is not maintained unless I stay me and he stays him." Women in the FW2 Generation could not have imagined making that statement, at least not in their early years of marriage. Maintaining a separate self after marriage would have been as alien as keeping our birth names (which

was to come later). We were barely individuals before we married. We welcomed rather than avoided the assimilation of our identity into our husband's identity. After all, fathers "gave away" daughters to husbands at their weddings. We were brought up to believe that husbands would take care of us.

The Old Love and Marriage versus the New Love and Marriage. In many households formed in the `60s, wives acceded to their husbands' requests. Most of our households were supported by husbands' salaries, which in itself conferred greater authority on their wishes. This is not to say that we were Victorian women with no legal rights and little education, married solely for economic and social reasons. FW2 women had input into decisions, but men had the final say. For example, when my first husband was considering job offers as he completed his MBA, I was on an extended trip with my parents. He wrote to me and described each offer. I responded with my assessment of each. One position meant moving to Chicago; I didn't consider that acceptable and told him so. A couple of letters later, he told me he had chosen the position in Chicago. In the `60s this was still unsurprising behavior since in the final analysis it was "the man's decision." Some

Roberta Katz, learning to be strong

My boyfriend gave me a hard time when I went away to college, not wanting me to go out. Right before my second year, I broke up with him. But his mother and my dad both died that year, which got us back together. We ended up marrying at the end of my junior year. I can't tell you how many people said to me, "Oh, are you going to finish school now that you're getting married?" There was never a question that I wouldn't finish college.

After we graduated, my husband went into the service. All that summer before leaving for Europe, he went to the racetrack and I began to realize that he had a gambling problem. We were overseas for three years. My first child was born there and my second child was born after we came back to the United States. My husband wasn't nice to my son and he started going to the racetrack again.

In 1972 I began taking my son to a psychiatrist who suggested that I also go into therapy. I was in group for about 4 months when I "got it" and told the therapist I was going back to school and wasn't coming back to group. He said, "Are you really going to go?" It was the

wives were fortunate in being able to turn the lemons of these decisions into lemonade. As my story continues, we moved to Evanston, a lovely suburb outside of Chicago, where I was able to get a job a few blocks away at Northwestern University, a position that led me into the doctoral program and a different life.

For FW2 Generation women who married later in life, whether for the first or a repeat time, there was a greater likelihood of preserving one's identity and valuing the person one had become. Therefore, I admit I was shocked to hear one of the 20-something participants in the 2005 television reality program *Hooking Up* say, "He wanted me to be his, and I wanted to be his." In maturity we come to value relationships in which love is given and received by forceful autonomous personalities.

"In successful relationships, this is something that couples know how to do: they know how to let their partner love them. It's very important," said Leonard Rosenblum to Cathleen Rountree in the joint interview with his FW2 wife June Reinisch, the first women to direct The Kinsey Institute.

Today, those of us fortunate to be in thriving relationships know better how to take care of them. And those who aren't in a love relationship

same reaction I got about continuing my education after I married. I answered, "Yeah, if I say I'm going to do it, I'm going to do it."

I went back to school to become a CPA. I wanted to get a divorce and knew I needed a career. Once I had my degree, I told my husband that if he didn't shape up the marriage was going to end. I really didn't want it to work because I didn't like him, but I thought I had to give him a chance. A few months later, I said, "This is just not working." It was hard because he didn't want to leave.

I was the first person of all our friends to get separated or divorced. It was just unheard of. I was very happy but I had no idea it would be so emotionally devastating. [*continued*]

are realizing, in Rountree's words, "It's never too late to fall in love, to be in love, to love. In fact, if love is the religion of one's youth, it deepens to become the spirituality of one's later years."

Understanding Relationships

The 1960s and 1970s—decades of early marriage for FW2 women—were Dark Ages in what we might call the psychosocial study of relationships. If young wives were trying to puzzle out a problem in their marriages in 1965, one of the books they would know about was the recently published *Games People Play* by psychiatrist Eric Berne. This manifesto of Transactional Analysis included a large number of Marital Games such as "Courtroom," "Frigid Woman," "Harried," "If It Weren't for You," and "Look How Hard I've Tried" as well as Life Games such as "Alcoholic" and "Kick Me." In every game the Parent, Adult, or Child in one person interacts with the Parent, Adult, or Child in another person. There are useful insights in Transactional Analysis, but it does not characterize relationships as a whole. Here are three later, more holistic views of relationships:

Love Is A Story. Psychologist and Yale professor Robert J. Sternberg proposed a narrative-based framework for studying relationships in

Roberta Katz, slipping back, moving forward

After I got my CPA, a man who interviewed me for a job asked me out. When I started dating him, several months later, it was like, "Oh gosh, here's the person pulling me out of the quicksand." I reverted to a person who was not confident that she could make it on her own. He began helping me handle the kids although he really wasn't nice to them. I just didn't know how "not nice" he was until later because I was used to so much nastiness.

We married in 1977 and moved to Brazil the next year. I thought it would be great for my kids. Brazil was wonderful except for the marriage. The kids went back to school in the U.S. in 1979. I finally left Brazil. My husband gave me a really hard time. He wanted me to choose between my kids and him. Can you imagine? You have to pick your kids. I said, "They come first."

I briefly moved back home but soon I got a job, a place to live, and a car. That showed I really could do it on my own. There was some help from my parents but definitely I could do it on my own. I took a position in accounting and worked there for some time.

his book *Love is a Story: A New Theory of Relationships*. Sternberg suggests that many theories look at the elements of relationships yet do not answer the fundamental questions of why we love one person and not another, and why we move in and out of love relationships. He writes, "The story gives the relationship meaning in the context of our lives." Sternberg's concepts are useful in analyzing the relationships of FW2 Generation women.

Sternberg contends that each of us has a story about what love is and about the role of each partner in the story. When two people have similar stories, they are more likely to create a shared story. He points out, however, that since a person may have more than one love story, a man or woman may leave a relationship when another person, sharing a more highly valued story, enters the scene.

There are many love stories, and Sternberg classifies them into five categories, stating that these stories function at the intuitive or experiential level.

- *The asymmetrical story.* The difference in role status between the partners is the basis of their relationship. Some couples, for example, have the equivalent of a teacher-student relationship or an employer-

A few years later, my next-door neighbor began telling me about country-western dancing because she knew I loved to dance. You're talking about a fairly sophisticated Jewish woman. Country-western dancing does not compute. Then I went on a ski trip and saw a group dancing to a country-western band. It looked like fun. I came back, called up my neighbor and said, "What about that free lesson?" I went and loved it. The guys were nice. They came to dance. They weren't hitting on you. Six months later, I met Joseph. We started dancing together and began teaching and competing. He is wonderful and a very caring man, so different from most of the men that I've met. In 1987, he asked me to marry him. He's always there for me and provides emotional support and care. I never had that before.

employee relationship. In most asymmetrical relationships, the man is in the more powerful role.

- *The object story.* The partner, or even the relationship itself, is valued for its function. For example, the physical characteristics of the partner are more important than the actual person. Today we hear of trophy wives.

- *The coordination story.* The partners view the relationship as evolving, as including adventures that both participate in. Couples in this type of story use the metaphor of travel or a journey to describe their relationship. Other coordination stories are business and garden stories.

- *The narrative story.* The relationship takes place within the context of an external text. For example, in a fantasy story, the couple

Martha Corelli's been searching for love her whole life

I was three years old when I came up with the dream of finding Prince Charming, the guy to give me unconditional love.

I thought my fiancé was that guy. He and I had a lot in common. We each were the eldest child in our families and we both had retarded younger siblings. His mother played the victim and mine was an alcoholic so we knew the traumas of dysfunctional family life.

You need to know that when I married I wanted to escape my mother's narcissistic rages that unfailingly caused me to retreat to my room, feeling like an empty shell with no reason to live. But on my wedding night, my husband went into a similar rage. His rages grew more frequent and intense with time. I kept thinking it would be okay. We had a son and daughter. Then, when our son was three, my husband started throwing him on the floor and screaming at him, "I'm going to kill you. I hate you." I'd gone from the frying pan into the fire. I finally took the babies and left him.

When I turned 40, I said to my best friend, "Oh my God, I'd better find somebody quick

assumes the roles of a fairy tale. Another narrative is the cookbook story in which the relationship needs certain ingredients added and combined in various ways.

- *The genre.* The mode dominates the relationship. A typical example is the war story where there is constant battling. Most of us have known at least one couple that always seems to be headed for a divorce because they not only argue in private but they make their differences known in public. For couples that share this story, the relationship successfully continues as long as the war rages.

FW2 Generation women undoubtedly had many love stories in their heads as they approached marriage. No single list of these stories exists. However, one frequently held love story is the Prince Charming narrative in which the woman thinks a man will answer all her needs, take her away from problems and free her from having to figure out her life.

Carol Lampton provides us with an example of a Prince Charming story. She thought a man would take care of her and she wouldn't have any financial responsibilities. As she explains, she clearly remembers sitting with her fiancé and discussing finances. He suggested that she

because I'm going to be over the hill." I went out and I found Howard. I just kind of threw myself at him. He was fresh out of divorce. I think he would have been quite content to live alone with his little dog. But much to my regret, I convinced him he would be a lot happier marrying me. I thought at last I'd found my dream, but he wasn't. The moment we got married it turned into a nightmare. On our honeymoon, he quit making love to me. I went to a therapist and I said, "What's going on? We just got married and my husband doesn't want to sleep with me." Two weeks had gone by and the therapist thought that was kind of alarming too. But two weeks wasn't anything compared to the six years that went by before I finally threw in the towel. You see his parents were alcoholics. There you are. I married someone from another dysfunctional family who had not healed himself either. [*continued*]

would need to work when they got married since his salary wouldn't be enough. At the time, she thought, "but you're supposed to take me away from all of that." She had never had a career plan and she believed that by getting married she wouldn't need one.

Some women recognized that their love story wouldn't lead to a particularly satisfactory life. In response, they changed the story. "I had this idea, explains Vickie Baker, "which my mother planted in my head, that my Prince Charming was going to come along and save me from having to decide what to do with my life. Somewhere along in the process, I realized I had bet-ter get my ducks in a row and figure out what I wanted to do with my life." After marriage and a child, she completed her law degree, practiced law for many years and is currently a judge.

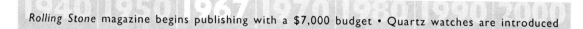

Martha Corelli's story concludes, finding Prince Charming

Five years after my second divorce, I met Robert. I knew the moment I saw him that he was the one I was looking for my entire life. He is a compassionate man, well respected in the community. He had been married for forty years. I had seen him with his wife around town. We were in the same social circles and our children were in the same school. We even lived a block away from each other. I used to look at them and envy her. That's the kind of life that I had dreamed of. I have been dreaming that my whole life.

All of a sudden Robert's wife died. After a while, we started dating and got married the following year. There it was and I was delirious with joy.

It took me 55 years to realize my dream. I found my Prince Charming and that's the happy ending to all of this. What a journey and what a road it's been but I had so much work, so much healing, to do in order to attract a man of his stature. I think that I've made a lot of progress in this lifetime. All of the challenges I've had have provoked a very deep kind of growth.

Loni Anderson,
Actor

"I'm about five minutes out of high school and I'm at this glamorous place with this wonderful guy [Bob Flick, a singer in The Brothers Four]. And in the middle of being dazzled, there's a new thought in my head. I want to be married to a celebrity. Now, I'm not thinking that I want to be a celebrity, I'm thinking instead of the kind of life I could have if I were married to one."

Marriage Enterprise Framework. Daniel Levinson provides a different framework for examining relationships. He conceptualizes marriage as an enterprise rather than an emotional and legal relationship or a cluster of stories. The Traditional Marriage Enterprise (TME) is the name he gives to the typical expectations of women who married during the 1960s and early 1970s. Two additional models—the Neo-Traditional Marriage Enterprise (NME) and the Egalitarian Marriage Enterprise (EME)—flesh out his framework and effectively describe the roles more mature and experienced FW2 women assumed in their subsequent marriages.

Traditional Marriage Enterprise. According to the TME model, a woman enters (buys into) a relationship (a business venture) in which she takes care of her husband, the household and children (job duties) in exchange for being taken care of (paid a salary). Most jobs have daily rewards that accrue independent of the paycheck, and a wife also has rewards independent of being cared for. For someone employed under the TME model, the love of husband and children, the joy of a beautiful home, the satisfaction of a job well done are

I finally have someone who understands how much my mother has hurt me. Robert is the kindest person in the world who never says anything negative. So it meant a great deal to me when he said, "I'm sorry. I cannot be in the same room with your mother. She is such a witch." My Prince Charming understands about the wicked step-mother, although she's my real mother. I'm still working on my relationship with my mother. I believe that love is the one thing that never truly dies. So I can now admit that I really don't like my mother, but I do still love her. But thanks to Robert, I now know that I don't have to put up with her shit anymore.

all examples of the daily rewards. We might add to Levinson's TME the concept of "sweat equity." Much more work is put into the marriage in the early years than rewards are taken out (job duties are high and salary is low). The justification, however, is that the stock options (future rewards) received for the extra effort will be more valuable later (loving relationship with adult children and husband, improved standard of living, free time for personal enjoyment later in life while being taken care of financially and emotionally by husband).

This might not be the enterprise that we saw in our own birth families, but we were sure that it was the way it was supposed to work. While marriage continues to be a strong institution, the TME with its assumptions was already a bankrupt concept by the early 1960s. We just didn't know it. Betty Friedan's 1963 book, *Feminine Mystique*, highlighted what she called "the problem that has no name." Using the terms of the TME framework, women gave up their personal development in order to perform their daily job duties. When the supposed reward of a wonderful relationship with their children and husband failed to materialize, which occurred all too frequently, women were left bankrupt.

Judge Judy,
Attorney Judith Sheindlin is also a popular television show host and author

"Instead of waiting for Prince Charming to sweep you off your feet, you do the 'sweeping' by dazzling yourself with your achievements. Instead of just getting by in the hope that something better will come along, live your life as though the better is already here."

Betty Donaldson, coordinated married life

Dave and I married after a whirlwind romance. We had only dated a month when we decided to get married at the beginning of my junior year. Neither of us had clear goals. After trying out five majors, I graduated and started teaching high school English to the dregs of the tenth grade. I was only 22 and I had five males who were 21. They were back in school after having gotten their girlfriends pregnant, dropped out to join the Army, but couldn't pass the test. That job was unbelievably tough but it was so incredibly rewarding that I became hooked on teaching.

Between 1965 and 1968, I had three children. Dave finished his master's degree and started teaching while working on his Ph.D. When I got pregnant the third time, Dave suggested that he put off his graduate work so that he could earn more money. I said, "Oh, no. You will not do that. We will get through this. Putting it off means you'll never finish." I knew that would be the case.

Alcoholism has been one of our challenges that Dave and I faced together. He really struggled with it for years. Places like AA would say, "Oh, you're too young to be an alcoholic."

For all too many women, the stock options turned out to be worthless when the husband, after accepting her work to care for him, the children and the household for 20-some years, decided he would rather fire (divorce) the 40-year-old and hire (marry) a 20- year-old. Then, without having developed herself and without skills she could use in other enterprises, the woman had to start over.

For women in the FW2 Generation confronting divorce, there were three ways to begin anew. One group was fortunate to find a fulfilling career, only sometimes remarrying. A second group was able to get employment but as office staff because they lacked the educational and employment backgrounds to move higher up the career ladder. The actions of both of these groups are admirable because they had thought of

He'd go to AA meetings just absolutely blown out of his mind, and they still didn't think he was an alcoholic. He was out of control and drinking was his cry for help. When we dated, he sometimes drank too much but other times that wasn't the case at all. I thought he just needed to grow up a little bit.

I continued to teach. As hard as it was, we worked things out together. We'd face the issues. We had financial difficulties, a lot from the fact that we didn't have much income and a lot from the fact that Dave's drinking was a huge drain. By 1970, he managed to say, "This is it." And he quit. Just dealing with all of that and doing it together is, in retrospect, something that really strengthened our relationship and strengthened our marriage. It strengthened our family tremendously. [*continued*]

themselves as wives and mothers but were able to transition into providers. The last group assessed their situation realistically and determined that their only marketable skills were those of wife and mother so they rapidly remarried. But even they coped as best they could given that they had put so much into their TME stock, a stock that bottomed out as decisively as if it had been Enron, WorldCom or Global Crossing.

Neo-Traditional Marriage Enterprise. Levinson's second marriage-enterprise model was usually initiated by the wife who sought to move beyond her role of wife and mother and wanted some assistance in the home so that she could have a career. Given their upbringing, FW2 Generation women rarely started with an NME relationship. Their younger Baby Boomer sisters, however, did begin to demand more. Some of the FW2 Generation women managed over time to evolve their TME into a NME, and often they entered into a second marriage with NME assumptions. In the Neo-Traditional Marriage Enterprise, the woman is still primarily responsible for the children and home but gets assistance from her husband. In exchange for this help, she contributes to the family income. However,

Gloria Feldt,
Executive Director of Planned Parenthood, 1996-2005

Raised in small Texas towns, Gloria recalls, "I just wanted to be a blonde, all-American, normal girl. That meant all I was thinking about was who I was going to marry." When she was 15, she dropped out of school to marry. By the age of 20, she had three children.

Betty Donaldson's story continues, working it out together

The year 1970 marked the beginning of real changes in our lives. Dave quit drinking for good and started looking for a job. He had a couple of offers, but for places we didn't want to go. Then the head of his department mentioned a position at SUNY, New Rochelle. They flew him out early one morning and he was back late that night. The kids were all in bed. It was about 11:00 PM. I was sitting at the kitchen table grading papers and sipping on a steaming cup of hot chocolate. He opens the door to our little rented house and says, "We're moving to New York. They offered me the job. I should have been coy and told them I wanted to think it over, but I said I'll take it."

In May, we took three days of leave from my job to find a place to live. We wanted to be in a small town and started looking in the countryside not too far from New Rochelle. We really didn't have any money. I don't know how we did it but we bought a house that first day. It was $4500 more than we expected. We had previously decided that I was going to take the year off. But Dave said, "I think we'd better find you a job."

should a family emergency come up, it is the woman who leaves work to take care of the crisis. This may sound quaint and old-fashioned, but FW2 Arlie Russell Hochschild wrote in *The Second Shift* that the burden of domestic responsibilities continued

South Vietnamese President Nguyen Van Thieu & Lyndon B. Johnson

to be the woman's in the late 1980s (when she first published her book) and as recently as the end of the 1990s when she updated the book.

Egalitarian Marriage Enterprise. It was even more unusual among FW2 Generation women to have begun married life with an Egalitarian Marriage Enterprise (EME). There are two versions of an EME. In the more rigid version, there is a 50/50 split with a fixed set of expectations (she does the dishes on Monday, Wednesday and Friday; he does the dishes on Tuesday, Thursday and Saturday; and they eat out on Sunday). In a more flexible or negotiated arrangement, partners do what they

That next day I interviewed for four jobs and ended up being offered three. I had been teaching high school, but one of the jobs was teaching seventh and eighth grades. Dave reminded me that I was burning the candle at both ends and said that maybe junior high would be easier for me. I agreed. The third day, we spent looking for childcare.

Then we went back to Iowa and worked like crazy for the next three months. Dave taught at the university and had another job at the Coca Cola bottling plant working odd hours to make money. Plus he was painting houses and I was teaching summer school. We had to manage the move and put some kind of down payment on this house. That was really a busy time. [*continued*]

prefer to do (she cooks; he cleans up the kitchen) and that is flexibly balanced against need (she needs to work late so he cooks; she cleans the kitchen afterwards).

Among women who were dissatisfied with their marriages, many sought either a NME or an EME the second time they got on the marriage road.

Consciousness Scale Framework. In the late 1970s, William Paisley and I developed a Consciousness Scale while studying women's portrayals in the mass media. The same scale provides insight into different levels of relationships.

Consciousness Level I—Put her down. A Level I marriage ranges from the subtlety of emotional abuse to the obviousness of physical abuse. Any type of abuse puts a woman down.

Charlyne Tucker was in a Level I marriage: "The emotional abuse began in earnest. He never hit me but since my self-esteem was not the best from the beginning of our marriage, I let him beat me down emotionally. According to him, I could do no right and I believed him."

Sometimes the "put down" became physical. Dolores Hernandez told me that the first time her husband beat her, she told him she would leave

Carlos Casteneda's *The Teachings of Don Juan* puts words to the mixture of spiritualism and drugs of the '60s

Betty Donaldson's story concludes, supporting each other

The three best things in my life are marrying Dave, facing and meeting challenges together, and establishing and meeting our goals together.

For example, in the late 1970s, I developed chronic ulcerative colitis. I was going from bad to worse. When the doctors started talking about a colostomy and me quitting work, I said, "Whoa, it's time to get serious here." I had a three-day talk with myself saying, "I've got to gain control." Dave and I talked about it a lot and he said, "Okay, if that's what you think." I told the doctor I wasn't caving into this. With new medications, I turned a corner.

I was also taking graduate courses and Dave helped out in many ways while I continued school part time. When I finished, it was like, "Okay, I don't need any more graduate school." I took one semester off and thought I would go out of my mind. Soon I decided I still needed to learn more. I was running down to the university and getting books all the time. After one semester off, I started taking classes again. Dave said, "I think we need to discuss this. Why are you just taking classes? Maybe you ought to have a plan here. Why don't you go ahead

if he did that again. "He never physically hit me again," she says, "but he did abuse me. He wouldn't hit me but if I went to bed and he was mad, he would pick up the mattress, throw me out of the bed, and physically abuse me that way. He abused me a lot."

Consciousness Level II—Keep her in her place. A Level II marriage ranges from the affirmation of a woman fulfilling the roles of wife and mother to the restriction or limitation of a woman to only those traditional roles.

Maureen Devlin's husband wanted her to focus exclusively on being a wife and mother. She eventually felt she had to leave for several months in order to make him realize that she needed something more, something for her. She explains, "When I was growing up, I had a horse in my garage, rode all over town and showed horses. I wanted to be involved with horses again. My mother had a riding school and offered me her first colt. My husband said, "Absolutely not. You cannot have a horse." So I finally left home saying, "Fine, then you take care of the children. I deserve a life." After three months, he decided maybe he would let me have a horse after all. He decided maybe I did deserve a life after all. I wasn't just a mother and a wife. I deserved some things for myself."

and get a Ph.D?" It had never entered my mind. I don't know why not. I think that must be a cultural thing.

Just prior to getting my Ph.D. in 1991, Dave said, "You know, you finish your degree and we'll just go any place in this country where you want to work." By this time, Dave was department chair and I was teaching middle-school English as well graduate education courses at the university. Other institutions were calling me to teach. I thought, "Why do I want to do a national search for a job?" I loved what I was doing. Fortunately, I was offered a job at a nearby college that was a perfect match for me.

Patricia Fisher's experience was somewhat different in that she wanted to go to work and had to find her own way around her husband's insistence that she maintain her role of wife and mother. "I did volunteer work," she says, "because my husband wouldn't let me go to work."

Consciousness Level III—Give her two places. A Level III marriage ranges from the willingness, even eagerness, to manage both home and work roles to the addition of a work role only because the husband wants his wife to work for needed additional money.

Carol Lampton says, "I had the kind of home situation in which my husband was fine with my working. It was 'whatever you want to do, however you want to run things, but you do it.' In addition to working, I had total home responsibility. Even things that a husband might traditionally do like pay bills or do yard work, he never did, ever. I had a full plate but it was the way I liked it and I wanted to grow professionally."

While Carol represents those women who took on the two roles of their own volition, Abbey Goldman, and many others like her, only took on the second role when her husband told her to go to work. "My son started college," recalls Abbey, "and then my husband told me it would be a good idea if I went to work and made some money to help with his expenses."

Barbara Mathias, if at first you don't succeed …

I married in high school and got pregnant right away. I would sit home and be sick while he was out drag racing. I found my husband with another girl and that made me feel both insecure and jealous. We divorced in 1961. The day the divorce was final I married his best friend. At the wedding party, my new husband tried to make out with my girlfriend so I ran away. That marriage only lasted two days.

To take care of my son and myself, I played piano in clubs. In my mind I thought you were supposed to be married, have children, and stay home. I knew my little boy needed a father so I talked myself into marrying a policeman who promptly quit working after I married him.

When I was six months pregnant with my second child, I had appendicitis. Because of the surgery, the insurance company where I worked told me I had to wait two months after my child was born before I could return. Since my husband didn't work, I had to work. When my daughter was five days old, I went to a temp agency and found out what a fast typist I am. My

Consciousness Level IV—Acknowledge that she is fully equal. A Level IV marriage is similar to Levinson's Egalitarian Marriage Enterprise. In acknowledging the wife and husband's equality, the marriage often is managed with each spouse contributing as equally as possible to the household income and responsibilities for home and children. Suzi Jeffers epitomizes the strict interpretation of "fully equal." As she explains, "When we eat out, my husband and I each pay for our own meal. This all started when we were dating and we've continued it."

Consciousness Level V—Recognize her individuality. A Level V marriage emphasizes individual strengths rather than gender-based stereotypes. Level V is the most difficult to achieve because stereotypes continue to get in the way. For example, in a marriage, the woman might have full responsibility for the children because she is "better" with them. But is she really better or is that just the assumption of the couple that has been shaped by societal values? Level V builds on Level IV but removes its rigidity. Both wife and husband contribute to their shared lives,

HUMPHREY FOR PRESIDENT

piano playing fingers could really fly. Soon I realized how much more I could make working for attorneys and court reporters.

About that time, I discovered drinking. This fellow I married drank a lot. I didn't realize just how sick he was. You see, I always worked hard and was involved in the work I did. I would think, "I'm buying this small bottle of whiskey and it's gone so quickly. I'll buy a bigger one and it will last longer." I didn't even know about addictions. The marriage was over in less than five years. I divorced him when I found him beating my little boy in the shower with a belt. When things would happen like this, I could never tell people how I felt. But if I took a drink I wasn't as afraid and I could speak my mind. [*continued*]

caring for the children, if any, being responsible for household chores and earning money. The difference is there is no sense of need for a daily 50/50 split on each item. No one is keeping score. While few FW2 women have ever reached this level, Claire Whitney describes how her Level II traditional "keep her in her place" marriage has grown into a Level V marriage. "I don't really remember how we adjusted at first after I went to work. It kind of evolved. At one point, I probably said, 'If you want dinner on time, you're going to have to help.' He got interested in cooking and started doing that. When his work hours changed, it became evident that he could do more. He said, 'You don't have to pick up the groceries on the way home from work. You write the grocery list, and I'll go to the store.' Later, when he had an even more flexible job, he would do the laundry during the day. I would come home at night and do the sorting and the putting away while he was at music rehearsal. It's still flexible. It's not a sit down and okay here's the list of things that need doing. You do your half, and I'll do mine."

Richard M. Nixon is elected President • Waterbeds are introduced and become popular on the West Coast

Barbara Mathias' story continues, a turn for the worse

In 1967, I met a very handsome, intelligent fellow. After seeing him two or three times, he took me prisoner for eleven months. There were beatings and real horror stories I don't want to get into. My mother had the children but no one knew what happened to me. This fellow was totally brilliant but insane. I was afraid to leave because he said he would kill my mother and children. He didn't want me looking at any men so he wouldn't even let me watch TV.

Not surprisingly, I got pregnant. I didn't think he would let me go to the hospital, but his dealer brought him drugs so he was in a good mood the day I went into labor. He insisted on a female doctor and nurses. I had bruises all over and told the hospital staff that I had been in a car wreck. As soon as I delivered, he bundled me up and we left. Several days later, he went to the hospital for the baby and then to my mother's home and told her that we'd been out of the country. He brought her and my children to the house with the new baby, then pulled out a gun and fired eleven shots, missing every one of us. All my fear of him fell away. In that instant I came alive, taking a huge metal lamp and hitting him until I knocked him out. I called my

Sally Jessy Raphael, Television talk-show host, Emmy award winner

During a time in the early 1960s when Sally was contributing to the family income, she realized that her husband did not support her decisions or believe in her. At that point, she asked herself, "Did I really want the power in my life to be in someone else's hands? The answer was no, and I determined from that moment on that I needed to live more on my own terms." Soon afterward, even though she had two young daughters, she divorced.

Uniqueness of the Marriage Situation for FW2 Generation Women

FW2 Generation women began their married life young, with little self-knowledge, few skills and the image of an idyllic future. What our generation couldn't know was that the future we envisioned, a replay of our mother's world, no longer existed. Moreover, it became clear to us in our young adulthood that many of our mothers had stayed married because they lacked good alternatives. World War II, the towering storm of our birth years, led to social, economic and political changes that would complicate our mothers' marriages as well as our own.

What are these changes that would make our marriages stand in contrast to those of our mothers?

- The postwar G.I. Bill changed the concept of education— first as an economic fact and later as a public perception—from a privilege of the few to an opportunity and, eventually, a necessity of the many, women as well as men. The reality of widespread educational access was

Vietnam death toll reaches 47,573—over 10,000 more than were killed in the Korean War

step-dad to come. I was afraid this fellow would come after me if I left, but my mother forced me to go. He did come by my mother's some, but I stayed inside for two months, afraid to go out. I always thought I was not afraid of anything and had a very strong mind, but I feared him. I found if I drank, I was not afraid of anything. I was not too stable and was a little crazy at that time.

He was killed a year later. The police said he died of a massive overdose of heroin in a motel room where he had been beaten from head to toe. [*continued*]

first felt in the 1960s with the construction of 2-year community colleges and additional 4-year colleges within commuting distance of day/night students (here in California the Master Plan for Higher Education, also known as the Donohoe Plan in honor of the Assemblywoman who promoted it tirelessly, was adopted in 1960 and led to a well-functioning system of 2-year, 4-year, and graduate-level campuses). Community colleges were criticized at first as "Grades 13 and 14" of the public school system. That's exactly what they were, but with transferable college credits. These educational opportunities that our parents thought would make us better mothers meant we were better educated than our parents when we married.

• When the Civil Rights Act finally marshaled the legal force of the U.S. Government against discrimination in employment (and public services), it was as much a response to the complaints of minorities and women who were already experiencing discrimination as it was a promissory note to youth still in school. Immediately after the formation of the National Organization for Women in 1966, NOW campaigned successfully against sex-segregated want ads. From the

First female undergraduates at Yale • Dept. of Agriculture bans DDT thanks to Rachel Carson

Barbara Mathias' story continues, trying to figure it out

The crazy fellow was 6'4" and handsome, so I married a short, bookworm fellow. Women had never paid him attention, but they did when he was with me. This went to his head and he told me he wanted to have an affair. I have not seen him since that day.

In 1970 I married an ironworker and had my fourth child. The marriage was okay until he fell at work, breaking his back. He became impossible to live with when addicted to prescription pain pills. I divorced him although I cared for him.

After a few years, he got better and we remarried. Then physical and mental problems caught up with me. After a tubal ligation, I bled for seven years. Doctors all said, "Don't worry about it." You could touch me and I'd bruise. I finally had a hysterectomy.

I started the rounds of mental hospitals to figure out why I did crazy things. They tried everything from sodium Pentothal to shock treatments, never realizing that I only did this wild stuff when I was drinking. I drank when things became too much for me. It could be months or even a year between episodes. My husband left about then.

Jane Adams,
Author of *Sex and the Single Parent* and other books

"My first personals ad [in 1978] described the man of my dreams but said almost nothing about me. Back then I thought that if I found Mr. Right and he gave me the specs, I could be whoever he wanted me to be. This time I knew better. Since the post-divorce frenzy, of which that first personal ad was a symbol, I'd created a life and furnished it with too much I value to make myself over to fit someone else's fantasy. I have an identity—independent, self-sufficient, successful."

mid-1960s onward, the promise of access to education and employment proved to be a potent stimulus for previously excluded groups. Taking advantage of the new work opportunities was likely to alter our interpretation of marriage.

- While earlier measures for family planning were widely known (as girls and young women we read the "diaphragm chapters" in *Goodbye Columbus* and *The Group*), the Pill so simplified contraception that it became a tipping point. And although it took some of us a while to get it right, the number and frequency of children was under our control, allowing us to complete educations and consider careers. We still couldn't give these matters the same dedication as a married man, but we could see a different inflection in our marriages than our mothers could expect.

- In retrospect, we can see that when no-fault divorce was added to this mix in the late-1960s, it was inevitable that marriages would be affected.

In 1980, I married a fellow who did leather work for bikers. Seeing me in a bad time, one biker said, "She's an alcoholic, why don't you send her to treatment?" That's the first time anyone put a label on my problem. I couldn't have made it without the psychiatrists and psychologists. I've always been considered very intelligent but I wasn't smart emotionally. I didn't take all their suggestions, thinking I was different. I had a hard time seeing where I was wrong or the part I played in what happened. In recovery, they say knowledge is not enough. I had knowledge, but didn't work through the problems. I also didn't stay sober. I came home from a funeral to find my husband with his usual drugs and bourbon. I picked up the bottle and was off again for two years. That fellow left and died shortly thereafter of liver failure. [*continued*]

The ledger of the 1960s shows: Biology is no longer destiny. Marriage is no longer indenture. Women are no longer silent in the public forum. (Who could ignore redoubtable figures like Betty Friedan and Bella Abzug?) Civil rights of access to education and employment are no longer denied.

More Choices

How did these factors coalesce in a unique way for FW2 Generation women? They gave us choices, but more... A "revolution of rising expectations" (newly coined phrase of this era) affected societies around the world. Food could be abundant; disease could be controlled; living standards could rise; disenfranchised groups could claim their rights. Individually, we were enjoying the last glow of postwar idealism before the darkness of Vietnam descended. In the 1960s "Be all that you can be" was not yet a military slogan; it still rang down the ages to us from its original proclamation by Jean-Jacques Rousseau.

But the most important level of change is often the mundane level, so I return to the fact that FW2 Generation women had choices. We could decide to have smaller families. We could even remain single with dignity.

500,000 people gather on 600-acre farm near Woodstock, NY, to hear rock music • *Sesame Street* debuts

Barbara Mathias' story concludes, satisfied

In 1983 I married a fellow in AA. We decided we didn't need AA, but we didn't need to drink either. He took a job that involved socializing and parties. Soon we were drinking and I was back to my problems, trying to run over people with my car. I worked for a nursing agency and the compassionate people there got me into treatment.

I had a counselor who handled the hardcore people. He helped me understand things that had happened in my life. You don't want people to rely on being a victim but once in a while it's the truth. He helped me see the parts I played and the parts others played. It was the turning point in my life. My husband went to AA and we're both still sober 17 years later. All was good until he went back to his ex-wife, after we'd been married twelve years. One day he just left.

I slid into a deep depression that continued for several years. Then in 1998, doctors found a tumor and removed my thyroid. It turned out that I had undiagnosed Hashimoto's disease. The endocrinologist said the disease probably triggered what I used to call my "weak moments" that led to drinking and wildness. After the operation, the depression ceased.

We could obtain education equal to our abilities. We could go to work outside the home with only manageable protest from husbands who, passing from the care of mother to wife, had not learned to do much of anything for themselves. We could free ourselves from alcoholic, abusive or unfaithful husbands. We were the first generation of women, perhaps in all history, to consider the roles of wife and mother as only part of our adult persona.

It is not surprising that the massive social, legal, economic and political changes in the 1960s would result in upheavals in marriages just as they did in every other arena. But rather than focus only on the rising divorce rate and its individual consequences, which we will hear about in Chapter 6, we should note that the freedom and dignity of a nonfraudulent divorce (prior to no-fault divorce, the majority of divorces were obtained with fraudulent declarations) actually focused new attention on the quality of marriage—a marriage that need not be endured should be more than endurable. Blazing trails into this new frontier of marriage, the FW2 Generation charted marital relationships that were marked by equality, mutual respect and the freedom of each partner to reach her or his own potential without restriction. Relationships were not to be regarded as zero-sum games in which the wins of one person entail losses for the

I married one more time to someone in AA who was a pathological liar. He was very successful and traveled all over the world, but he liked other women. Then I became sick and that's not what he wanted. They thought I had a stroke but they found blocked arteries. I'm without insurance now, and I can't work two or three jobs at a time like I could before.

In AA, two years ago, I met a fellow musician who's had bad luck with women, like I have with men. He's the nicest person I've ever been around.

An ex-husband and son have been clean and sober for seven years after seeing the change in me. If the bad parts of my life were necessary to give either one of them a chance to find a better way, I guess I'm satisfied.

other. Partners who help each other are both enriched. Many relationship problems were identified as communication problems that had teachable solutions. The center of gravity in marriage counseling shifted from "save this failing marriage" to "make this good marriage even better."

CBS's Walter Cronkite reporting from Vietnam

Rock-A-Bye Baby:
The FW2 Generation Gives Birth

When I Was Little

I imagined I'd grow up, get married and have four sons even though I played with girl dolls. Hanna, my favorite, was the size of a one-year old. I dressed her in my own baby clothes that I found in a dusty box in the attic. My grandmother made a beautiful quilt for her using fabric scraps from previous sewing projects. I still recall the feeling of pure bliss as I wrapped Hanna in her multi-colored quilt. Yet not many years later, I dreamed of sons.

I wanted four sons and I got four sons. But it took twelve years, two marriages, and a blended family to fulfill the dream. I came out of my first marriage with two wonderful sons, Ken and Edward. My second marriage brought a stepson, Andy, who was wedged in age between my sons. The arrangement with Andy was fairly typical for the period. He spent every other weekend and parts of vacations and holidays with us. Although I loved having the three boys around, there were some rocky times with Andy. It's not surprising since he was trying to make his way between two quite different households. Fortunately, as Andy and I both grew older and wiser, the relationship improved and today we have a strong bond. My fourth son, Will, came along a few years later.

Home smoke detectors introduced • April 22 designated Earth Day • FW2 Margaret Court Smith wins Grand Slam

Terry Sherman, independent and self-confident

I was the youngest of four children, probably an afterthought. My parents were very devoted to us but weren't what you would call doting. They raised all of us to be pretty independent. They had done all the PTA stuff and school thing with my siblings and that wasn't their deal by the time I came along. From that standpoint, and I appreciated this in hindsight very much, meals were a sharing time. However, my parents weren't in every aspect of my life.

I was 11 when we moved from the Midwest to the East coast. You might think that would have been a real shakeup of my world. I never remember it being anything but just another step. I pretty much have taken that perspective all through life. It is just another step. If I don't know how to do something, I'll figure it out. I've never worried about things like that.

I had a very solid family upbringing. My parents raised me with very few restrictions. There were never curfews. I was just told to use my best judgment. I probably was a Goody Two-Shoes because of it. I didn't want to lose those privileges.

Raising children takes a village and a lot of work and time from the parents. The joy is amazing and the love overflows, but that doesn't alter the amount of effort required. I was very lucky to have Thelma, a wonderful neighbor, who helped raise my children as if they were part of her family. Our boys played with her three children after school and on holidays while my husband and I worked. She lived across the street and our children felt equally at home in both houses. Later Thelma went back to work, and I was fortunate to find another special person, Ana Maria, a woman from Guatemala whose husband was working on his Ph.D. Ana Maria, her husband, and their three children became Will's second family. They lived in married-student housing on the Stanford campus and as Will got older, he biked between his dad's office and Ana Maria's apartment, believing the whole campus was his backyard.

FW2 Generation women had no role models for how to manage careers or college studies while raising children and vice versa. Most of our mothers hadn't worked since they married or had children. Should we stay home? Could we go back to college? Would it be OK to continue working? In the 1960s, many FW2 women who taught found that they were required to quit once they were pregnant, or at least

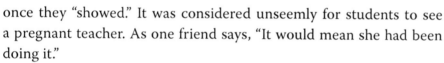

once they "showed." It was considered unseemly for students to see a pregnant teacher. As one friend says, "It would mean she had been doing it."

So how was I going to manage with another child? Will arrived late in the evening of June 2, 1975. My husband and I were preparing our research proposal to the National Cancer Institute for a study on effective public communication campaigns that had to go out by FedEx no later than 6 PM. With the deadline in mind, I arranged to meet my doctor at Stanford Hospital at 7 PM when she would induce labor. The proposal went off on time; the baby was born on time; the next day we stopped by our offices to introduce him to our colleagues as we made our way from the hospital to home; and I was back at full-time work on June 4 with a two-day-old son in my arms, wrapped in the well-worn quilt I had used with Ken and Edward when they were infants and, originally, my doll Hanna.

Originally introduced in 1923, the Equal Rights Amendment is reintroduced into Congress • Beatles break up

Louise Moran, childhood self-sufficiency carries her through adult

I look back at my childhood and marvel. My dad taught me how to change a tire. There are not a lot of girls that changed tires in the 1950s. A girlfriend and I mowed yards occasionally. My mom taught me how to cook, plant seeds, and cultivate flowers. They both taught me the meaning of a dollar. My parents never put limits on me, limits on what I could do. That didn't mean I could do everything. I didn't stay out late and that kind of thing. I'm talking about limits on what I was capable of doing. I think that's really been a big influence on my being self-sufficient.

Once I was an adult, they supported my decisions. I can still remember when I told them I was going to get a divorce. I expected them to be very upset and they weren't. They had never said what they thought about my husband and the way he was. They kind of went, "It's about time."

Barbara Ehrenreich, Social commentator and prolific author

"No culture on earth outside of mid-century suburban America has ever deployed one woman per child without simultaneously assigning her such major productive activities as weaving, farming, gathering, temple maintenance, or tent-building. The reason is that full-time, one-on-one child-raising is not good for women or children."

I can still smell the exotic perfume of Star Jasmine in the air when we arrived at our offices that warm June morning. We found a huge cardboard greeting affixed to the door that I still have. It read, "We lost a future female feminist struggler, but we gained another supporter in the enemy camp." The department's female students had been hoping to hear the words "It's a woman, a baby woman." from the Doonesbury cartoon of a few years earlier.

FW2 Generation women who decided to "do it all" usually felt incredibly lucky to have the opportunity to be actively engaged in so many facets of life. I was doubly lucky because I was an academic at the time, one of the professions where it was not as difficult to mix career and motherhood. Will easily settled into an office routine—a crib in my husband's office where he kept a watchful eye on him and changed his diaper before bringing him to me to nurse. In the mid-1970s we were keenly aware of sex-role stereotypes and wanted to lead both private and public lives that addressed the biased attitudes and behaviors that were prevalent. We even gave our son a hyphenated last name, Butler-Paisley, and later told

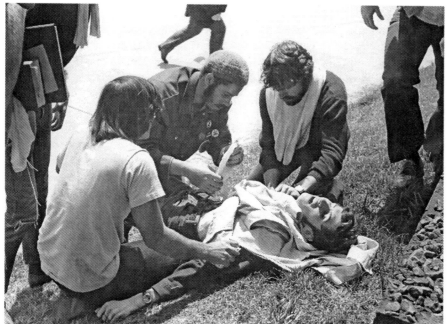

Victim of National Guard shooting at Kent State

him that he could choose either last name when he was older. He eventually dropped Butler, a decision that was fine since Paisley is the name of the Scottish town where his grandfather was born. Will, on his 30th birthday, casually mentioned he's using the hyphenated Butler-Paisley as a pen name.

Expert Voices

FW2 Generation women knew little about parenting and had few resources. The paucity of information led FW2 Ellen Galinsky to conduct early research on this topic that she published in her 1987 landmark book, *The Six Stages of Parenthood.* Parents cannot exercise control over all life events that occur during these stages. But they can help build skills that enable children to handle the twists and turns of life rather than to fade in the face of adversity. Edith Grotberg researched the skills children need to become resilient. In her book, *Tapping Your Inner Strength*, Grotberg

National Guard kills 4, wounds 9 at Kent State; 4 million students at 900+ campuses strike • FW2 Janis Joplin dies

Barbara Mathias, her childhood spills over to her children

My stepfather was a child molester and a drunk. Let me explain. My mother was an orphan and married an orphan who abandoned us. We moved in with my aunt who had many different men in and out. There were a lot of secrets. My mother dated a married man for 10 years and they married when I was 11. It was just chaos. He molested me from the time I was very young until I learned to run and hide to avoid him. I told my mother, but she didn't believe me.

But the real heartache is that he also bothered my little girls. My adult son said, "How could you leave my sisters there knowing that he would abuse them?" I responded, "You don't understand, I didn't know about people like him. I didn't know it was forever." Somehow, I thought that it was only me. I never had any idea or dreamed he would bother anyone else. It seems so naïve now with all the knowledge in the world but when we were younger there was nothing. You would never talk about it, about anything like that. It was my deep dark secret for a number of years. It's affected my younger daughter. One daughter just overlooked it. It

shows how parents and caregivers can help children develop a sense of *I HAVE* (external support network of people they can trust), *I AM* (inner resources of their personal positive traits), and *I CAN* (problem solving skills and perseverance).

Baby and Child Care, the bible we all consulted, was first published by Dr. Benjamin Spock in 1946, just in time for the post-war baby boom. His revolutionary book rocked both conventional wisdom and the pediatric establishment when he urged affection and flexibility instead of the strict discipline and rigid schedules previously used to prepare children for a harsh world. Spock, with his radical new approach, told parents, actually his early editions told *mothers*, to trust themselves because "You know more than you think you do." Spock's guidance was important in that it changed the way children were raised but it perpetuated the myth that parents naturally know how to raise children.

Consider other "natural" talents such as athletic, musical, and dramatic ability where innate aptitude is important. Then consider how many famous people in those fields would even be known without the benefit of teachers and coaches, without education and studying, without the purposeful and systematic development of their talent. Yet we still

didn't affect her very much, so she says, but then it turned out that he even bothered his great granddaughters.

    I finally had to do something. When I first found out my stepfather bothered my daughters and granddaughters, I wanted to kill him. But I knew that the appropriate way to handle this was to call the social agencies that handle such matters and make sure no children were ever allowed in their house again. Of course, this didn't go over well with my mother and my brother. You see, when I was in high school, my mother and stepfather had a son. This was his real father so the accusations were awkward. He still doesn't believe it. It just became a nightmare, but I knew that all children are too precious to allow that to continue to happen.

believe that parents just naturally know how to raise children to be the best that they can be, to fully develop their abilities, to function well in a complex society. It is hard to imagine a job more important or demanding than being a parent. But it is the one profession for which no credentialing is required. As the rocket engineer Wernher Von Braun said, "Man [sic] is the best computer we can put aboard a spacecraft, and the only one that can be mass produced with unskilled labor."

Our Childhoods Influenced Our Child Raising Behaviors

The social and political times, our spouses, our personalities, even location influenced the way we raised our children. But perhaps the most important determinant was our childhoods. This is not a psychoanalytic memoir, as I am primarily interested in the adult lives of FW2 Generation women. But stories of childhoods spilled out, sometimes in the first five minutes of an interview. It became apparent that to understand our child raising experiences, we needed to look at circumstances that shaped our early years.

Stephanie Coontz,
Professor, social historian, and author

"[G]rowing up in the 1950s … was not so much a matter of being protected from the harsh realities of the outside world as preventing the outside world from learning the harsh realities of family life. Few would have guessed that radiant Marilyn Van Derbur, crowned Miss America in 1958, had been sexually violated by her wealthy, respectable father from the time she was five."

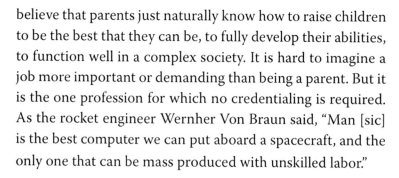

Jury finds Chicago Seven not guilty of conspiracy charges in 1968 Democratic National Convention riot

Martha Corelli, handicapped because she was healthy

When I was two and my mother was pregnant, my father joined the Army. When the war was over, my mother put us on the first ship taking dependent families to Germany. The conditions on the ship were atrocious. My sister became ill with what was later diagnosed as encephalitis. She was in agony and screamed for five days straight. We got to Germany and it was all so sad. My sister became retarded and epileptic. This is really the center of my life—my sister.

Several years later, the doctor told my mother to send my sister to a home for retarded children. She was very disruptive and uncontrollable, and it was truly a nightmare trying to live with her. About that time, my mother began drinking and became an alcoholic.

Then when I was 11, my brother was born. That was a highlight. We needed that boost because things were sad in our family. He was very bright and precocious. I just adored him. My father was transferred to Germany, and the weirdest thing happened. On the ship going across the Atlantic Ocean my brother began having a hard time. When we got to Frankfurt, he had a massive convulsion and nearly died.

Dorothy, the adopted orphan in the *Wizard of Oz*, is lonely and frequently ignored by Auntie Em and Uncle Henry. She is dismayed that they may give away her dog at the insistence of a cranky neighbor. In the famous 1939 movie version, she laments her predicament to her dog Toto saying that there must be "some place where there isn't any trouble" before launching into song. Many of the women I interviewed, like Dorothy, believed that: *Somewhere over the rainbow... dreams... really do come true.*

But the dreams didn't come true, at least not for those with unhappy childhoods. Many situations and events of childhood led a person to feel that she had a *happy* or *unhappy* childhood. Did her family help her to build self-confidence or did they demean her? Did they project positive life attitudes

Richard M. Nixon meeting with Elvis Presley

My sister died when she was 14. Of course, she was living in an institution. My parents never told my brother about her. I was on a skiing trip at the time. When I came home, she was lying in an open coffin next to the Christmas tree. It was so shocking because I hadn't seen her for years. She looked a great deal like me. My brother just lost it. He was basically saying, "What am I? Chopped liver in this family?" Very shortly thereafter he began convulsing. He, too, became an epileptic. The message I always got was that I was the weird one, the handicapped one, because I was the only one who was healthy. I had these two handicapped siblings, and all the attention of my parents went to them. I never felt that I was worth much. [*continued*]

and behaviors or dysfunctional ones? Was childhood scarred by a parent's death or other tragedies? Did she experience unconditional love, rationed love, or little affection at all?

Unhappy and Traumatic Childhoods

During the early 1940s when the FW2 Generation was being born, the psychologist Abraham Maslow departed from conventional scientific research to look at "healthy" individuals to understand behavior. His resulting theory, published in 1943, explains that individuals have needs they must fulfill before they can move to higher levels. His five need levels are:

- *Physiological* such as air and food;
- *Safety* such as secure shelter and health;
- *Belonging* such as satisfying relationships;
- *Self-esteem* such as feelings of worth, and
- *Self-actualization* such as pursuing goals or having a sense of purpose.

Parents who do not adequately meet the lower level needs of their children primarily create unhappy and traumatic childhoods. This is clearest when parents physically or emotionally abuse their children and deprive them of both physiological and safety/security needs.

House approves ERA (354-24) • Nat'l Women's Political Caucus founded • Nasdaq debuts • Coco Chanel dies

Martha Corelli's story concludes, searching for her mother

My life was extremely chaotic, constantly moving from place to place. By the time I was in eighth grade I had been to 11 schools in three countries. I don't know how I survived it at all. I did think a lot about suicide when I was a child because I felt I didn't belong and I wasn't good enough. My mother always said, "Well you know one always loves the bird with the broken wing more than the healthy bird." That was the message. I think my mother could never love me because it would betray her love for my sister.

I used to try to be sick. I was successful in having a great deal of upper respiratory infections. My grandmother would come and read to me by the hour when I had pneumonia. Those were wonderful times. You have to have one good supportive person in your life in order to survive. The early part of my life was truly about survival.

My mother abused me terribly as a child with her temper tantrums. She would not stop until I was emotionally demeaned. I felt as though I'd been murdered psychologically. That's why I thought of suicide. I'd be like an empty shell, and there would seem to be no reason to

Emotionally and Physically Abusing Children

Children with abusive parents always bear the emotional and, in some cases, the physical scars. In Harriet's unhappy childhood, her mother abused her so extensively that her adult health has been permanently damaged.

When Harriet Magill was five, her mother took her from New York to Reno for the six-week residency necessary to obtain a divorce. Then, rather than returning as agreed, she took Harriet to California. "This really caused quite a rift," explains Harriet. "It marked the end of any relationship I could have with my father. From then on it was, 'You don't really want to send a birthday card to your father, do you?' If I said, 'Yes,' I got a beating. I learned very quickly to say 'No.'

"When I was nine she sent me away for the summer and had remarried by the time I returned. She had three sons over the next five years. My stepfather was an old-fashioned, old-world German who believed all the terrible things my mother said about me. She told me that I was incorrigible. I didn't know what that word meant. I just knew I was afraid. She said, 'Your stepfather doesn't like you being here and will send you away if you misbehave.' Since I knew my father didn't want me, I had

live because she hated me so much. She really hated me.

My childhood set it up so that the rest of my life I would spend healing myself and seeking self-actualization. I had to look deep within myself in order to fulfill my goal, my dream. I can't say the words 'my dream' without crying because it has been such an enormous journey to get there, to find the happiness that I was looking for, to find unconditional love. I spent my life searching for my mother. I kept looking for my mother to love me but that was a dead-end search. As a result, I had no idea how to be a mother because I hadn't healed myself of this wound from my childhood by the time I had children.

nowhere to go. I was raised with this uncertainty. I just never knew where the love was going to come from. And the hitting continued. She'd slap me and yank me up by one arm and kick me in my lower back."

When Harriet was 10, she met a neighborhood boy who, after many years of being a playmate and then a best friend, became her lifelong sweetheart. They married in 1964 and in describing the next part of her life she says, "I have had a wonderful, wonderful marriage. I have been very blessed. He is my support system, and I am his."

Their first child, possibly as the result of her mother's physical abuse, was born multiply handicapped with four heart problems, deafness, visual impairment, and severe mental retardation.

I asked Harriet how she survived. She responded that when their child was born and they learned of her massive health problems, she and her husband realized they had to get away from the bad environment created by not only her mother, but now also by his parents. By then her mother-in-law was an alcoholic and her father-in-law was distracted with his new wife.

Fortunately, Harriet had finished her certification as a registered nurse. "We decided I would work; he would work," she explains. "We would take

Angela Harlan, alcoholism creates a dysfunctional childhood

By the time I was eight, I knew something was not right about my dad, and when I was 13 I knew he drank too much. I didn't understand it, and, in true 1950's fashion, my mom never talked about it. So I became the perfect daughter, doing well academically in spite of being sleep deprived. Because of my dad, I was very dependent on my mom for stability and was crushed when our financial situation forced her to go to work. Every day I came home after school to an empty house and waited every night to see if my dad would be drunk or sober. All the surrounding insecurities really marked me.

My life journey has been colored by early events over which I had no control. Later, I knew I had control over some things. I vowed I would never stay married to an alcoholic, would stay home with my kids, would do everything to avoid conflict, and would make home a happy, safe place. These things underlie everything in my life.

Joe and I married when I was teaching and he was getting an MBA. Soon I was under pressure to have a child because he didn't want to be drafted. Being a good girl, I said, "Sure,"

care of our daughter; do the best we could for her. We would get away from all the discord. We moved away. That probably saved us."

Her first-born died despite years of dedication to her, and eventually Harriet and her husband had two healthy children. "We've deliberately kept our children away from those people. The four of us—our daughter, our son, my husband, and me—formed a tight unit."

Alcoholism Creates Dysfunctional Families

Alcoholism might be considered another form of abuse, but it has its own distinctive problems. Alcoholic parents ruled and ruined many homes yet alcoholism was rarely acknowledged or discussed in the 1950s. Although Alcoholics Anonymous was started in the mid-1930s, it spread slowly. Children of alcoholics often need control in their lives in order to compensate for the lack of control they have over the chaotic home life. Today there are programs such as Al-Anon and Alateen that can help to mitigate the damage of an alcoholic parent. But these resources weren't available to the FW2 Generation when we were young. Alcoholism, much like abuse, was one of the family secrets that burdened our childhoods.

and became pregnant immediately. The next few years were difficult; the only saving grace was my wonderful son.

In 1970 my husband went back to school, and I went back to teaching. It was the happiest time in my life but I was trapped, trapped in those ideas that I should be there for my family. My son asked if we were going to have a baby. I said, "Yes." I felt I couldn't break that promise. And there you go. I was having this really great experience teaching and then we're off to my husband's new job and I have a daughter. It was a time of real conflict because I wanted to be the perfect mom and the perfect wife and I wanted to live up to all those things that I had professed as being important but I was really not terribly happy myself. [*continued*]

Managing in the Face of the Unimaginable

Sometimes events that create an unhappy childhood are outside anyone's control. "I lost both my parents when I was 12," Joanne Perry says. "My mom was 48 and my dad was 50. One night, at a party, my mom dropped dead. One week later, to the day, my father died of a massive heart attack. They said it was a broken heart."

Although her mother's sister took her in, Joanne was separated from her brother because her aunt wouldn't also take him. She herself had been in an automobile accident and didn't really "mother" Joanne. "When you're a normal 12-year-old, psychologically all you want is acceptance. That's the time in life when you just want to belong. After the tragedy there was this hush-hush over my life. I felt like saying, 'Please don't treat me differently. I don't know why this happened. I don't know what to do.' There was never any therapy. You just didn't in those days. So what did I do? I strove really hard to be very good, to please everybody so that no one would not like me."

Faye Dunaway,
Academy Award winning actor

"…I always tried to understand why my father was the way he was [alcoholic womanizer]. …When I heard that he had been beaten severely by his father, it helped me understand a bit more. But, you know, as Albert Camus said, a human being is responsible for his face. Childhood experience can help those who love you to understand, but each of us is responsible for who we are."

Angela Harlan's story concludes, not taking care of herself

My precious daughter developed a problem and eventually was sent to a child psychologist. Finally, I called him up, "How do you know it's the child that needs therapy and not the mother?" He said, "Well, sometimes therapy can help you both." The psychologist enabled me to see that my anger and turmoil were related to my childhood. Gaining some insights, I went back to school. But I became pregnant again and was so nauseous that I quit. I had this lovely third child but it was a hard time for her to come into our family.

I sank into a deep depression, becoming suicidal. I'd think about hanging myself from the attic rafters. I started seeing my therapist twice a week and was on two anti-depressants. My goal each day was to be dressed so the kids wouldn't know how bad it was. It was like walking through water, just unbelievable. I'm a mind over matter person and just couldn't figure it out. I didn't understand why I was thinking about suicide. I had this great family and this husband who wasn't an alcoholic. But I had a lot of stuff in my head that I couldn't leave my kids, couldn't take off in any sense of the word, and still be a good mom.

Happy and Self-Actualizing Childhoods

As far as I know, no childhood totally escapes bad situations or events, which means that all adults bear some burden of bad memories from childhood. But unhappy parts seem to recede in importance over time in the memory of those who had generally happy childhoods.

Creating Independence and Self-Confidence

The death of a parent in one home may create havoc and result in a dysfunctional family. In another, the remaining parent may help the child develop positive self-esteem. "My father died of cancer when I was four," recalls Laura McGown. "It was just my mother and me all the years I was growing up. Financially we weren't well off. My mother had to go to work, but she always gave me a real sense of belonging. She was working from the time I was in third grade so I was pretty much a latchkey kid. By the time I was 12, it wasn't unusual for me to take a bus downtown and go shopping on my own. I've always had strong self-esteem."

Instilling Positive Life Attitudes and Values

Another type of happy childhood is the result of parents instilling positive attitudes and values. "I was baptized in the Catholic Church

Finally, I pulled myself out of the depression and got off the medication. Unfortunately, my older daughter told me she's bulimic. She had become quite overweight. You wouldn't think they'd go together but they do. She's on a lot of anti-depressant medication and has just started Weight Watchers. Looking back, in high school she would make plans with friends and then tell me she was too tired. I was tired and sleeping a lot and it made sense. If I'd had clearer eyes back then I might have seen that we were both depressed.

on the day that Pearl Harbor was bombed" says Christie Dowling. "I was raised in a small town and had a great traditional family and an idyllic childhood. As my siblings and I became teenagers, our dad got us jobs picking prunes on the local ranches. This required getting up at 4 AM on August mornings so the majority of the picking could occur before the temperature rose to 100-plus degrees. It was hard work, made difficult by the heat and uncomfortable by the dirt clods we knelt on. We'd fill a bucket, carry it to the road, empty the prunes into the box, and mark our special number in chalk. It took two or more buckets to fill a box, which brought the handsome sum of 20 cents. Even if we made money babysitting in the winter, we still had to pick prunes in the summer. It wasn't about the money; it was about learning to work. We all possess incredibly strong work ethics and have been successful in our various endeavors because of the experiences our parents made us have."

Margo Howard, Syndicated advice columnist, "Dear Prudence"

"…we were extremely close. I had no siblings and my mother [columnist Ann Landers] was heavily invested in me, emotionally. … [A] recurring pattern [in her letters] is her thanking me for my letters, loving them, asking for more, and apologizing that hers were not longer/better/neater. Her concern for my well-being, my children's, and whichever husband was in the picture shines like a beacon from one decade to the next."

Supreme Court backs the *New York Times* publication of Pentagon Papers • Walt Disney World opens in Florida

JoEllen Brown, learning positive life attitudes

My father was 45 when my parents married. My mother was 37 and they had me very quickly because back then that was pretty old to be having a first child. My dad was already an established professional, very successful and was at the point in his life where he could take time to do things with me. My mom stayed at home and was a really nice mother. I had a lovely childhood. It was an idyllic, wonderful life.

I learned from my dad the value of education. My dad's father had emigrated from Italy and was uneducated. My dad was one of 11 children and they all got an education and did something with their lives. I grew up in a household where we were very cognizant of being citizens of a great country and of the freedom and responsibility involved in that. They believed in charity, that if you do well you have a moral and ethical obligation to give back. For example, I remember my father being active in a fundraising effort to send money to victims of a catastrophe in Italy.

Because my dad changed careers so many times, we had a lot of change in our lives. I had no fear, whatsoever, of change. Change was no big deal. That was another good

Providing Unconditional Love and Support

Some children looked in vain for unconditional love most of their lives while others experienced an abundance of parental love and support that gave them a solid foundation. "Growing up in Vermont was magical and safe," says Frances Judson. "I wish everyone could have the wonderful childhood I had. When I was a freshman in high school we moved to a place that I thought was icky. I was way too smart for the school I was in. By my junior year, my wonderful parents let me go away to boarding school. I thought I'd died and gone to heaven because finally I was in a community of people that valued what I thought was important. That was a happy time."

In describing her childhood as one of the best things in her life, Frances says, "How much better could it be? I'm a lucky girl. I had that fabulous childhood with really supportive, wonderful parents. My brother, sister and I all did incredibly stupid things and made incredibly stupid choices. But our folks were there for us saying, 'Everybody makes mistakes. Let's just move on.'"

Parents who are more than just adequate provide for their children in numerous and complex ways. Ruth Spiro remembers how her father was

thing about the way my parents raised me. We'd just pick up and move. It was nothing. We always enjoyed it. It always worked out, and nobody ever complained. We were not a family of complainers.

I grew up thinking you can do anything you want to do, thinking everything is open to you. The way my parents raised me is responsible for a lot of the drive that I have.

supportive during her teenage years. "He absolutely focused his desire on giving us a good sense of values. He was an immigrant who mastered English at a late age and went on to complete medical and dental school. He was an extraordinary man. I remember that when I sat in Civil Rights picket lines he questioned me long and hard about what the repercussions might be. If I could justify it, he would agree. He might walk down with a watermelon at 10 o'clock at night to make sure I was okay or he might help in the background. He was incredibly supportive."

From Childhood to Motherhood

Unhappy childhoods show what goes wrong but not necessarily how to prevent it. Happy childhoods show what works well but not necessarily how to achieve it. There is still an intuitive leap between our childhood experiences and our later parenting wisdom.

As a parent, I had no consistent philosophy except to love the children because I felt that I had been well loved. Probably we all raise a first child using some principles derived from our own childhoods, and then we raise later children with guidance from the good and bad experiences of our first child. My eldest son Ken, for example, joined Little League.

Katherine Campbell, getting unconditional love

I was the youngest, but I don't think my parents pushed any of us. They approved of everything we did. I had unusual parents because they always gave about the closest you can come to unqualified love. They were mostly approving unless you were doing something really stupid.

When I was 4, we moved from the Southwest to the East coast. That was both a negative and a positive influence on me. I really never got to know my grandparents or other relatives very well. That was negative. The positive side of that, the flip side, is that if I had known them better I would have ended up prejudiced like they were. It seems that my father was prejudiced until he met someone after we moved who was more progressive and who changed my dad's life forever. We have a letter in which he writes about this change. You can't overestimate the impact of that on my life.

My parents never expressed any particular expectations about my life. But I think this story will tell you about my father and how supportive he was. At dad's funeral, my brother spoke

Fanny Howe, Professor, poet and author

"…after their father and I broke up, survival for my children and myself as their only caretaker was all that drove me. I learned how to bend the rules, to prevaricate, to be crooked, to get something for as little as nothing, to take now and pay later, to fake facts in exchange for safety, … to find the free clinics, the kind people, the food stamp outlet, … The potential for corruption that is in all of us is certainly triggered by the feeling of being absolutely alone in a desperate situation. I would do anything for my children."

He had every parent's nightmare of a coach, an equal opportunity bully—yelling at players, parents, umpires, and the opposing team's coach. The coach used only his best players, leaving some children on the bench game after game. Ken didn't enjoy it and didn't sign up again. Our reaction was to keep our next son, Edward, out of Little League. It didn't occur to us that Ken's coach might have been the only bad apple in the coaching barrel. If we had been more astute, we would also have known that we could move Edward to another team if the coach didn't work out. So Edward might have had a great Little League experience but was denied that opportunity by us.

Will, meanwhile, was the kind of child who just demanded to play baseball. He came home one day and told us that he had signed up and the coach would be calling that evening. He started with T-ball, moved on to pitching machine the next year, and was an early draft pick for majors the following year. Thanks to Will's experience in the majors, we saw how the right coach can contribute to

about the lack of a generation gap in our family. If any of us were interested in something, dad always made sure that he read about it so that he could talk with us. This was true even if dad might not agree. Dad never said, "Don't do that."

My parents always wanted the three of us to stay close. One of the things they did was rent a place at the beach in the summer and invite me, my siblings, and our families. We always spent that week together. Then we celebrated Christmas and Thanksgiving together. My parents made a real effort to have a family, to have some continuity. They put a lot of effort into raising us and keeping us together.

a child's development. On the first night, when the parents were gathered in the Little League coach's home, we were told, "I'll never bench your child for a physical mistake, they're just children. But I will bench them for a thinking mistake. I'll teach them to be focused on the game, to know what to do on the field, and to anticipate different outcomes."

Will's coach played all team members, independent of their talents. He worked with a few children at a time throughout the year, seeking to hone their skills. He got the team to the playoffs year after year. Edward, eight years older than Will, served as the assistant coach one summer and finally got some on-field experience.

We are still a long way from a science of parenting even in the 21st century. We don't know how to help all children develop their full potential. I don't think I've ever met a parent who is satisfied with every decision she made. We FW2 women were raised in the middle of a major shift in child-raising philosophies ourselves, and

FW2 Aretha Franklin wins Grammy (Best Female Rhythm & Blues Vocal Performance) • Apollo 14 lands on moon

we were frequently uncertain about the right course of action to follow with our own children.

Having and Not Having Children

Controlling the number and the timing of pregnancies is a conflicted issue—frowned on and yet practiced throughout history—linen condoms were used in ancient Egypt by 1000 BCE and coitus interruptus even earlier, perhaps 1500 BCE.

Our Great Grandmothers and Pregnancies. Just a few years before our great grandmothers began giving birth, Congress passed the Comstock Act of 1873 making it illegal to send contraceptive information or devices through the mail "on the grounds that such was obscene, lewd, lascivious, filthy, indecent and disgusting." (History records that Anthony Comstock was an obsessed gun-toting vigilante of "purity.")

Gloria Feldt,
Executive Director of
Planned Parenthood,
1996-2005

"It is not an overstatement—
it's a jubilant statement of
fact—to say that fertility
control gives women nothing
short of control over their
lives."

Despite the lack of information and education, documents
show that our great grandmothers used coitus interruptus,
abstinence during fertile times, prolonged nursing (an ineffective method practiced even by some of the FW2 Generation), condoms, douching syringes and solutions, vaginal sponges,
cervical caps, and various herbal remedies. Since some methods were
ineffective and others were not easily available, abortion, as in all periods
of history, was also used to limit family size. Much of the nation was still
rural, and the social milieu promoted large families. Given these factors,
it is no surprise that my maternal Great Grandmother had ten children
and my paternal Great Grandmother had twelve children.

Our Grandmothers and Pregnancy. The Federal Comstock Act
and the passage of similarly worded acts in most states never slowed down

Kate Michelman, in her memoir *Liberty and Justice for All: A Life Spent Protecting the Right to Choose*, tells the story of her abortion in the years before *Roe v. Wade*. In a story like many other young women coming of age in the early 1960s, Kate married fairly young, at the age of 20. Much in love and a practicing Catholic, she found herself the mother of three daughters in just three years. The third pregnancy was plagued by health problems and her physician urged her to not have additional children. Kate agreed. Since she believed in the Church's position that birth control was a sin, she and her husband practiced what is called natural birth control.

Kate's role as wife and mother was typical for the time. She considered herself "busy, frazzled, happy." Her husband's career was the primary focus and she played the important supporting role of taking care of the home and children. A role she enjoyed and for which she received the expected social support.

women's [and men's] desire and need to limit the number of children although they led to imprisonments and made it difficult to get information and devices. Just three years before my grandmother was born, a German physician developed the diaphragm, which could not legally be imported into the US. In 1916, Margaret Sanger began bringing diaphragms into the US for use in her birth-control (a term she coined) clinics. Limited availability of the diaphragm, combined with the need to have it fitted by a physician and the age of our grandmothers, meant few of them used this contraceptive although it eventually became a reliable birth control method for later generations. Reflecting the emerging pattern of smaller family size that was still influenced by urban and rural differences, my maternal grandmother, who lived in towns, had four children and my paternal grandmother, who lived on a farm, gave birth to eight sons. (She also raised two orphaned nephews.) [*See photo p. 118*]

Our Mothers and Pregnancy. In 1925, a few years before our mothers entered their childbearing years, Margaret Sanger's husband funded Holland-Rantos Company to manufacture diaphragms in America, making this birth-control device more widely available although still illegal. By the time my mother married, the Depression had made plain the ne-

When her daughters were five, four, and three and life was progressing according to plan, Kate found herself alone one evening, waiting for her husband. Worried when he didn't arrive, she stayed up all night. As evening turned to morning, she called the hospital to see if any accident victims matching his description had been admitted; she called the police to see if there were any reports of accidents. She was desperate and frightened.

The next morning, her husband walked in. That was both the good news and the bad news. He told her that he was in love with another woman and wanted a divorce. She writes, "I was stunned. Waves of pain, fear, shock, anger, and an overwhelming sense of disbelief rocked my world." She pleaded with him to think of the children, to consider the life they were building together, to see the impact on her. When nothing budged him, she asked him to seek counseling so that they could work out any problems. He was adamant about leaving and moved out immediately.

cessity of small families. Studies from the early 1930s indicate that birth control was used by about 60 percent of white, married women. (Comparable data for unmarried women and for different races and ethnicities is not available.) The two most frequently cited methods were coitus interruptus and the condom, both requiring male cooperation. Andrea Tone, in the *Journal of Social History*, describes ads that appeared around this time in women's magazines for "feminine hygiene" products promising "protection," "security," and "dependability." Such products, widely known as birth-control methods but unregulated because they were just for hygiene, included douche powders and liquids, suppositories, and foaming tablets. By the late 1930s, these female contraceptives, sold in stores, marketed door-to-door, and obtained by mail order, outnumbered sales of condoms five-to-one suggesting the desire of women to have personal control over pregnancies. Only in 1937 did the American Medical Association reverse its stand and recognize birth control as a legitimate part of medical education and practice. My mother continued the trend toward smaller families, having two children. [*See photo p. 119*]

FW2 Generation and Pregnancy. It is impossible to recreate the mood, attitude, and (lack of) knowledge of the FW2 Generation

Kate Michelman continues with her story in *Liberty and Justice for All: A Life Spent Protecting the Right to Choose*. She writes about her feelings in that time after her husband leaves, "In an instant, my life changed from that of a typical young mother to complete turmoil. I was devastated, frightened. My self-esteem was destroyed; my identity crushed; my life shattered. I had been rejected by the person I loved. I had no money or job. Our family was disintegrating before my eyes, and I blamed myself."

What could make the situation worse? Several weeks later, while Kate was still trying to figure out how she would manage to provide emotionally and financially for her three daughters, she received another shock. A shock that would change the direction of her life. She was pregnant. Could she cope with another child? What would be the impact of a fourth child on her three small daughters? How would she manage financially?

A sense of desperation led her to attempt suicide. Discovered in time by her neighbor and rushed to the hospital, Kate recovered.

Faye Wattleton,
First female president of Planned Parenthood, 1978-1992

"[Even in the mid-Sixties,] unless you were preparing for marriage, contraception was not discussed. After all, why would virgins need birth control? So, all alone, like so many other single women with boyfriends, I worried about pregnancy. Though I was surrounded by obstetricians and gynecologists every day and human sexuality was the substance of my work, I was still too embarrassed to discuss contraception with anyone."

about sexuality and birth control. Just as we were being born, Sanger's early organization became the Planned Parenthood Federation of America and began a major expansion. By the way, after Sanger, males assumed leadership until 1978 when FW2 Faye Wattleton became not only the first female president but also the first African-American president of the organization. I don't remember anyone mentioning Planned Parenthood, certainly not our mothers. If they said anything about sex or birth control, it was often the rhetorical question, "Why would he marry you if he can get it for free?" If that wasn't a sufficient threat, they told us that if you "did it" you would get pregnant. The twin virtues of staying a virgin were clear—a husband and no disgraceful pregnancy. But, the FW2 Generation was like the Roman god Janus with one face looking out on secret sexual experimentation and a second face looking the other way, pretending there was only virginity. Of course, we didn't talk about sexual activities, even with friends. No one wanted to be considered a "bad girl."

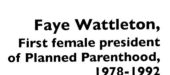

Title IX of Education Amendment prohibits discrimination & changes face of athletic programs • 1ˢᵗ cell phone call

Her doctor, learning the reason for her actions, told her that a therapeutic abortion was possible. Her case would need to be brought before the hospital review board and they would have to determine if she was unfit to be a mother and therefore able to have a legal abortion. Her other option, of course, was an illegal abortion.

After much soul searching, she decided to pursue the former option. Although terrified by the situation, she met with the all-male hospital review board. As frightening as they and their questions were, having a fourth child as a single mother was even more frightening. The board asked her many personal questions that she characterizes as "humiliating" and said they would soon make a decision. But instead of a decision, the board called her back for a second meeting with more questions. Finally, one doctor said, "We have considered your case carefully and have decided you may have the abortion." But even then, the story was not over.

Laws, including the long cultural shadows of overturned laws, public attitudes, and inadequate information influenced the thinking and actions of the FW2 Generation. In 1960, the year the FDA approved the Pill, 30 states still had laws prohibiting or limiting the marketing and sale of contraceptives, even to married women, and in 1964 eight states still banned contraceptive sales. The Pill helped change the acceptance of birth control and bring contraception to married and unmarried women. At that time, however, unmarried women were often embarrassed to ask a physician about any method of birth control because it revealed they were sexually active.

FW2 Generation women, among the earliest takers of the Pill, used the high dosage Enovid pill with 10 milligrams progesterone and 150 micrograms estrogen. Today, the Pill women typically use has 1 milligram progesterone and 20 micrograms estrogen. Grateful though we were for birth control, we now realize we were guinea pigs for high dosage birth-control pills just as later, in our 50s, we were guinea pigs for high-dosage hormone replacement therapy.

Gloria Feldt

"…I was barely twenty. Two method failures and one episode of magical thinking and, bingo, I had three children. … I had severe anemia with my last two pregnancies….The Pill had reached Odessa, Texas, by then and I started popping those high hormone Enovid E's like they were candy. The hell with the side effects. I knew that having another child right then would send me over the brink, physically and emotionally."

Kate Michelman's story, told in her memoir *Liberty and Justice for All*, reflects not only the legal times but also the state of technology. In the 60s, we were still a decade away from inexpensive home pregnancy tests available without prescription at most drug, grocery, and convenience stories. Consequently, it took much longer than it does today to learn if we were pregnant. Weeks passed while we waited to see if perhaps we were just "late." Then, suspecting a pregnancy, more time would pass before we could get an appointment with the doctor. Even after the appointment, we waited days until a phone call from the doctor's office let us know if the "rabbit had died," meaning we were pregnant. [Actually, the rabbit always died. The change/non-change in the female rabbit's ovaries that indicated a pregnancy could only be determined by killing the animal and inspecting the ovaries. However, the shorthand for a positive pregnancy test became the "rabbit died."]

Aware that the clock was ticking away the days during which it would be safe for an abortion, Kate Michelman set up an appointment at the hospital a few days after the review

Tess Gallagher,
Poet, short story writer,
novelist, playwright

"It was very present to me and painfully clear from photographs and film coverage at the time [of Vietnam war] that we were bombing the children of another country and I really couldn't conscience being able to carry a child of my own, knowing this, that I was a part of why this was happening, and that my own husband was over there, asked to perform this cruel act by our government."

FW2 Generation Experiences with Children: Then and Now

For FW2 women who had experienced inadequate parenting themselves, the struggle to raise a child was sometimes too much, causing them to ignore or leave their children even though they loved them. For a second group of women, a growing awareness of the inadequacies of their childhoods caused them to break with the past and parent in different ways. A third group of women had moderate to wonderful childhoods and sought to give their children similar experiences.

Period I: Having Children

Planned and Unplanned Pregnancies

The path to parenthood was far from trouble free. Problems with conceiving or successfully carrying a baby to term still seem fresh to these women, even 35 to 40 years later.

Some difficulties can be attributed to health problems that weren't easily identified for FW2 Generation women although they

board had finally approved the procedure for her.

Without saying what she was doing, Kate got a friend to stay with her daughters. At the hospital, she was prepared for the therapeutic abortion. A nurse came into her room with papers to be signed. Almost casually, the nurse inquired if Kate's divorce was final. The financial terms had not been worked out and Kate responded, "No." The nurse told Kate that they had failed to mention that she must have her husband's signature on the document to show that he agreed to the abortion.

Kate Michelman was furious and frustrated. But the requirements of state law meant that her protestations were for naught. She redressed and left the hospital. Kate contacted her husband, they met, and he signed the necessary document. Finally, a few days later, she was able to get the abortion that would allow her to move forward with her life. A life that eventually led her to the presidency of NARAL Pro-Choice America from 1985-2004 and has made her a sought after speaker and advisor.

probably would be today. "I had ten pregnancies and seven miscarriages in the first ten years we were married," says Harriet Magill. "I couldn't avoid pregnancy no matter what we did. I kept getting pregnant and kept miscarrying. It was years later that we found out I have a really bad thyroid."

For other women, pregnancies created health problems. "My first pregnancy did not go well and I ended up with a severe kidney problem," says Linda Bixford. "The baby died so there was a lot of trauma in my life. I was so naïve at the age of 20 that it never occurred to me that babies didn't get born perfectly healthy. The three children I have living were my 5th, 6th and 7th pregnancies."

Frequent birth control failures meant that many children were unplanned. This quote is typical: "We had three children quickly and didn't plan a single one of them. The first two were diaphragm babies. *Obviously* the diaphragm didn't work. The doctor thought I should try the Pill. That wasn't exactly foolproof either as the third child was a Pill baby. Finally I had a tubal ligation."

Adrienne Barbeau,
Award-winning Actor

"I was frightened. I was nearly thirty years old. I'd dated nine men in eleven years, not one of them interested in a long-term commitment. I didn't care about getting married but I was ready for a long term relationship and I wanted children."

Pamela Ratcliffe, a supermom who was old before she was young

I was pregnant when I got married at 16, and the school forced me to leave halfway through my junior year. I had three children by the time I was 21. Then I took on three foster children. It was Easter. A neighbor was sitting in his car just up the hill from all our homes. He must have been in his usual alcoholic stupor when his wife walked up to get him for dinner. She got in the car, and he took off, crashing into a tree. They were both critically injured; she was in the hospital for six months.

Their children were eight, ten, and eleven. Around 7 PM, they were still walking around the neighborhood and had nowhere to go. I said, "You might as well come on in, and we'll see what's going to happen." It turns out their relatives didn't want to be burdened with them. Then their father died a few days later, and I was the one who had to tell them. I never thought of myself as young. I was old before I was young. I took them, and that was that. They stayed with me until their mother got out of the hospital. Eventually two of my neighbors started coming over to help. We'd set up ironing boards in the living room. This was when girls wore ironed cotton dresses to school every day. Instead of a coffee klatch, we'd have an ironing klatch.

Period II: Raising Children

Parents enter the Raising Children Period in stages, but primary parenting focus shifts to this period when there is no longer any emphasis on babies. Parental responsibilities of these years include not only loving, setting standards and goals, disciplining, and providing for children's material needs but also volunteering at school, chauffeuring children to extracurricular activities, assisting with schoolwork, providing advice and guidance for teenage decisions, and myriad other ways that parents are involved in raising children. The range of experiences of women I interviewed led me to characterize them as Supermoms, Perfect Moms, Flawed Moms, and Regular Moms.

I had my fourth child in 1966. At about the same time, my daughters had two girlfriends whose mother had died suddenly of cancer. Their father fell apart, so they came and stayed with me for most of a year.

Then I took in two teenage boys who had problems. The mother of one boy had died suddenly, and he had nowhere to go. Another boy was considered a delinquent and had major problems with his dad. They were friends of my daughters in school so they just kind of drifted in too and lived with us. It was kind of an unusual situation. [*continued*]

Supermoms: Parenting One's Own and Other People's Children

A few women enlarged their vision of motherhood to include parenting other people's children in addition to their own. They became Supermoms.

In the aftermath of her mother's unexpected death, 21-year-old Sandra Ray took charge of her 15-year-old sister and 8-year-old brother when her son was just 13 months old. Dolores Hermandez volunteered to raise her step-daughter's child who was born within months of her own baby. Pamela Ratcliffe became the neighborhood mother for children whose family life was even worse than that of her own alcoholic-father/narcissistic-mother childhood. Other women liked raising children so much, feeling they had something special to offer, that they added adopted children to their families.

Perfect Moms: Doing it All

Many women believed they *should* be Perfect Mothers. After all, they had been told that a college education would make

Doris Kearns Goodwin,
Author and presidential historian

"I took my oldest son, Richard, to spring training ... I taught my two youngest sons, Michael and Joe, how to keep score, bought season tickets, and took them to dozens of games every year. ... Sometimes, sitting in the park with my boys, I imagine myself back at Ebbets Field, a young girl once more in the presence of my father ... There is magic in these moments, for when I open my eyes and see my sons in the place where my father once sat, I feel an invisible bond among our three generations."

Five Watergate break-in defendants plead guilty • Senate Watergate hearings televised • "I am not a crook" –Nixon

Pamela Ratcliffe's story concludes, when old finally needs to be young

I finally needed something for me and so went to work as a waitress. I looked forward to every night just incredibly. I would work all day long to make sure that I could be ready to leave at 6 o'clock. I had dinner on the table; had the laundry done; had the kids fed and bathed. Everything was done so I could walk out of the house and go to work. I remember how much fun that job was.

[*Pamela eventually teams up with a business partner, and they open a bar. When he wants out, she buys his interest in what becomes a highly successful venture. At that point, her husband quits his job and says she has to hire him. A few years later, everything becomes more than she can bear.*] At the end of 1975, I left home. I just couldn't do it anymore. I wanted something for me. I made an incredible financial sacrifice because I felt I had never done anything except what was always expected of me even though I had my own successful business. I just felt like I had never had a life except for everyone else. It's not that I begrudge it but I just never had it. I signed everything over to my ex-husband, and he took custody of

them better mothers. "I had to be the perfect mother," recalls Brenda Dunlap. "I did everything. I never realized that maybe my husband could do some of it."

JoEllen Brown expresses the dual desire to fulfill the traditionally accepted mother role *and* to accomplish goals in her career role. "[In the late 1970s] I pushed myself to the limit to try to be the wife that I had been brought up to be, the career woman that I had been trained to be, and the mother that I was trying to be. We all went through that—remember the ads with the woman saying, 'I can bring home the bacon, fry it up in a pan, and never, never, never let you forget you're a man.' I was going to do it all. And for a while I did."

Flawed Moms: Struggling Through, Leaving Home

Some women had children but didn't want them or didn't know how to be a mother. "I got pregnant at 18," said Canda Mitans.

the children. I went from never looking at a price tag to living in a basement apartment working as a waitress.

I stayed in the area so I could see the kids. The reason I left was the growing sense that there was no room for me there. I didn't know what I was going to do. I didn't have a plan. I just did it. I think I felt the plan would come later but I needed to get away. Once it was over I can remember this incredible sigh of relief.

"I was totally unprepared. I was a good parent in that I did all the things you were supposed to do but I didn't have any clue about what it really meant. That was not a good thing to happen to me or for my kids to have that parent." Similarly, Helen Young looks back and says, "I know I wasn't fair to my first child. It wasn't his fault that I got pregnant but he was an unwanted child and I didn't always control my temper with him. I probably made him feel unwanted. You learn as you get older, and that's why it is so important for people to wait to have children until they have more maturity. Some people do fine, but I wasn't ready for it."

Sometimes the struggle with family was more than they could take. They tried to be good mothers, but they finally had to leave to take care of themselves. Most continued contact with their children, but they turned major responsibility over to their husbands or parents. Not everyone who thought about leaving actually did. Patricia Fisher, for example, says, "I remember thinking, 'Would I be able to go create a new identity for myself? Disappear and become someone else?' But I knew I never would really do it because I would never leave my kids."

Gloria Feldt

"For only when equals come together can both men and women be free to follow their hearts and their minds in making families that are right for them. … I am blessed with such a marriage…. Though we have given birth to no children together, we have blended our families into a new mix that is enriched by each member and woven into a whole cloth by love."

World Trade Center opens in NYC as world's tallest building • Federal Express begins delivery operations

Lois Cameron, a supermom with so much to give

We had four children and thought they were just the best. We believed we had a lot to offer so when the older ones were adolescents we decided to adopt a brother and sister. Seven-year-old Brian was hyperactive. Today we'd say he has ADHD, although we didn't know that at the time. As he grew older and larger, he continually badgered and sometimes physically threatened me. Many times I said to my husband, "If you come home and can't find me, look in the closets. I might be tied up somewhere." We took him to counseling, but that didn't help. It was total hell.

His sister Marsha was 5 and very quiet at first. Later, she began to steal from us. We had to put padlocks on the outside of our bedroom doors. It was an awful way to live. My health went down drastically. I developed high blood pressure, and the doctor repeatedly told me, "You've got to do something. You've got to get the children removed. You're dying a slow death." My body was shutting down because I felt so trapped. I had no place to go.

Regular Moms: Doing the Best They Could

The Supermom, Perfect Mom, and Flawed Mom were more the exception than the rule—often the product of difficult childhoods. Most were just Regular Moms. Somehow they balanced child-raising responsibilities with the rest of their lives. Regular Moms were more likely to have had "normal" childhoods.

The Unimaginable Happens: Losing a Child

Unfortunately, being a mother of any kind does not make one immune to the tragedies of life. When asked, "What are the three worst things that have happened to you?" a number of women said, "The worst thing that could happen would be to lose your child. That never happened to me so I can't really say anything bad happened." But some women did lose a child—in infancy, in those difficult teenage years, or even as young adults.

Julie Ash shares her story. "As the children grew I developed a very strong relationship with them. There were just the three of us. I drove a school bus so I could be home with the kids when they were little. I continued to learn from my kids as they matured. I even enjoyed them

We really did love these two children. We went through counseling, but nobody seemed to help. To make matters worse, our youngest child got caught up in this. We had so many problems to deal with that we unknowingly harmed her. A few years ago, she said, "I feel like I've been dead since I was five years old." I won't forget that as long as I live.

It's an unfinished story. Our relationship with Brian is good. There was a time when he thought we could do no right. Now he thinks we can do no wrong. Marsha, on the other hand, has made awful accusations that are both untrue and scary. She called one night when she was high on drugs and threatened to kill us. We felt we had to keep our doors locked and check behind us constantly. We told people about her threat so they would know to look for us if we were missing. It's hard because we have given so much of our lives to these children.

as teenagers. When my older son went away to college, I got to know my second son as a person apart from his brother. Then the worst thing in my life happened. My older son died. It was devastating. He fell off a balcony and was instantly killed. They took him to the hospital and tried to get his heart going but the doctor just said to forget it. I always admired the doctor because it's a hard decision to make. He didn't know that my son had a living Will. He didn't want to be kept alive. Now, when things get bad, I know that nothing can really be as bad as what I've already been through."

Louise Moran also lost her son. Both women have tried to deal with the tragedy; both know it has changed them forever. "The major event in my life happened February 9, 1993. My 16-year-old son was spending the night at my ex-husband's house. He and a friend drove to the store to get snacks. They were returning home at 9 PM when he hit a tree. Both were killed. I joined Compassionate Friends, a group for bereaved parents, and went for a couple of years. One woman in the group, whose child had been dead for several years, said, 'I always feel like I'm standing alone.' I have that feeling even now. I don't fit a lot of places. I've had a real hard time."

American Indian Movement (AIM) occupies Wounded Knee, SD for 72 days • Gender bias in language examined

Mary Jackson, leaving the children at home

My defining story is that my mother died when I was a high-school senior. My parents were divorced, and I had a difficult relationship with my father. I just wanted to get the heck away. In college, I was looking for an older person, a parent figure. I got engaged to a man who was four and a half years older than me who seemed worldly and sophisticated. We married two weeks after graduation.

After my first son was born, I had an extended postpartum depression. By 1972, I'd had three sons. I was delighted to not have a daughter. All my cousins were girls and my mother had three sisters and they were constantly in bitter battles. It was just such a relief to have these cuddly boys who adored their mother.

Meanwhile, I was struggling to come out of depression and went to a psychiatrist three times a week. Once I began to feel better, I got interested in painting again. As I gained confidence in my own thoughts and experience, I decided I was going to give painting a serious try. My focus was on being a pretty good mom, keeping the house going, and furthering my art. But the more

Period III: Relating to Adult Children

Once children are adults, mothers become alternately friends, coaches, nurturers, cheerleaders, and silent observers. The positive, in-transition, and negative adult-adult relationships show three child-raising outcomes.

If all goes well, there is a positive relationship between a mother and her adult child or children. No one goes through the years of raising children without making mistakes. What matters is that the mistakes were minor, or occurred within a stable, loving (single or dual parent) family where compensating factors overcame the mistakes, or led to insights. Once mothers raised children to adulthood, we arrived at the portal of adult-adult relationships, which sometimes opened smoothly but frequently had squeaky hinges in the form of unforgiven prior mistakes and new miscommunications.

You Give 100 Percent

Figuring out the right "light touch" as a parent of adult children can be wonderfully rewarding. Unknowingly, many FW2 women had followed the advice of Yogi Berra, "You give 100 percent in the first half ... and

I self-actualized, the less my husband and I had in common. He was always uncomfortable with my artistic side. That was one of the reasons that ultimately led us to split.

Then everything changed in the early 1980s. I decided that I couldn't stand the marriage any longer. I knew that my husband would never give up the kids. I knew that he probably wouldn't survive. I knew that he would just go to pieces if he had to live by himself.

I was the one who wanted to leave so I moved out. By this time our eldest was in college; our middle child was a sophomore. It was just awful to leave because I adored my boys. I told them in January that I was going to leave at the end of the school year. That was a terrible time. It was hard on everybody but it was hardest on the youngest.

if that isn't enough in the second half you give what's left." Although education and work took a great deal of energy and time, FW2 women gave another 100 percent of themselves to raising their children. Some found they had to give still more to their adult children, but for many, the outcome was positive. "I have a great relationship with all four of my children, my son and daughter and two stepsons," remarks Kate Shapiro Chen. "The hardest thing is to back off from parenting and let them each to relate to me as an adult." Another woman, Shirley Olson , worked for six years as the sole support for her children, and during this time they developed a close unit. "We had to count on each other," she says. "I used to tell them that it was their job to go to school, get good grades, and not get in trouble. It was my job to go to work and earn money. Everybody has their job, and let's just all do it." She speaks glowingly about her adult children: "They refer to me as their best friend, which makes me feel great. I was fortunate. I never had the horrible problems with my children that a lot of people have. Now we are more friends than mother/daughter."

Shere Hite,
Author and director of Hite Research

"Every family is a 'normal' family—no matter whether it has one parent, two or no children at all. A family can be made up of any combination of people, heterosexual or homosexual, who share their lives in an intimate (not necessarily sexual) way… Wherever there is lasting love, there is a family."

VP Spiro Agnew resigns (income tax evasion)—replaced by Gerald Ford • Barcode invented • Gas: 40 cents gal.

Frances Judson, problems with teenagers resolve into joyous adult relationships

The kids went through horrible teenage times. There were moments when you really just wanted to say, "I'm sorry; someone's made a mistake here. I have the wrong children. Take them away. I'm a nice person. I've done what I thought was right, and they're being vile." My daughter was a vile teenager. That's the only word to describe it.

Despite Virginia's vile adolescence we have such a fun time with her now. She is just a joy. She is so thoughtful. She travels a lot and always calls when she is leaving town. She keeps in touch. She is funny. She sent me a Mother's Day card two years ago that said, "Thank you for not giving me away when I was a teenager."

My son wasn't quite as bad but I do remember saying to him, "Richard, this whole adolescence thing is a process. You must go through it in order to be a normal grown up but don't expect me to like it because I don't. You're not fun to be with, and I don't like being called those bad names. Get over it." He is still inventing himself as a grown up. I would say our relationship with him is very good when he's around. But we are cautious; we don't intrude too much.

Erica Jong,
Author

"I look at my daughter and her friends in their twenties and they are reveling in their sexuality. They don't feel guilty, and why should they? … But I would be happier if my daughter and her friends were crashing through the glass ceiling instead of the sexual ceiling...." [continued]

Dee Johnson felt lucky to have a stepson living with them and then a "surprise" daughter later in life. "I have a very loving, very close, very warm relationship with both my daughter and son. My daughter came home after she graduated from college a few months ago. She quickly decided she should move out. I think she was right although I was kind of sad to see her go. She tells me a lot, more than I really want to know sometimes. We love each other dearly. We email each other every day and talk most days. My daughter and I squabble sometimes but mothers and daughters always do. We laugh about it. My son and I talk frequently but not as often as my daughter because he's busy with a wife, child, and job."

Sometimes good relationships are forged even when there have been major traumas. Lynn Sullivan shares her story with us. "I get along wonderfully with my children. I let them live their own lives because they deserve it. We just have a great relationship. My youngest daughter is almost like a soul mate to me. They've had a lot to work through. My sister-in-law's husband molested them, which was one of the reasons I divorced my husband. He wouldn't believe our daughters and wouldn't

When he calls we'll do a dinner. My husband will go and have lunch with him at work. He called yesterday because he was working on a project and needed some ideas. He said, "Can you brainstorm with me?" Of course, we'll jump in and do that, but we're still treading a little lightly with him.

talk to his sister. Her husband went on to molest the other children in the family before ending up in prison. I can't believe that I didn't see it."

It Ain't Over

Relationships are more like movies than snapshots so assigning them to a single category may not be appropriate. Or, as Yogi Berra said, "It ain't over, 'til it's over." One woman says she and her daughter were close. Her daughter called her regularly and they'd have lunch or shop. "It was all hugs and kisses. Now, she's met some guy and all she wants from me is a greeting card relationship. It's the pits." A few months from now, they may again feel close. That's the changing nature of these relationships.

Jessica Kleinman had many miscarriages after the birth of her son. She wanted another child and perhaps this partially explains why she struggles to let go of the child-adult relationship. "Having a child was a miracle. He's a great kid although he has his problems. I try very hard to not give a lot of advice, but sometimes I can't help

Erica Jong
[*concludes*]
"…Being able to have an orgasm with a man you don't love or having *Sex and the City* on television, that is not liberation. … the problem is: You're not going to elect Carrie to the Senate or to run your company. Let's see the Senate fifty percent female; let's see women in decision-making positions—that's power. Sexual freedom can be a smokescreen for how far we haven't come."

Electricity rates increase by 30% • Mexican-American Women's National Association formed • Digital watches

Gage Worth, looking toward the parent-adult child relationship

I was very happy I wasn't on one of the planes that crashed [on 9/11] because I haven't gone full cycle with my daughter yet. I really pray that nothing happens to her and nothing happens to me while we're estranged. I always thought I was a successful parent and I even thought it was the most successful thing I ever did. It was easy to evaluate on a day-to-day basis that it was a success. I had a great relationship with her, but now she's rebelled and is a willful 19 year old.

I start to question everything. I should have had more time with her. I shouldn't have worked so hard. I don't know. We didn't communicate enough. I know that it will end and come out the other side, but we're not there yet. I was a disciplinarian, and to be a disciplinarian in today's world with all the permissiveness, it makes you the mortal enemy of other parents and kids too. Now she is pulling away and wants to be on her own. She doesn't want me to give her any instructions, any limits, anything. So she is at college where she needs to be, and we don't talk that much. I'm just assuming there will be another time when she gets back into what we used to have.

doing it. I've gotten to the point where I've removed myself from feeling responsible for him. If he blows it yet again, it's just too bad. He currently has a good job but over the years he made some bad choices about women and financial matters. I can go back and figure out why he's done *x* or *y* but as my brother says, 'You can take too much blame for the bad and too little credit for the good.' My attitude now is 'Okay, kiddo, we're here for you but you need to take care of yourself.' That's working for now."

Wrong Mistakes

Relationships with children change over time, and it is tempting to call all situations "transitional." However, at any given time, some relationships are negative and may not change much in the future. There are times when the Yogi-ism "we made too many wrong mistakes" seems uncannily appropriate.

Familial relationships were strained in Pamela Ratcliffe's birth family and, not surprisingly, in her own family. She says, "Losing the custody of my children is the worst thing in my life." But a lifelong pattern of alienation from her parents and siblings seems to be replicating itself in the relationships with two of her daughters. "I'm alienated from two of my children. With my oldest

I guess you have to have a certain amount of perspective like my husband has. He raised three before he helped me raise this one. When you're in the middle of it you think this is the way it is going to be forever and what did I do wrong. I'm very sure that it will get better. I can see glimpses of what it is going to be like.

,,

daughter, we may never bridge our differences. My second daughter won't initiate anything. I have to be the one to make the effort."

Uniqueness of Child Raising for FW2 Generation Women

Our mothers, grandmothers, and great grand-mothers primarily raised their children with help from their mothers because they lived nearby. The FW2 Generation didn't. Many of us moved to other parts of the country as our husbands pursued their careers. We had few resources—professionals, organizations or books—to help us figure out what to do. Those of us who went to work found our-selves sorely lacking role models for guidance. When divorce came to many of us, we needed to figure out single-parent strategies, often in new locations and circumstances. Some of us

Richard M. Nixon departs before Gerald Ford is sworn in

Paula Conley, an early abortion, later leaving the children

I had an abortion before they were legal. It was horrible. I was picked up at the Empire movie theater in a black sedan. There were three other girls in the car as well as a man and a woman. Periodically they made us put our heads down and cover our eyes. The driver took us to an abortion factory in the country.

Until then, I'd been Goody Two-Shoes. I didn't have many boyfriends. I went to parties, but if a boy touched me I wouldn't go out with him again. I was a prude. When I met James, I was a virgin. We fell in love and planned to marry. When I got pregnant, I told my parents. My fiancé never told his parents; to this day they don't know. My parents made all the arrangements. But I also knew that I couldn't be pregnant. James was still in college and wasn't ready to get married. He wasn't supportive afterward. He never wanted to even mention it.

After we married, we had two children. It turns out all James did was take up time and space. He didn't support us the way I expected so I went to work as a secretary. He beat me up one time. That was enough. That's when I left. He never told his parents why, and I didn't

were trying to succeed in demanding careers and needed the assistance of loving trustworthy child care workers and other helpers. God is in the details, they say, and the details required a great deal of attention even while we were trying to understand who we were and how to how to raise children in the turbulent `60s and `70s.

Conclusion: "I know, but that was different"

My children have mostly forgiven me for the times I was particularly inept. One August afternoon, for example, I failed to go to the airport to meet Edward when he returned from a month with his dad. He was nine years old, and the flight attendant called our home when I didn't show up. I thought Edward was returning the next day. I was in the middle of a long phone conversation when the person Edward called after not reaching me came by and slipped a note in front of me: *Edward is at the airport.* I dropped the phone and dashed to the airport an hour away. Edward and I are very close so I don't mind how often he good-naturedly retells this story of abandonment.

Raising children who grow up to be happy and successful (by their own criteria) ranks just above the State Lottery as a sure thing. FW2

think it was right for me to tell them. They think I'm the bad person who left him. We finally divorced, and the kids and I moved into an inexpensive townhouse.

Later, I left the kids with their father. I didn't have any money. I had to beg my in-laws basically to buy shoes for the kids. I just had had enough. I was tired of trying to figure out where the next meal was coming from. On the verge of a nervous breakdown, I moved away. The children came down every six weeks, or I went up there. I was never really out of touch with them. Their father ended up having a nervous breakdown, so the boys lived with his parents. I love my children but I probably should never have had children.

women who have now reached a plateau of reflection between the 2nd third and the 3rd third of our lives have much to be thankful for and at least a few things to regret. High on my thankful list stand my children. They have crafted their own lives and become, to echo the words of Shirley Olson, "the kind of people I would want to have as friends, even if they were not my children. I think they are the most interesting people and among the funniest people I know."

We are children; we are parents of children; we are parents of children who are parents. We struggled for independence and even distance from our parents yet we want to hold our children close. When I interviewed Wendy Henderson, she expressed exactly my thoughts about this dilemma. Wendy and her husband live on the west coast with a son in Chicago and a daughter on the east coast. The children return home when they can, but given their busy schedules that isn't often. Wendy told me that she was pouting about not having her children nearby when a friend said, "That's exactly what you did to your parents." Wendy responded, as many of us have, "I know, but that was different."

FW2s Faye Dunaway (*Chinatown*) and Valerie Perrine (*Lenny*) are Best Actress nominees • Patty Hearst kidnapped

Heigh Ho, It's Off to Work We Go: The FW2 Generation Goes to Work

Once Upon a Time

In the spring of 1970, as I was finishing my doctorate at Northwestern University and looking for employment, my dissertation advisor said, "If you don't get a job, you'll still be a great hostess." I laughed. I was married, had two small children, and liked to give dinner parties. However, that didn't mean I'd be satisfied with anything less than a career that would allow me to use the knowledge I had worked hard to acquire.

But the story is incomplete if I leave it there. My advisor was Donald T. Campbell, a leading psychologist, a brilliant man who *The New York Times*, upon his death in 1996, called a "social scientist who left his mark on half a dozen disciplines and who helped revolutionize the fundamental principles of scientific inquiry." Don hired me as his research assistant in 1966 when the ink was still wet on my M.A. degree, after I accompanied my husband from Stanford to Chicago for his first post-MBA job. Two years later, Don recommended my admission to the Ph.D. program with a National Institute of Mental Health fellowship. He was a caring man, and I feel honored to have studied with him. But let's face it: Don would never have said to a male student, "If you don't get a job, you'll still be a great host." He and most other

US troops leave; Saigon falls to Communists • Bill Gates & Paul Allen start Microsoft; write BASIC for PCs

Virginia Garfield, divorce changes part-time work to full time

A friend of mine opened a claims adjusting business and asked me to help him. That was 1976, and I had two young daughters. Previously, I'd run a nursery school for a year and a half but I was a stay-at-home mom doing my volunteer work. It seemed I was so busy. I said if I got a dime an hour I'd be a rich person.

I worked out of my house and handled the claims adjusting reports. My husband and I were beginning not to get along. It just wasn't a good situation so the work was a nice outlet for me.

I found myself a single mom in 1985 when my husband and I split up. I had an 18-year-old, a 16-year-old and a 10-year-old. I started working full time. I'd drop my son off at the bus stop in the morning and go on to work. I arranged with my boss that I could be home when my son returned from school.

I enjoyed my work as an insurance investigator, handling claims and investigating accidents. Some of these were routine and boring but others were fascinating. No two days

Lore Harp,
Co-founder, Vector
Graphic, Inc.

"I guess I've been somewhat headstrong and determined all my life but I don't know where that came from. I think sometimes the combination of everything in your life is such that you do things you hadn't really contemplated doing. As things develop you meet the challenges and stand up to them, and if people respond to what you're doing, then it feeds on itself."

people at that time thought the statement was not inappropriate when said to a female. Don, bless his memory, was grounded in the values and attitudes of his generation.

Even that is not the end of the story. A dozen years later, in an unforeseen twist of events for a man of his well-accustomed ways, he found himself divorced and remarried to a well-known anthropologist who couldn't find employment at Northwestern University, where Don had worked most of his professional career. When she received a tenure offer at Lehigh University, Don gave up his position and moved with her to Bethlehem, Pennsylvania so she could pursue her career. By 1982, women were an important part of the workforce and their needs were becoming a factor in the life equation of married couples.

Many women have stories more dramatic than mine, stories of not being taken seriously, stories of discouragement, stories of being paid less because a woman "didn't have to support a family" even when she did, stories of blatant discrimination, and stories of sexual harassment. But FW2 Generation women took it all in stride and continued to make employment inroads both in numbers and variety of occupations.

were ever alike. I met everybody from ditch diggers and ice-cream cart drivers to presidents of corporations, police chiefs, fire chiefs and everybody in between. Eventually I took the licensing test, passed it, and was on my way.

I saw a high-school friend this summer at the class reunion and told her what I had been doing. She said, "You always wanted to be Nancy Drew. You got to be Nancy Drew." Yeah, in a way I did.

Yet these were not anticipated inroads. When I asked FW2 women about their life goals when they left high school, 78 percent said, "marriage and children." Another 10 percent recalled no expectation about their future. Only 12 percent had career goals, and these were primarily traditional aspirations of executive secretary, nurse, artist. One woman in this career group wanted to be a doctor but then married after two years of college and never pursued that goal. In actual fact, approximately 98 percent of FW2 women worked, most for a large number of their adult years.

Sex-Segregated Employment Opportunities

Girl Friday Wanted—Must Have 10 Years Experience

Help Wanted ads are only one way to find employment opportunities. However, when they were sex-segregated, they reflected the value and place of women and men in the workforce. A lawsuit protesting the sex-segregated listings documented a typical ad,

Cokie Roberts,
Senior news analyst for NPR and political commentator for ABC News

"What I didn't anticipate was the real and blatant discrimination that greeted me upon my graduation from college. It was 1964; the civil rights bill was passed that summer. I think that it is something young women really don't understand, which is that it made all the difference in the world to have the law on our side....The help-wanted ads were white and Negro, male and female."

FW2 Annie Dillard wins Pulitzer for book *Pilgrim at Tinker Creek* • Mood rings & pet rocks • Postage: 13 cents

Jobs—Male Interest		Jobs—Female Interest	
Acad. Instructors	$13,000	Acad. Instructors	$13,000
Accountants	$10,000	Accountants	$ 6,000
Adm. Ass't, CPA	$15,000	Bookkeeper Ins.	$ 5,000
Advertising Mgr.	$10,000	Clerk-Typist	$ 4,200
Bookkeeper F-C	$ 9,000	Draftsman	$ 6,000
Financial Consultant	$12,000	Keypunch D.T.	$ 6,720
Land Development	$30,000	Keypunch Beginner	$ 4,500
Marketing Manager	$15,000	Proofreader	$ 4,900
Management Trainee	$ 8,400	Secretary	$ 4,800

placed in *The Pittsburgh Press* by an employment agency in 1970, five years after passage of the Civil Rights Act that forbade discrimination in employment. I alphabetized the lists for ease in comparing the number and types of positions open to men versus those open to women and added an average at the bottom of each column to show the difference in salaries. [*See table above and on facing page.*]

In the 1960s, if you weren't married or if your husband was still in school, then you worked. You worked in spite of the questions that doubted your seriousness and the required typing test even when you weren't seeking a secretarial position. Typically you were asked, "What are your marital plans? Do you have a boyfriend? Will you continue to work if you get married?" Sometimes it got much more personal as Susie Clark remembers, "When I was being interviewed for jobs in the mid-1960s, I was asked what kind of birth control I was using, and I answered. My daughter and her friends are appalled that anyone would ask that kind of a question."

I recently found an old 1966 *Harper's Magazine* article by well-known business management consultant Peter Drucker. He wrote, "Most graduate students, while far from rich, live well above the poverty line. Their

Jobs—Male Interest		Jobs—Female Interest	
Office Mgr. Trainee	$ 7,200	Secretary D. T.	$ 5,400
Product Manager	$18,000	Secretary, Equal Oppor.	$ 6,000
Retail Manager	$15,000	Secretary, Executive	$ 6,300
Sales-Advertising	$ 8,400	Typist-Statistical	$ 5,000
Sales-Consumer	$ 9,600		
Sales-Industrial	$12,000		
Sales-Machinery	$ 8,400		
Average:	$12,562	Average:	$ 5,986

income, however, comes from fellowships or grants rather than from wages. If there is a wage earner in the family, it is the wife rather than the husband." Notice how graduate students were assumed to be males. This is the way the world worked then, and we didn't think to question it.

Law versus Culture

As the FW2 Generation began seeking jobs, discrimination in employment became illegal under the provisions of the Civil Rights Act of 1964. But just because it was illegal didn't mean that it ceased to exist. Some women spoke about subtle and not so subtle discrimination when trying to get a job. Ann Baxter told me, "I was looking for a university job, and the guy I talked to said, 'There is a position within the Oceanography Department but they go out on cruises, and you wouldn't want to do that.' Of course, I just sat there saying, 'Oh, okay.' I was too naïve to know any different." But others didn't take "no" or "you can't" as the final word. As Katherine Campbell, recalls, "After I got my master's degree in chemistry and worked for a few years, I sought a position at a large chemical company. The recruiter told me

Billie Jean King,
Tennis trailblazer

"Wimbledon is one of the most respected events in all of sports and now with women and men paid on an equal scale [2007 announcement], it demonstrates to the rest of the world that this is the right thing to do for the sport, the tournament and the world."

Jean Woods, sexual harassment is a hurdle, not a barrier

In the mid-1960s, the high-school principal where I taught put the make on me. Because I wouldn't come through for him, he got pissed. It got to the point that I either had to quit or he was going to fire me. This was just before awareness of women's rights issues. I went to a family friend, a big gun in the school system, who told me, "You've got a good case and you could go to court and win. But you'd be blacklisted and never get another teaching job in the state." So I quit.

I traveled a bit and came back wanting to teach. I ended up in a school in an unsafe area. I didn't care where it was or what it was or who the kids were. I just wanted the job. It turned out to be a great position. I couldn't have children so all the energy I would have put into raising children I put into the students. I was teaching in a primarily black community in a continuation school for students who'd been kicked out of other schools. Drugs were rampant; gangs were beginning to grow like crazy.

I worked on an individual basis with these kids in a team-teaching approach. I had some confrontations with them. One very angry young man threatened me, and threw a tire iron

Judith Richards Hope,
First female partner in a major international corporate law firm in Washington, DC.

"After hearing a lawyer speak about his profession during a high school career day, I told my parents, 'I'm going to be a lawyer.'… They just said, 'Let's talk about it at dinner, after you've practiced your piano.' Their treating as ordinary what, in 1953, was their daughter's out-of-the-ordinary ambition was one of the luckiest things that ever happened. If they had said, 'Girls can't be lawyers,' I would probably have given up right then."

that if I had a Ph.D. I could get a job but that there weren't any jobs for women who didn't have Ph.D.s. It was only because I pursued the matter that I found out this was not true."

The Civil Rights Act created the Equal Employment Opportunity Commission (EEOC) and authorized it to investigate cases of employment discrimination. The Commission initially focused on racial discrimination, as that had been the intent of the bill when first drafted in 1963. *Sex* had been added to the Civil Rights Act at the last minute, and the motives for its inclusion are still being debated—as a "poison pill" to doom the bill, or as a genuine response to women's demands for fair play? In EEOC's first year, one third of the 8,852 charges were filed by women claiming sex discrimination. However, it took several years before the EEOC began seriously investigating these charges. The Chair of the EEOC, when testifying before Congress, even asked that the word "sex" be removed from the act. Fortunately, EEOC Commissioners Aileen Hernandez and Richard Graham and attorney Sonia Pressman Fuentes actively worked to enforce the prohibition on sex discrimination.

at me. The last time I had anything to do with him—and this was about his coming to class and being on time—he grabbed me and started shaking. The school insisted I file an assault charge. In court, I testified against him. I realized afterward I shouldn't have. In a dream, I was driving and saw him sitting behind a bush with a gun. He shot me. That's when reality hit. I never did that again. A lot of reality came to me with that, understanding how you deal with these kids and how you perceive them. I became a coach. I involved myself totally with them, got the kids involved in sports programs.

Teaching was a very important part of my life for 30 years.

During an interview with journalist Betty Friedan, Fuentes spoke passionately about the EEOC's lack of willingness to address sex discrimination and suggested that women needed an organization that would have a role similar to the NAACP. Because the EEOC was not taking sex discrimination seriously, Betty Friedan and a small group of women founded the National Organization for Women in 1966.

Did Sex-Segregated, Help-Wanted Ads Matter?

What does all this have to do with the FW2 Generation and the generations of women that followed? To answer that question, let's return to the discussion of sex-segregated help-wanted ads. The EEOC determined that it was unlawful to run ads separately for whites and blacks. However, EEOC's guidelines allowed newspapers to continue to run ads separately for female and male positions as long as there was a statement that this was "a service to the community" and that jobs were open to both sexes. Newspapers argued that the ads merely reflected differing interests of the sexes. Over

Sarah Weddington,
Lawyer, argued and won
Roe v. Wade

"The [high-school] players on one side of the court would work their way, two dribbles at a time, to the center of the court, where they would pass the ball to teammates three inches away, who would head for the goal two dribbles at a time….[as a P.E. teacher explained,] 'Young women must preserve their reproductive capacity; after all it is their meal ticket.' I took a silent vow that I would have a meal ticket other than reproductive capacity."

Christie Dowling, networking overcomes lack of mentors and role models

When my daughters started school, I went to work in a furniture store as bookkeeper/office manager. Occasionally I was asked to assist in sales and discovered my innate ability to sell. Leaving the numbers behind, and going out on the floor of a major national furniture chain, I realized that I excelled, and quickly became top salesperson.

In my early 40s, I got the career mid-life itch. Feeling like I had accomplished all I could in furniture sales, I turned to an insurance company. They tell me life insurance is a difficult product to sell, but I won "Rookie of the Year" in our office and placed eighth in the Western Region. I found I was quite competitive and loved it. I was enthusiastic, energetic, and positive. I was making lots of money.

Management encouraged me to join professional women's groups. Networking was the key word at this time. I happened upon an organization called The National Association of Professional Saleswomen (NAPS). I attended the inaugural meeting and was so inspired

time, some newspapers changed the headings to *Jobs—Male Interest* and *Jobs—Female Interest* in the hopes of avoiding discrimination lawsuits. NOW worked to convince the EEOC that sex-segregated ads do make a difference, and the EEOC ruled in 1968 that these ads violate the Civil Rights Act.

Forty years later, we might wonder what the fuss was all about. Did sex-segregated help-wanted ads restrict opportunities for women? Stanford University researchers Sandra Bem and Daryl Bem investigated this question in two studies. Their findings were used in successful lawsuits against *The Pittsburgh Press* and AT&T, the former for "aiding and abetting" sex discrimination by continuing the practice of sex-segregated ads, and the latter for producing ads and recruiting brochures with copy that appealed to only one sex. In the experimental studies, the Bems demonstrated that "sex-biased job advertisements discourage men and women from applying for 'opposite-sex' jobs."

In 1971, the Pennsylvania state court ruled that *The Pittsburgh Press* and the *Post Gazette* must discontinue the practice of sex-segregated help-wanted ads. *The Pittsburgh Press* appealed, and in 1973 the Supreme Court ruled against the newspaper, thus ending sex-segregated

that I immediately joined and spread the word to others. There were seven women in the initial group and within three years, the year I was president, we had 389 members.

You need to remember that at this time women in sales were pioneers in their fields. In many cases, they were the only female in sales in their firm. They were fighting an uphill battle to survive, let alone do well, in a "man's world." There was no assistance from anyone. Then, along came NAPS.

It was indeed a heady time. I started a networking group of 10 people with a variety of sales backgrounds, with the common goal of generating leads of firms that were moving to new headquarters. We were with real estate, moving, computer, phone systems, furniture, and space planning companies. At our break-fast meetings, we would each bring in three leads, and after discussion of the contacts, every member would walk away with 30 pre-qualified bona fide leads. Our approach was innovative and was written up in *Sales & Marketing Magazine.*

President Ford '76

advertising at that newspaper and establishing a precedent that eventually ended the practice in all newspapers.

AT&T, in its 1973 $38 million settlement with the EEOC and Department of Labor, paid back wages to women and agreed to change their recruiting policies and advertising to attract both women and men into non-traditional positions within the company.

Ann Piestrup,
Founder The Learning Company, children's education software

"I was a very intense little girl. I was looking for the meaning of life, and I wanted to make the world better."

You've Come a Long Way, Baby?

Impressive progress against gender discrimination has been made since the FW2 Generation began working. Women are pursuing their dreams of successful careers in all fields of endeavor. They can even choose to teach, nurse, and work in an office with the tremendous advantage over their predecessors that advancement opportunities in these traditional fields are open to women—a teacher can rise through the ranks of the school district; a nurse can become a nurse practitioner or hospital administrator; an office worker can train for management. When the boundaries for advancement are permeable, no field is undesirable.

FW2s Faye Dunaway (Best Actress) & Barbra Streisand (Best Music) win Oscars • Toronto Blue Jays team created

Phyllis Zimmer, wanting a different life

I never envisioned a picket fence or a home full of children. My English teacher, whose husband had died young, encouraged female students to have a career "in case" things didn't work out. Another influence was my mother's dependence. I didn't view myself that way, but it was hard to be different because it was pre-women's lib. In college, a man I dated wanted to marry me. I said, "I want to be on my own; I want to work." He responded, "I'll let you work." It pissed me off. I'm thinking, "What do you mean you'll *let* me work? Who's *letting* you work?"

I worked as one of the few female business reporters. I enjoyed it, but there were no mentors, no role models. Then another woman was hired; we became lifelong friends. When my boss left, they promoted an uncommunicative man. My friend quit, saying I should have been promoted. I thought, "How could I be bureau chief? I'm the only woman; I'm not that experienced. I've only been here two years." You don't see doubts like that in women today, partly because of those of us who paved the way, paved it pretty well.

There was a more idealistic time when many of us thought it was as simple as 1-2-3: progress individually, help other women along, and wait until the generation of patronizing and often nasty male bosses departed from the scene. We believed that, once our generation of highly qualified women achieved some power, we would see the end of sex discrimination. We imagined other minor miracles in that future time of equal opportunity, such as plentiful and affordable childcare and husbands who were willing to shoulder a fair share of the household and family responsibilities so that we would have opportunities roughly equal to theirs to make contributions to the family and society in the same ways that they did. We were partly right.

There are still cultural barriers and much gender stereotyping to overcome. When legislation brought sex discrimination barriers down, sexual harassment went up. When women complained, men retaliated. A sampling of recent lawsuits shows there is still progress to be made. In 2001, the EEOC filed a lawsuit against Morgan Stanley on behalf of 100 women who received lower compensation than their male co-workers and were limited in their professional advancement. In 2004, Home Depot (Colorado) made a $5.5 million out-of-court

I needed to break away from my family and spread my wings. A woman couldn't be on her own when she had a perfectly good home with her parents. So I took a job I didn't want, just to move out of state. Eventually I found a marketing job where I would get the experience of traveling as a woman on an expense account.

In the 1970s, I had a paid sabbatical working for a journalist who treated me like a gofer. I told his second in command, "I'm ready to quit. I thought I'd be writing for [his] column. I'm not interested in going for the guy's lunch." He replied, "Wait. Don't quit." He told his boss I was the best intern they had. Actually he said I was the best female intern they had. They'd had a bad experience with a woman and weren't going to hire another female. I was there for my whole gender. They agreed to change my responsibilities so I stayed as a writer and reporter. [*continued*]

settlement for a race, sex, and national origin harassment and retaliation lawsuit. In that same year, Smith Barney agreed to pay $54 million to settle a sex discrimination lawsuit. Currently, there is a class-action lawsuit covering 1.6 million women against Wal-Mart, the country's largest non-governmental employer.

Betty Ford speaks at a Candidates' Luncheon, Chicago

We're not there yet. The frontiers of gender equality are moving beyond the region of protests, statutes, and lawsuits. Even before statutes and collective action gave women some legal and political leverage, we were engaged in "consciousness raising"—a term we used in women's gatherings in the 1960s. Now, when we are well into the legal and social revolution that we sought, it seems

California enacts "right-to-die" law • FW2 Penny Marshall stars in *Laverne and Shirley* • US celebrates Bicentennial

Phyllis Zimmer's story concludes with promotions and prestige, but still "different"

Twelve years later, I'd topped out in my job. I wanted a managerial position with a multi-million dollar budget and a company car. I knew the president of a labor union and liked his honesty. He hired me to reposition the company. After three years, bargaining time was approaching. I'd "been there/done that." However, I was still there during contract negotiations. One evening my boss called and said, "I want you to announce the strike. I'm not coming." I would be on all networks and identified with the union. I thought, "I'll never get another job." But you do the best you can with the hand you're dealt. A few nights later, when I'm working horrendous hours, I thought, "Why, dear God? What am I supposed to be learning?" I got a smile, ear to ear. If I could do this, I could do anything.

I did get the job I wanted, VP of corporate communication. In my first two months a politically motivated group staged a media attack, infighting on the board caused the cancellation of a major meeting, and the board fired the president. Talk about the need for an image turnaround. I was there six years and loved it.

to be time for consciousness-raising again. Gender conservatives who want to dial the clock back say that "a woman's place is in the home." That choice is up to each woman, we say. In a free country, no one else has the right to tell me where my "place" is. A second line of resistance is voiced by people who think they are being fair-minded: "Women think they can have it all, but no one can have it all." That's certainly true, and we'll settle for the same amount of "all" that men have always enjoyed—an unchallenged right to work as well as a life partner and a family if desired. The details of shared and divided responsibilities and tasks need to be worked out within each family unit, just as they are now.

I was recruited to head an organization and did everything from running it to merging it. I turned to consulting and helped launch a new media business and worked on marketing with other companies. Then I realized I had to have a job job. My credit card company started botching my bills. I wanted to switch, but was turned down by three places even though I was earning money and had good credit.

So, I'm working for an industry group to develop a multi-media campaign and am still here after a year and a half because I'm running into age discrimination in job interviews. That's troubling because I know that I'm high energy, a really good worker who surpasses goals. I may go back to consulting. You can do that at any age.

In spite of all the recognition and awards I've gotten over the years, I remember my mother saying, "You know, we love you anyway, even though you're different."

Careers Created Without a List of Ingredients

Putting a Career Together Piecemeal

Even women who did not experience sex discrimination had to figure out how to have a career in a society that expected them to stay home. Some FW2 Generation women had an early vision of their goals and moved straight toward them. This was an advantage for them, because someone who knows what she wants is less likely to be deflected by the biased and ignorant advice that we all received. However, for every clear-sighted visionary, there were at least a hundred women who put their lives together as if they were sewing patchwork quilts or cooking dinner based on whatever ingredients they found in the house.

Women's career and volunteer activities are as varied as quilting patterns. I have a quilt that my great-grandmother pieced, my grand-mother quilted, and my Mother gave to me. Called the Log Cabin, it's made of blocks with strips sewn in sequence around the four sides. These blocks can be sewn together in numerous ways, making it impossible to describe all the potential pattern variations. The more common combinations have their own names—Barn Raising, Sunshine and

Susie Clark, patchwork quilt of paid and volunteer work

The office where I worked in the late 1960s had many career accountants. The men were allowed to bring coffee to their desks but women weren't. The men were better paid than the women. Sometimes a woman would get promoted or leave her job and they would upgrade her job, which meant a man would be hired. I worked there for four years until I had my first child.

When my son was three, I put him in a co-op nursery school. I agreed to be the parent volunteer coordinator, which was a major turning point. I started heavy, serious volunteering. I enjoyed it; I loved it. It gave me an outlet because I liked to organize and run things. I loved my children but I wanted something for my brain. We became active in the church, and I started volunteering there. My whole life went over to volunteering. I was on the PTA although I had no children in school yet. I became superintendent of Sunday school, president of the Episcopal Church women, Cub Scout leader, Brownie Scout leader. I had nine volunteer jobs. At night I would sit at the dining room table and spread out the paperwork that I had to do.

Shadow, Straight Furrow. Similarly, FW2 Generation women pieced their lives together with blocks of careers, family life, volunteerism, social involvements, personal passions, adventures, etc. in unique patterns.

You may remember Joanne Perry from the previous chapter. Her parents died when she was just 12. In Joanne's patchwork adult life, she returned to teaching once her children were in school. Throughout her interview, she frequently mentions that her family always came first. She had a half-time position, which further indicates the size of the family pieces she put into her life quilt. She then adds, "I helped three friends in a floral design and wedding business. That was fun too. It was a little cottage industry that grew. We became popular and busy. I really learned a lot about that business." And then she describes her involvement in various volunteer groups.

Like many FW2 Generation women, Joanne has always had considerable energy. Therefore she is unaware of any incongruity her "family first" statements and her many other activities. Her volunteerism led to her selection as Citizen of the Year, which she understandably views as a major life highlight.

Plus I was doing everything in the house and with the kids. Volunteering was a way to create my identity.

By the mid-80s, my son was in private school, and we would soon have college tuition bills. I got a job, just 15 hours a week. I left for work after the kids went to school and was back before they were, so it was a perfect job except that I have this personality that I couldn't leave it at 15 hours. I had to do everything, and ended up running the office. I worked there 10 years and took on more and more responsibility and was working 30-35 hours a week when I quit. The people adored me and kept giving me great raises because they didn't want me to leave. Of course, I continued volunteering all those years.

The Making of an FW2 Judge

While many women sewed patchwork quilt careers, some developed all their expertise in one area. But not even they began with a diagram or list of steps to be followed. Martha Daughtrey, called Cissy by her friends, will remind you of many FW2 women who made professional strides unknown in their mothers' generation.

Cissy started law school as part of the 3-woman quota in her class. For a while, however, it looked as if she might not complete her degree. She married, had a daughter, and dropped out of school. Her husband's salary as a young professional was minimal so she needed to figure out how to manage her time, responsibilities, and finances in order to get back to school. She did and graduated from Vanderbilt Law School with honors.

But law-school honors did little to help her secure a job. The Nashville firms were male-only dominions, and none would hire her. Professional positions in banks were also reserved for men; one bank manager actually suggested she

Alison Gordon,
First woman reporter to cover professional baseball

"The obsession with the locker rooms ... ignored the most serious problem of being a woman reporter in those early days. For us, the real challenge of the job was having to do it better than anyone else or risk failure on behalf of the whole female sex. An inexperienced male reporter could ask a dumb question... An eyebrow would be raised here and there... If a woman asked the same question, it would be further proof that broads didn't know anything about baseball."

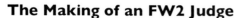

FW2 Diane von Furstenberg's wrap dress design sells 5 million, featured on *Newsweek* cover • Movie: *Network*

Lucy Ewing, patchwork quilt of incongruous pieces

I had a wonderful time for three years as a hotel banquet salesperson, doing all the weddings. I was the only woman on the sales staff, and felt I was breaking ground for women in the hotel business. I made good money. That was crucial because my husband was in school, and I was providing for our children as well.

I quit when my husband took his first foreign assignment. Upon returning, I became a stay-at-home mom, launching my volunteer career. I'd grown up with my mother's stories that the Bronx of her childhood was a pleasant suburb until the subway came. I learned the subway was coming near our house and wanted to be sure that story didn't repeat. I authored the citizens' report describing our bulls-eye concept of development concentrated around the metro station and tapering off to the neighborhoods. The county staff used the document to help define their planning. Then I was elected the civic association's president and became president of my sorority's local alumni association.

When we no longer had foreign assignments, the older children were in college and I finished the undergraduate degree I'd started 20 years earlier. I volunteered in the career center,

apply for a teller's position because he wouldn't consider her for the attorney's position. Even passing the Tennessee bar did nothing to help her find employment. Moving was not considered an option since her husband was developing his career in Nashville.

So Cissy went into private practice. It wasn't easy getting clients, but she soon made a name for herself. "It was all so difficult," she remembers, "but eventually the U.S. Attorney hired me. He was the only person in town who was willing to take a chance on giving me a job. I really hadn't thought about going into criminal law because the folks at the law school had told me that women could either practice family law or get into estates and trust. I was told to 'work in a nice trust department in a bank.' Yet, here I was going into prosecution work at a time when there never had been a female prosecutor in the history of the state. All the juries were still male. All the judges were male. All the prosecutors were male. All the defense attorneys were male. It was a very, very male world that I walked into. I was in that position for only a year because a Democrat had hired me and the Democrats lost the election that fall. In those days, it wasn't just the US Attorney who left when the administration in Washington changed. In the smaller of-

Supreme Court rules woman's abortion decision cannot be vetoed by husband • Naval Academy accepts 1st women

figuring if I hung around I'd decide to pursue a law degree or something else. The career center offered me a half-time job, which was fine. My daughter was in high school. It was wonderful to get paid after 14 years. A new Dean of Arts and Sciences hired me to start an A&S alumni association. I was also chairing the parent advisory committee at my daughter's school, and was chair of the budget committee of the county council of PTAs.

Soon I was a full-time administrator, work was fabulous. Throughout these years, I stayed involved with my sorority. When work changed in ways that isolated me from other university activities, I quit. I became my sorority's regional alumnae director for the southeastern states, which helped fill the void. Interestingly enough, the head of university relations hired me as project director for the commencement program. Now I'm a freelance writer for the university magazine.

fices, at least, everybody left. I was out of a job, but I had demonstrated that a woman could try a criminal case and the jury wouldn't acquit just because the prosecutor was a woman. So the State District Attorney hired me."

Cissy's career began to take off—first female assistant U.S. attorney in Nashville; first female assistant district attorney for Davidson

Liz Carpenter, Rosalynn Carter, Betty Ford, Elly Peterson

County, making her the first female prosecutor in Tennessee's state courts; first woman appointed to the faculty of Vanderbilt University School of Law; first female judge on the Tennessee Court of Criminal Appeals; first female Associate Justice on the Tennessee Supreme Court; first female Tennessee judge on the Sixth Circuit U.S. Court of Appeals.

President Carter urges energy conservation • Nat'l debt: $718 billion • Movie: *Star Wars* • Disco music

Lucile Templeton, commingling domestic and professional roles

I knew the name of the city manager in high school. How many students know something like that? But it took 17 years to begin my city government career. I married right after high school, had two children, and was a stay-at-home mom. I got involved in a neighborhood group that successfully lobbied for an overpass so that a new expressway didn't separate our homes from the nearby school. It was a real growth experience finding I had good organizational skills. I started junior college, knowing that whatever I wanted to do, I'd ultimately need a college education.

By the time I focused on city management, it was the early 1970s. I completed junior college and transferred to nearby USC. My spouse and I were beginning to grow apart. Then, unexpectedly, he announced he wanted a divorce. This was my first semester at USC. I was taking care of my children, worrying about going to a prestigious college, trying to see if I could compete with these bright kids when I'm in my 30s. Suddenly I'm a single mother; it was really traumatic. I went through a bad time of weeping and being ticked off. Finally, I pulled myself together and graduated with honors.

Cissy vividly recalls the experience of running for elected office. "Some women lawyers came to me saying, 'We need a woman on the Supreme Court and want your name on the ticket.' I spent the next six months campaigning to get the Democratic nomination. I had never done any campaigning before, and I had a hard time going around to the members of the Democratic Executive Committee and saying, 'I need your vote.' Friends who had helped others run for political office sat me down and told me how to do it. They made me learn to look somebody in the eye and say, 'I need your vote.' It worked, and I was elected."

With a career's worth of bruises from knocking down doors, Cissy is determined to keep doors open for other women. Many of her activities have focused on improving the status of women in the legal profession, including service on the ABA Commission on the Status of Women in the Profession. She also served as President of three organizations—Middle Tennessee Lawyers Association for Women, Women Judges' Fund for Justice, and National Association of Women Judges.

In addition to promoting greater opportunities for *women* in law, Cissy has been in demand to serve the profession in ways that help both women and men—guest faculty positions, service on the board of editors

My field required a master's, and I chose Syracuse, one of only three universities offering the Public Administration degree with an emphasis on local government. I had to rent my home, find an apartment near good schools and activities for my kids, and get myself established in graduate school. This doesn't seem like a big deal, but after all, until the age of 27, I'd never even driven more than 30 miles by myself. I got my graduate degree in a year and a half, receiving an award for outstanding graduate student in urban administration.

Arizona's Community Services Department hired me as an Administrative Analyst. I was the first female, non-clerical employee at the city yard. I learned about trucks, garbage, diesel engines and sidewalk maintenance as well as how to supervise the motor fleet division. This was stuff girls don't normally learn about. By the late 1970s, I'd advanced to Administrative Assistant in the City Manager's Office. [*continued*]

of the *ABA Journal*, involvement with professional association committees and delegations, and more.

As you might expect, her professionalism and hard work have earned her numerous awards and honors. Early in her career the *Ladies Home Journal* named her one of the Ten Outstanding Young Women of America. A few years ago, I had the privilege of seeing her receive the American Bar Association's Margaret Brent Award. This award, named for the earliest (1648) woman to practice law in America, honors female lawyers who have "influenced other women to pursue legal careers, opened doors for women lawyers that historically were closed to them, and advanced opportunities for women within a practice area." At this event Cissy was praised for her "intelligence, perspective, perspicuity, tenacity, and commitment of energy—all qualities that have enabled her to achieve so much in a low key, non-threatening manner, with good humor."

"Making Partner the Hard Way"

What happened to women who didn't present a non-threatening face? Was female assertiveness praised like male assertiveness? Ann Branigar

Mary M. Schroeder,
First female Chief Justice of the 9th Circuit Court of Appeals

"The role of women is not to feminize the courts, but to humanize them."

First woman ordained as Episcopal priest • Discrimination against those with disabilities banned by HEW

Lucile Templeton's story concludes, managing reality and striving for dreams

Trying to make my way in a man's world. That's how I characterize my 40s. For every position I've ever held, I was always the first woman. I learned to work in an organizational setting, to be supervised, to supervise others, to manage office politics. Being a mom and going to school, that's all my experience had been

I became Assistant to the City Manager and three years later the Assistant City Manager. Life was good personally and professionally. My children went off to college and I remarried. I had success in my career and was using my skills to improve the community. In 1992, I received a statewide award for the Outstanding Assistant City Manager.

But soon afterwards, I realized I wasn't going to reach my career goal of being a city manager. I wasn't strong in finance and, while most city managers are generalists, the our city council wanted a manager with extensive financial training and experience. Also I didn't fit the mold of authoritarian leadership style that the city council had grown accustomed to. My leadership style was more what women do -- team development. A position in another town

Hopkins tells how difficult it was to get into the "men's clubs," professions dominated by males, especially if you were an assertive female. Ann rose quickly in various positions in large corporations and was eventually hired as a senior manager by Price Waterhouse. Over a two year period, she brought in and managed contracts totaling more than $40 million. She seemed to be on the fast track to becoming a partner.

In 1982, a senior partner told Ann that he was going to recommend her for a partnership. She was the only female in a group of 88 candidates. At that time, she had brought more money into the firm and had more billable hours for two consecutive years than any other candidate.

In March, Ann was told that her candidacy had been placed on hold but that she would be considered the following year. In evaluating her, various partners had described her as a woman who was "macho," who "overcompensated for being a woman," and who should take "a course at charm school." One partner who "supported" her candidacy made comments clearly indicating she was being judged by standards applied to women, but not men. He said, she "had matured from a tough-talking somewhat masculine hard-nosed manager to an authoritative, formidable, but more much appealing lady partner candidate."

was not a possibility, as my husband didn't want to move. I wasn't going to reach my goal for both personal and situational reasons. That was my ultimate professional disappointment.

I'd gotten into political trouble with the city clerk, and had retreated from the conflict. I was an only child and didn't grow up with conflict. I thought, "We're financially stable. I don't need to work. I'll retire."

When you're retired everybody calls on you. I decided to only do those things that I had a strong interest in or where I was uniquely qualified. I took on a number of community projects those first few years. Three years ago I served for a year as foreman of the grand jury. That was an absolutely fantastic experience that probably wouldn't have been possible if I hadn't retired.

At this point, Ann was advised that she could increase her chances of becoming a partner by softening her image. Specifically, her mentor suggested that she "look toward appearing more feminine," dress less in "power blues," and "not carry a briefcase." She was told to "walk more femininely, talk more femininely, dress more femininely, wear make-up, have your hair styled, and wear jewelry." In December, Ann was informed that the senior partners had reconsidered, and she would not be proposed again for a partnership.

Denial of a partnership is tantamount to being fired. Ann could stay as a senior manager, but her income potential would be restricted and she would wear the "denied partnership" equivalent of Hester Prynne's scarlet letter A. She left Price Waterhouse and started a management consulting company, actions that would be expected under the circumstances. However, this is when she took the unusual step of filing a lawsuit against her former employer, claiming sex discrimination. She sought not just back pay but also reinstatement as a partner.

Jane Harman,
Congresswoman

"Friends and colleagues often ask me why a middle-aged mother of four wants to serve in the U.S. Congress. To me, the answer is simple: to add value, to make a difference. To know, at the end of the day, that I've done everything I can to make our country and the world better, safer places."

Theresa Goddard, the importance of a plan

Beginning when I was 11, I worked as a Mother's Helper each summer. When I was 15, I worked at a florist. One year, because I had good grades, I got to leave school a week before Christmas vacation to work full time at the department store. I continued working there through the summers and holidays until college. In school, I felt stifled. I remember telling my high-school counselor that I wanted to take drafting. She said, "Only boys can take that because they need the skill for their adult work."

I always worked part-time while in college, even after I married in my junior year. But after college, I became a stay-at-home mom and wife. Well, sort of. I did fundraising for and became president of a co-op nursery school.

When my youngest child began kindergarten, I practically ran to a nearby clinic to work in the hematology lab. The Med-Tech job was great because I worked with wonderful women and the pay was good. Yes, in those days, only women were Med-Techs. After three years, I saw there wasn't a career path. I decided I needed to learn business so I joined the phone

U.S. Supreme Court: Price Waterhouse v. [Ann] Hopkins, 490 U.S. 228, 1989, Section C, Paragraph 2:

"An employer who objects to aggressiveness in women but whose positions require this trait places women in an intolerable and impermissible catch 22: out of a job if they behave aggressively and out of a job if they do not. Title VII lifts women out of this bind."

Her case eventually went to the Supreme Court. Six years after filing her lawsuit, the courts made a final decision. Price Waterhouse was ordered to hire Ann as a partner and to pay her $370,000 in back pay. Most women would have taken the money and left. Yet Ann, using the same determination and strength of character that caused the "old boys" to deny her entrance into their domain, persevered—working for twelve years as a partner in the firm. Ann documented her story in *So Ordered: Making Partner the Hard Way*. She travels throughout the country speaking to business and legal groups about her experiences, helping to open the way for women in the professions who seek to break glass ceilings.

Using "WomanPower" in the Senate

How do women bridge the stereotyped differences between the genders in leadership roles? Researchers Dorothy Cantor and Toni Bernay, in *Women in Power: The Secrets of Leadership*, examined this question. They studied 25 women politically active at the local, state, and federal level and concluded that these women are self-confident, use creative

company, which had great training programs. I hoped to find something I could aspire to. Working there, I realized I had an aptitude for technology and a talent for sales. Learning that AT&T thought Rolm would be a big competitor on the equipment side of the company, I developed a five-year plan to work for Rolm, make more money, and have a real career rather than just a job.

Around this time, the mid-70s, my husband was having an affair with someone at work. I confronted him and he said he'd stop, but he didn't. When I found out the second time, I said, "I don't need this and I don't need you." By that point I honestly had put my plan into motion. I had paid off my bills and was saving money. I was doing well in my job and thought, "I can do this; I can take care of myself and my kids." That's why I didn't hesitate. I had a career plan. [*continued*]

aggression, and activate *WomanPower*, the "power used to advance an agenda and make a difference in society."

They pursue different political agendas, but FW2 women Kay Bailey Hutchison and Barbara Boxer are good examples of Senators who have learned to work around the constraints of sex discrimination in order to make a difference.

Barbara Boxer grew up in Brooklyn. Her mother, who never completed high school because she had to work, nonetheless instilled a sense of pride of achievement in her daughter, telling her that nothing could stop her from accomplishing her goals. As proof, she told Boxer that there was even a woman in the Senate. Her father, the son of Russian immigrants, studied at night and became a lawyer when he was 40. His example inspired Boxer.

Typical of FW2 women, Boxer married immediately after college and worked to put her husband through law school. She left her position as researcher and stockbroker in 1965 when her husband accepted a job that meant moving to California. During the next seven years, she had two children and focused on raising them. However, her activism from earlier years was never far from her thoughts and actions. She began organizing neighborhood groups and then ran for the Marin County Board of Supervisors.

Theresa Goddard's story concludes, from high tech to high touch

Right on plan, I moved to ComPath. The women I worked with felt telecommunications was the only industry where females were encouraged. We were thrilled to have broken into a field that had traditionally been male only. I was in high tech before most people even knew what that meant. I sold Rolm's largest CBX to Four Phase, and they offered me a job managing the system with a big salary increase. While friendly to women, telecommunications was still a male-dominated field. Fortunately, my manager became my mentor, helping me to plot my future. I'm forever grateful.

I moved to Zylog with another large pay raise. The people were great, and I was able to make a difference, saving the company a considerable amount of money. In the 1980s, I achieved my goal of working at Rolm. I thrived in the dynamic environment and didn't mind the almost non-stop travel because this was the success I wanted. It was a great time to be at Rolm, an excitement that I've never seen or felt anywhere else. After eight years, I accepted an early retirement package. The corporate environment was changing; my children were

Barbara Boxer,
Senator from California

"My husband thought he married Debbie Reynolds and he woke up with Eleanor Roosevelt."

Barbara Boxer

"If you were married, they thought you were neglecting your family; if you were single, they thought something was wrong with you; and if you were divorced, they were scared of you."

Boxer says campaigning as "a woman ... was almost a masochistic experience, a series of setbacks with not a lot of rewards. If I was strong in my expression of the issues, I was strident; if I expressed any emotion as I spoke about the environment or the problems of the mentally ill, I was soft; if I spoke about economics, I had to be perfect, and then I ran the risk of being 'too much like a man.'" Boxer lost that election when politically motivated letters were published in the newspaper, complaining that she would be abandoning her children if she were elected (the position she sought was a part-time job).

Looking for another avenue of expression, she became a newspaper reporter. Two years later she was hired as Representative John Burton's aide. Then in 1976, Boxer ran for the Board of Supervisors and served in that position for six years, becoming its first female president. In 1982, she ran for the U.S. House of Representatives to fill the seat vacated by retiring Representative John Burton. And 10 years later, she successfully ran for the U.S. Senate.

Apple II best selling computer, others: Commodore Pet & TRS-80 • Elvis Presley dies • Yogurt is popular

having children; my parents' health was failing. I felt like I was all over the place. I took a position at Sun Microsystems where I was involved in innovative customer support programs. Unfortunately, my father died a year later and my mother started having health problems. I realized I couldn't do it all, feeling "this is long enough."

After my mother died, I started an interior design and real-estate staging business. All my life I've been driven by the left-brain. I never thought I was creative, but all of a sudden, I find I have a good eye and a latent ability to make things pretty.

It's been a wonderful journey. I met some great people who took me under their wing. I tried, in turn, to do that for people who worked for me. Last summer, at a Rolm reunion, two women who had worked for me told me how much they appreciated that I mentored and encouraged them in their career aspirations. I was very touched.

People associate nurturance with women and therefore contend that they should be home with their children. But women who have become politicians believe their desire to nurture is fulfilled in their efforts on behalf of social issues, the environment, peace, and myriad other concerns of the national "family."

Kay Bailey Hutchison grew up in the small Texas town of La Marque and credits her parents with giving her a sense of integrity, honesty, and faith. Like most FW2 women when asked about their high school goals and aspirations, she replies, "I always thought ... that I would just be a mom, that I would have a family and just be a mom. It was never contemplated or discussed that I would do anything else. It was always assumed that I would go to college, because Mother and Daddy had both graduated from the University of Texas. ... But I never intended to go beyond that and actually have a career."

Because she wasn't getting married after college, she decided to go to law school. "I was one of only five women in my class of five hundred at the University of Texas School of Law. I loved law school. It was the first time I really enjoyed school as school. It was the first time I had ever been intellectually stimulated and challenged. When I graduated

Denise Richardson, setting goals

I needed to work but the only two jobs I'd ever had were newspaper writing and teaching. I tried to get a college job but was told, "Retirees fill all our vacancies; they work cheaply without expectations about tenure, raises or benefits."

I was totally desperate, and the only newspaper job I could get was "stringer," making $5 an inch for copy they published and $5 per picture they ran. I worked really hard, discovered I loved it. That was the beginning of a wonderful 13-year career.

I became a reporter in 1972 covering city hall and writing features. A year later I moved to the police beat until the point in my pregnancy that the police didn't like me at crime scenes. Back to city hall beats and, in what might be called "shades of Brenda Starr," I became an investigative journalist. Before I was 30, I had achieved a career goal that I wouldn't have thought possible for another 10 years.

After a brief maternity leave, I returned as a weekly columnist and police reporter. I helped put together one of the first cable news programs in Florida, frequently writing copy for the

in 1969, I couldn't wait to get out and prove myself. I was completely unprepared for what happened next. Even though my male classmates were getting hired by all of the big law firms, I was running into a wall. I interviewed with about thirty firms, and the response was always the same. They would compliment me on having graduated from law school, and tell me they were sure I'd make a fine lawyer. Then they'd give me the speech: 'We have to invest so much in starting lawyers, and we lose money on a woman. Training is expensive, and you will get married and move away, or get married and get pregnant, and we can't afford to put all that money in and not get a return. Sorry...'"

Roots begins on ABC • FW2 Sharon Pratt Dixon Kelly 1st woman on Democratic National Committee from D.C.

newspaper deadline and then dashing several miles to the television studio where I "ripped and read" on the air. I received numerous Best Story awards, which meant I got to write longer features for the *Sunday Magazine*, and by 1977 was its editor. I took it from an attractive vehicle for color ads to one of the best-read sections in the paper.

I learned to manage staff, production schedules, and legal issues. The success of the *Sunday Magazine* is something that was incredibly exciting to me. I edited and published a major investigative piece on the Church of Scientology, which earned the two reporters the Pulitzer Prize.

By 1983, I was finding my success hard to fit into family life. I couldn't keep accepting better positions and more responsibility because that meant more time away from home. I was taking on way too much. I was really invested in my career, my husband's success, and my daughter's participation in multiple educational experiences, lessons, and sports. I was truthfully just exhausted. [*continued*]

"One day, after yet another disappointing interview, I was driving home and I passed TV station KPRC, the NBC Houston affiliate. On a lark, I pulled into the lot, went inside, and asked the receptionist if I could speak to someone about a job." Several weeks later she was hired. "Because of my law degree, he decided to experiment by assigning me to cover the state legislature in Austin. It was the first time a local TV station had set up a state capital bureau. It was also the genesis of my life in government—the start of a career path I could never have predicted."

Hutchison learned about politics, and the public learned about her through her nightly television reporting. She says, "When the Harris County Republican chairman asked me to consider running for the legislature, I was surprised. Then the idea started growing on me. I realized that I wanted to do it." She continued her accomplishments in *politics*—first Republican woman elected to the state House of Representatives, first Republican woman ever elected to a statewide office in Texas, first woman from Texas to be elected to the U.S. Senate, and Vice Chair of the Senate Republican Conference

Kay Bailey Hutchison, First female Senator from Texas

"So when I'm asked, 'Does it make a difference that women are part of the process?' I say, 'You bet. We bring our life experiences to the table. Nobody fought for homemakers to have retirement accounts until we did in the Senate in 1993, for God's sake.'"

Denise Richardson's story continues, persevering

I cried when I quit the newspaper. My husband had started a new bank. My decision to become his VP Marketing was really stupid. I'd been running a section of the paper and was highly respected, a peer to major people in the industry. The gap between what journalists and bankers think about is huge. His executives couldn't relate to my freewheeling do-what-you-have-to-do to get-what-you-need-to-get-done spirit. When you're an investigative journalist, if you have to rent a plane to fly through the jungle, that's what you do. My husband said, "If you're going to be a banker, you've got to start thinking like a banker." I would rather die.

I founded a medical practice management company because our bank was adjacent to a medical complex. Doctors didn't know how to run their businesses. I didn't either except, having been a journalist, I knew that anything you wanted to know you could learn. I was fearless, relentless and persevering. I said, "I can do this, I'm going to do this," and I did do this. Everything became easier. I could take an hour off to do something with my daughter. My husband and I could talk about non-banking topics.

Kay Bailey Hutchison

"When I entered the field in 1969, it was the first time a local television station, in Houston, Texas, had a woman news reporter. I covered for both radio and television, but was once told that women's voices were not really suitable for anchor work, especially in radio."

making her the only woman in the top five leadership positions of the Senate Republicans—and in *business*—bank co-founder and small business owner.

During her tenure in the legislature, Hutchison married a fellow member of the Texas House of Representatives. When she was 58, in pure FW2 style, she and her husband adopted an infant daughter and just four months later adopted a 3-month-old son.

No Recipe but Good Results

The stories of Cissy Daughtrey, Ann Braniger Hopkins, Barbara Boxer, and Kay Bailey Hutchison are repeated, with variations, many times. Such is, in fact, the complex pattern of FW2 employment. These profiles illustrate the nontraditional employment paths that many FW2 Generation women chose and finally claimed as their own.

Denise Richardson and other FW2 Generation women who worked in traditional fields still made their mark in nontraditional ways—continuing to work when previous generations would have returned home,

Soon I had a list of clients and a staff of 50. Unfortunately, I was available 24/7. Before I knew it, I was totally exhausted, but I didn't know an ethical, moral, and responsible way to leave. I decided to gut it out for six years until the multi-year contracts expired. The key was *not* taking new clients. Then a friend called to say he had a new client for me. We'd worked on civic boards together so I felt I had to meet the doctor.

The psychiatrist became my client and had a major impact on my life. His practice, based on the Mind, Consciousness, and Thought philosophy, had an extremely high success rate. I realized that most of my work was crisis management—something goes wrong for a client and I ride into town ready for the shootout. I wasn't creating a healthy family, healthy work environment, healthy working relationships with my clients, or a sense of peace in myself. I changed and the next decade was wonderful for me and my company. [*continued*]

seeking advancement rather than settling for the accepted female positions lower on the ladder, and performing their work in nontraditional locations such as other countries. These women, who say they never intended to have careers, nevertheless created paths, opened doors, and climbed ladders as no group of women had done before.

Uniqueness of Careers for the FW2 Generation

Apart from our energy, our educational readiness, and the postwar optimism that nothing is impossible, five factors contributed to the distinctive work histories of FW2 Generation women—which of course are still ongoing:

1. We wanted control over our lives. Although we were kept busy handling both home and work, these activities were under our direction. Our mothers were dependent on our fathers for their success in life—a dependency that left many of them stranded by death or divorce. We wanted more control over the outcomes.

Patricia Schroeder,
First woman to represent Colorado in Congress

[Response in 1972 to constant press questions about how she could serve in Congress and take care of her children at the same time:]

"Jim and I get up very early—about 6 A.M. We bathe and dress the children and feed them a wonderful breakfast. Then we put them in the freezer, leave for work, and when we come home, we defrost them. And we all have a lovely dinner together. They're great."

Denise Richardson's story concludes, finding satisfaction

I'd come to love the medical practice management business, but my goals changed. In 1991, I sold the company to the staff. They were very good at what they did and wanted to continue. I began working with a consulting firm dedicated to Psychology of Mind/Health Realization. By the mid-90s, I was director of the business division and developing programs focused on the principles of innate health. A medical school dean sent his leadership group to my seminars, and attended one himself. Later, he invited me to the university to meet with groups at the hospital and medical school. At the end of the week, he said, "What would it take to get you to move here?" I responded, "Send a moving truck."

In 1998, I became an Assistant Professor, teaching in the public health program. The dean said, "I don't know what you're going to do but you're going to find a way to bring the philosophy of innate health into the medical school." The concept evolved; we successfully raised money to endow an institute based on a new paradigm in leadership, decision-making and health policy initiatives. We focused on understanding the nature of thought, the

Sadat, Carter & Begin, Camp David Accords Ceremony

2. We had no role models for success in the workplace. Nor, as children, had we participated in organized sports—rules of the game, "playing fields of Eton," and all that. So we made up our own rules, seeking guidance from our peers rather than older mentors who, if they were present at all, might be "Queen Bees," as they were called, protecting their hives.

3. We wanted to open doors closed to women. We were outsiders and wanted to become insiders. But insiders controlled our access. Even when we met the objective criteria such as education, we still had to meet subjective criteria or be passed over. That usually meant being perceived as non-threatening. We were nice; we ignored many slights and harassments.

4. We wanted to help other women following us. Perhaps the natural female response to "tend and befriend" explains our behavior. Perhaps we had learned the importance of mentors and wanted to mentor younger women.

unrecognized capacity of people to see the role of thought in the creation of their moment-to-moment experience, and the implications of that understanding as a source of change, creativity and effectiveness. In 2000, I became the Institute's director.

Remember the psychiatrist who changed my life? He once told me, "It's my dream that the philosophy of innate health is integrated into a medical school, but I don't think I'll live to see it happen." After leaving Florida, I'd run into him occasionally at professional meetings. When we established this Institute, I reconnected with him. He is now the medical director of the Institute and on the faculty. It's almost hilarious that I have been the one to help him realize his dream. This work is the most thrilling and wonderful thing that I've done in my life. Last night I had dinner with a guy who's my age and thinking about retiring. He asked me when I was going to retire. I responded, "Why would I want to do that?"

5. And on a different dimension, it was a heady, exhilarating time for FW2 Generation women. It was exciting to be the first women in the positions we won access to. It was exciting to be told "you can't do that" and then do it. It was exciting to figure out how to manage both work life and home life. It was exciting to belong to something called a "sisterhood"—the power of mutual support has been a lifelong satisfaction to us. *I get by with a little help from my friends / ... gonna try with a little help from my friends* was our song, after all.

Early Training of an FW2 Entrepreneur

I've been an entrepreneur from the time I was seven. That summer I made Mud Pies from water and dirt in tiny aluminum pans with a flower blossom on top. I offered them for sale on the front sidewalk. When I was 10, I charged fellow Waldemar campers a dime to wash and iron the silk neck scarves we wore. My innovative ironing technique was to spread the wet scarves on a wall; they came off stiff but smooth.

Isabel Allende, Novelist

"I had two guardian angels—an adopted grandmother and my mother-in-law—who helped raise my kids while I juggled three jobs. And I had an understanding husband. He did not stand in my way, and for that I am grateful, but he didn't share any of the domestic chores. Maintaining the household and raising the kids were my responsibilities alone. One had to be a superwoman to cope with that life. The obstacles seemed immense to the women of my generation, but so was our energy."

Dan White assassinates George Moscone & Harvey Milk; Dianne Feinstein named mayor • Intel's 16-bit processor

Georgia Lafferty, a nod to the Civil Rights Act

My boss at directory assistance, where I worked in the summers, called and said, "We're getting ready to do something really amazing here. We're going to bring women into management." This was 1964. The phone company had seen the proverbial handwriting on the wall. I was hired, in the first group of women managers, to forecast the need for operators.

By 1965, I was Group Chief Operator. The following year, they wanted to promote me but the positions above were filled. I took a temporary, nine-month position in New York so they could bring me back and promote me around those just above me. After that, I got the first in a series of positions that had never been occupied by a woman. I was third in command, supervising chief operators. There were no role models and no one to mentor me. When my supervisor left, I became second in command. The management style was the same one used when the dinosaurs roamed the earth. It was an autocratic style in which you kept information to yourself. There was no way in God's green earth I was going to be able to do that. Finally, I decided that if they wanted an imitation man they should have gone out and

So it's not surprising that I continued my entrepreneurial experiments in adulthood, whenever my daytime positions permitted this kind of recreation. My first such effort was a journal printed on our own offset press. It was not exactly Virginia and Leonard Woolf's Hogarth Press, but we had a subscriber list. During that period, I had to sit on my hands at parties since the ink from the offset press was always under my nails. Later I started a computer school for children. The staff wrote educational software during non-class times, but the prize-winning Atari 800, a marvelous machine for its time, lost its marketplace when schools adopted the Apple II computer. I moved on to create a company that developed business software utilizing the new CD-ROM technol-

Nancy Landon Kassebaum 1st woman elected to Senate • First cell phone tests • Postage rises to 15 cents

hired a real one. I evolved a more feminine, collaborative style that worked a lot better with the chief operators.

By 1969, I was bored and realized the company would pay for my MBA. In one class, I saw how a computer could do the task of predicting the need for operators. To prove it, I bought a Fortran book and my neighbor, who worked for GE, got an OK for me to use his computer lab at night. I wrote the program, making every mistake known to man or God. I told a senior manager about the program and he said it was "truly impossible" that a computer could do the task, but asked for a demonstration. Each person who saw the program was so impressed that they wanted it shown to the next higher management level. Soon AT&T adopted the program nationwide, which eliminated 20,000 force assistant positions. [*continued*]

ogy. Being on the bleeding edge (yes, you read that right) of technology was stressful, but I thrived on the challenges of building that company for ten exciting years until I sold it.

My mother also had entrepreneurial aspirations. She said wistfully, "When I married, I wanted to open a shop where I'd design and make women's hats." But her dreams were blocked in many ways. What would people say? Would her husband feel that she had overstepped? How in the world would she get started? There are always difficult questions that can't be answered until a person decides "I will do it" and "I will take the first step tomorrow morning." Many FW2 women figured out their steps on their own. Others were fortunate in having friends in the sisterhood who were starting all kinds of ventures. Any financial, logistic, or legal question could probably be answered within two or three phone calls.

Portia Isaacson Bass, Co-founder of The Micro Store, one of the first computer stores, and founder of Future Computing

"What an entrepreneur does is 100 things and 99 of them fail—usually in such small, minor ways that the world doesn't even notice they were ever trying anything. And finally they get one of them right."

The Power of Any Role Model or Precedent

I thought about a number of careers over the years. When I was young I briefly wanted to be a minister, but I had never seen or heard of a female

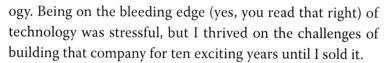

Georgia Lafferty's story continues, moving on, moving up

I was stymied by 1973. I dearly loved my job, but saw no advancement. They usually bump people ahead by assigning them to New York City. I knew I could handle it although this time it would be for two years. My boss said, "I can't send you because I'd be responsible for wrecking your marriage." I thought, "You may very well be right, but gee whiz, I deserve the right to make that decision."

My husband, Bob, suggested we sail for a year. It was a bit crazy, but my boss agreed to a leave. We sailed from Florida, working our way toward San Francisco. There were adventures and misadventures, and I occasionally called in to extend my leave. Finally, my boss said, "You're needed to handle a disaster brewing in the Pacific Telephone Company." I flew from Costa Rica, and Bob agreed to sail the boat to San Francisco. He sped up his return when he learned about an opportunity in Memphis. I was not yet through developing the methods and training program for a newly installed automated directory assistance system so he went to Memphis first. One morning, in the new home, Bob was chatting with the phone installer who

minister, so I discarded that idea. As a teenager, I decided I would become a lawyer. I went as far as to meet with the Dean of the Law School, but I didn't know any female lawyers so it seemed too improbable. In college, I thought it would be interesting to work as a geologist, a well respected profession in an oil-rich state. However, I learned that as a female geologist I could do lab work but not fieldwork, which was of course the focus of my romantic vision. There were other "dream careers" contemplated along the way before I acquired my present aliases—researcher, academic, manager, entrepreneur, writer. Even now I am working on new career plans and anticipate more aliases in the years to come.

Role models and precedents can be defined too narrowly, such as "another

Iranians seize US Embassy & take 66 American hostages (90 people) • Three Mile Island nuclear disaster

said, "You know, things are really changing around this place. I've heard there's some woman coming in." Knowing this was me, Bob said, "No kidding. You looking forward to that?" The guy responded, "I'm going to kill myself. It's going to be the end of life as I've known it."

I transferred to Memphis after a successful cutover in San Francisco. They needed me as a plant manager because they had to put women into non-traditional jobs. A woman in management was such a rarity that the workers often found excuses to bring their wives and girlfriends by just to show that they weren't kidding when they said there was a woman in charge. I attended pole-climbing school and every other kind of training I could get. But it was frustrating because without adequate training, I felt I couldn't contribute significantly. To get the stimulation I missed at work, I got my second master's degree in the Industrial Organization Psych program and began my Ph.D. [*continued*]

woman who has already succeeded at something we want to try." That definition often leaves us without role models and precedents in the specific ventures that we are considering. For example, when I began my CD-ROM software/publishing company, I didn't know of any other female entrepreneurs in that field. However, I did know women who had founded successful educational software companies and book publishing companies. These role models provided me with few details about my planned venture but much motivation.

If a woman has had a fortunate but not privileged upbringing and has seen enough of the world to understand it a little, then she can muster enthusiasm and confidence for all kinds of ventures. Her role models and precedents can be very general, even metaphorical—"I have to make some tough decisions tomorrow: what would Amelia Earhart do?" "I don't know if I can handle this challenge: what would Jane Goodall do?" "People are really criticizing me for that decision, even though I think it's the right one: how would Eleanor Roosevelt respond?"

In another respect, though, the best role models are not icons but real people we have known well. They may know nothing about our specialized fields, but that doesn't matter. We choose them because we want

Georgia Lafferty's story concludes, taking her career a new way

Bob told me Holiday Inn was ready to install a computerized reservation system but had no training program. I got the job. My challenge was training the central agency staff and establishing procedures for every front desk person worldwide. It was a fascinating period, but once the training was running smoothly, I was bored again. Bob took a position with Harrah's in Atlantic City, and I was hired by Playboy to train 5,000 people in their new hotel and casino. Looking back, I'm glad I did it. But we didn't realize casinos were a nasty business. My situation deteriorated, and I lost my job. Bob was in an equally stressful position.

He took a job in New Orleans, and I got a two-semester job at the University of New Orleans. It was perfect. I thought it would give me time to look for a *real job*. In fact, I was having a wonderful time. I was offered a corporate job but turned it down on Bob's good advice. I discussed options with the department chair who said that if I got a Ph.D., he'd hire me permanently. I entered a doctoral program about 80 miles away while continuing to teach full time.

to do our work the way we know they would do it if it was their work. We picture their facial expressions and body language as they settle down to hard tasks. We see their handiwork. We hear their spoken thoughts. They are very satisfactory role models.

I have had two such sources of inspiration. My paternal grandmother, Harriet Matilda Rigsby Butler, was in my life from the beginning. I loved sitting by her foot stool and hearing her stories of riding back and forth in a covered wagon from Illinois to the Indian Territory where her father sold fruit trees. She instilled in me a sense of adventure. She was perhaps best known in the family for refusing to speak ill of anyone. For instance, when all in the room criticized her brother, she'd quietly and firmly say, "But he was a really good milker." I learned that no harm is done by speaking generously of others.

The first such role model outside my family was Connie Douglas Reeves who taught me how to ride horses at Camp Waldemar when I was 10 years old. Connie wasn't a typical teenage counselor; she was 51 that summer and already a legend. When she taught us to "saddle your own horse," she was teaching us the importance of self-reliance and responsibility for our actions.

Bob was getting more depressed and finally told me that he was moving to Florida, turning down my offer to join him. We probably weren't right for each other at that point, but he's a great guy and it killed me. In 1985, I found myself divorced. Everything changed, I didn't even have credit in my own name. The following year, I finished my Ph.D., became an assistant, and soon was an associate professor. Beginning in the 1990s, my career really bloomed. I received multiple teaching and research honors, was named Distinguished Professor, and served as president of the Southwest Academy of Management. Teaching at an entrepreneurial university gave me the opportunity to help start a series of executive MBA programs in various locations. It's wonderful.

Interestingly, I'm still learning from Connie. In 2003, I was visiting with a friend I had not seen in many years. Polly told me about a recent trip to the Texas hill country where along the way she took her husband to Camp Waldemar on the Guadalupe River so that she could show him the place that held wonderful memories for her. It was autumn, and giggles

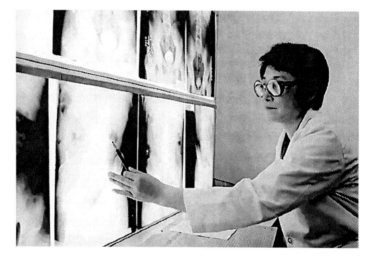

and shrieks of girls no longer filled the air. Walking across the quiet, open field, Polly saw a woman, legs stretched across the dashboard, snoozing in a golf cart. As she moved closer to make her presence known, the woman woke up. You guessed it. Connie was 99, still slim, wearing the familiar blue jeans and sporting the same large silver belt buckle. Her eyesight wasn't great, and Polly had to speak a bit loudly to be heard. Connie told her she was still head of horseback riding at Waldemar but had given up

Jane Friedman, First and only female CEO of a global publishing house [HarperCollins]

I was an English major, but I was always very good with numbers. When I graduated from college, I decided that I was either going to go to Wall Street or be a publisher. The summer that I graduated, I worked in a securities house and hated it, and I walked into Random House and got a job as a Dictaphone typist.... So I am really the person who has gone from the proverbial mailroom to the CEO. ...nothing was too demeaning to me. I opened mail, and I still to this day say to young women, "Open the mail and read it. You will learn so much. Answer the phone and ask if you can help." I started in publicity, but then I went into marketing, advertising, promotion, and publishing itself. I was able to just keep crafting as I went along. I was very fortunate. That is not something that everybody has, but it's also not something that everybody takes advantage of.

Judge Judy,
Attorney Judith
Sheindlin, popular
television show host and
author

"I had a little chat with a woman recently ... She'd just turned sixty—and had also just graduated from medical school. 'A dream fulfilled' the doctor told me. ... She radiated energy and life."

active teaching when she was 96. She continued to supervise the staff, ride with some classes, and give tips to the young girls. And we thought she was ancient in 1952!

Since Polly told me this story, I've followed news of Connie. At the age of 100, she saddled her horse and rode in the parade celebrating the National Cowgirl Hall of Fame's new building in Ft. Worth. Two years later and just one month shy of her 102nd birthday, her favorite horse, Dr. Pepper, threw her. While in the hospital, Connie remarked to the camp owner, "I think Dr. Pepper has made our decision. It's time for us to retire. I just wish I'd done it more gracefully." She died a few days later.

Like finding an unexpected treasure, here was Connie giving me lessons 50 years later. She, like most of us, was sometimes thrown by life. A newly shod Dr. Pepper had even kicked her when she was 84, shattering her thighbone. But Connie's energy, determination, and strength of character brought real meaning to the lyrics: pick yourself up, dust yourself off, and start all over again. She inspires me to keep doing what I love, and perhaps most importantly, to accept that I might not go gracefully.

On the Road Again:
The FW2 Generation Divorces

Facing Up to Divorce

When I first married in the early 1960s, I assumed it was "until death do us part." I didn't know anyone who was divorced. Or, I thought I didn't. In 1995, 25 years after my divorce, I was looking through old family pictures and documents while visiting my parents. Halfway through the stack, I saw my maternal grandfather's death certificate. Interested in family medical history, I carefully read the document. When I saw that the surviving wife was not my grandmother's name, I couldn't imagine whose death certificate I was reading. Maybe my great-grandfather? Deciding this couldn't be a clerical error, I asked my father. Yes, my grandparents had divorced and that had angered my mother so much that she never spoke to her father again, even shutting the front door on him when he visited many years later, hoping to reconcile.

When I was young I must have known people who were divorced, but divorce was socially unacceptable and mentioned only when necessary.

The Hero Within

FW2 Generation women were reared on tales of wedded bliss. The plot line of 1950s romantic comedies consisted of laughable misunderstandings

Valerie Bradford, ignoring his affair

It happened when he went to Japan on a business trip. I called him in his hotel and commented on a noise in the background. He told me there was a group of people in his room. It just didn't sound right to me.

Several months later, I walked in my husband's office and he put something in his drawer very quickly. I thought, "That's not right." The next morning, after taking my son to school, I got the keys to his office. I looked in the drawer and found a letter he was writing. It said things like "I would crawl to California to see you." My heart jumped out of my skin about three feet. I went to the library across the street, copied the letter, put the original back in the drawer, and went home. I thought I was a really good detective.

That afternoon I confronted him with the letter. He told me it didn't have anything to do with me. I thought sarcastically, "Of course it doesn't." I screamed and I yelled. He took the paper, tore it up, and threw it down the commode. He never denied it. If there was another woman, I wasn't going to let her have my family.

Judge Judy,
Attorney Judith Sheindlin, popular television show host and author

"In the story of my life, I am the hero. I am the one who saves the day—not with brute strength but with wit and intelligence. ... Everyone else in your life is merely a supporting player.... If you have a healthy spirit, a positive outlook, and a sense of personal accomplishment and importance, you will be a better partner, friend, and mother. ... It's about being responsible for your own happiness.

and at least one memorable fight in the acquaintance of two young stars who would seal the movie's end with a kiss. These movies, we imagined, were the backstory of the wedding announcements we read with great interest in the newspaper. The dating tips we read in *Seventeen* (which debuted with us in 1944) were our guide to avoiding unnecessary and time-wasting detours on our own primrose paths to marriage. And indeed, we did fall in love and marry.

But we soon learned marriage and divorce go together almost as often as love and marriage. We were the first generation to use the no-fault divorce option in large numbers. Three new circumstances—our educational attainments, effective birth control, and improving employment opportunities—enabled us to divorce when marriage was unsustainable.

Most of the women I interviewed had wanted to remain in their marriages. When you read their stories, you'll see that they often overlooked faults, forgave affairs, and attempted to accommodate to bad situations. They were anything but

I had to reestablish the feeling that my husband was entirely mine. I don't like sharing. He would never admit to the affair. But I knew it was one of two women. To this day I can recite their names. I forget a lot but not those.

I always hope that women who go through this sort of thing will give it time. My sister's husband was killed. She tells me these days that she has no one to talk to about her children. She's married to another man, very happily married, but she says she envies us talking about the times that we had with our children when they were small. When I think of people divorcing I think they should give it time. You do get through your bad times.

casual about divorce; it was a last resort. Contrary to those who point to no-fault divorce as the major factor in the breakdown of the family, I have come to believe that no-fault divorce was the tool that finally enabled women to defend the institution of marriage. It enabled them to say, "This isn't a real marriage when you behave like this, and I won't take it any longer." When divorce is difficult to obtain, women try to live with the fact that their bodies, emotions, and trust are being abused. They can't prevent the demeaning of marriage when they are also trying to protect themselves within the travesty of a marriage.

I believe that many FW2 women who divorced were heroes in the classical sense of the term—that is, the multi-step story sequence (the hero's journey) as described by Joseph Campbell, Carol Pearson, Maureen Murdock and others who have studied mythology across cultures. These FW2 women defended the institution of marriage even when it meant leaving their own marriage. Their steps echo those of the hero's journey:

Maureen Reagan,
Women's rights advocate

"[Political consultant] Bill Roberts came to our apartment to discuss ...what was happening with the exploratory committee [to nominate Reagan for governor of California]. ... [His firm] believed that the divorce issue had been the cause of Rockefeller's defeat in 1964, and they were determined not to make the same mistake twice. The consultants were very nervous about Dad's previous marriage... In fact, Stu Spencer later suggested to my husband that I dig a hole and pull the dirt in over me until after the election."

Iran hostage rescue fails • FW2 designer Norma Kamali makes popular fashion statement with sweatshirt fabric

Louise Moran, living, for a while, with his affair

"I'm making my contacts." That's what my husband always said when I asked why he stayed out so late. He often did not come home until 10, 11, even 2 A.M.

In 1986, I found out he had a girlfriend. One day, he told me about a client who was getting a divorce. A few days later, he told me he had gone by her house to get some papers signed. Then one day, he came home and said that she had a vodka tonic waiting for him in the freezer when he got there. I said, "You know, I don't think that sounds very professional." He never mentioned her name again. Never.

Around then, I joined a health club. I looked up where this woman lived and saw that I could get to my health club by going down her street. I drove by her home at 9 A.M. once and there was his car. Acting like a detective, I hovered in several different areas. I got tired of waiting for him to leave so I went to the health club and then home. I called his office and said, "Where have you been?" He told me he'd been out looking for a car for our daughter's six-teenth birthday present. I snapped back, "No you haven't." He said, "Yes I have." I repeated,

1. Leaving ordinary lives to begin a journey—the marriage journey;
2. Encountering difficulties and challenges—alcoholism, emotional and physical abuse, and adultery;
3. Finding a teacher or mentor who provides the skills needed to overcome the problems—friend, minister, rabbi, marriage coun-selor, etc.;
4. Using these skills to face the challenge—defending their belief that marriage means *something*—love, a partnership, honesty, and respect—rather than *anything*—abuse, cheating, and alcoholism;
5. Returning home or re-emerging in society, changed by the experi-ence—finding growth in their employment and parenting roles and often finding happiness in a second marriage.

Consider Marsha's story. Marsha believes her childhood was ideal. She and her younger sister were cherished in a close-knit family of four. She even chose a college in the nearby town so that she could easily return home on holidays and many weekends. Soon after graduation, she married Bob, a fellow student she met during her junior year.

Unexpectedly, the simple "I do" thrust Marsha into a major life journey. She felt the loss of her loving family as she made her way

"No you haven't. You've been at Karen Nadler's house." After a long silence, he said, "Oh, are you going to be home?" He came home and said nothing was going on. I told him, "I don't want to live like that." He kept repeating that there was nothing going on. This went on for a year and a half. [*continued*]

in the early years of her marriage but looked forward to this new phase of her life. Marsha and Bob moved more than 1600 miles from her sister and parents so that he could take a job that would provide them with a stable household. She imagined that she would be the perfect wife, and over the years friends and family thought she had achieved her goal. She had a successful husband, a beautiful home, two wonderful children, a career in advertising, everything. But her marital journey was not what it appeared. When Bob drank, as he increasingly did, his suppressed anger came tumbling out. He belittled her; he ignored the children; and he eventually spent many weekends away from the home after he started gambling. The dark voice in Marsha made her feel that her husband's failures were her fault.

Louise Moran's story concludes, a lesson learned from divorce

On weekends, my husband would tell me he was going to play golf or he was going to the office. I'd call the club or his office and he wasn't there. I started my detective work again. A girlfriend told me she saw him carrying flowers into an apartment house. I knew he had represented some apartments that were in foreclosure. The next Sunday, when he said he was going to work, I drove down to these apartments. I saw his car parked out front and I took a white shoe polish dauber and wrote on his back window *bastard*. I got back in the car and drive home.

I was working in the flowerbeds when he came home, walked up to me, and said, "Did you write that on my car?" I went, "Yeah, I did." He said, "Why?" I answered, "Because I'm tired of you visiting your girlfriend in your apartment." He said, "I don't have an apartment." Well, I knew he did. I had figured it out. When he finished that deal, he told me he was not getting as much money as he had thought. I finally realized he traded his services for the apartment. That was when I made him move out.

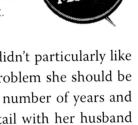

Marsha couldn't turn to her parents, as they didn't particularly like Bob. Besides, she believed this was the kind of problem she should be able to handle on her own. After struggling for a number of years and trying a variety of solutions, from having a cocktail with her husband each evening to threatening to leave, she realized that she needed outside help.

She turned to her minister who said, "I'm sure you're exaggerating. Perhaps you're tired and need a vacation. Why don't you and Bob get away on a little trip?" The minister knew her husband was a staunch member of the church and community, although it seemed that he was frequently away on business even on the weekends. Perhaps Marsha was just dissatisfied with her life and blamed Bob. A few weeks later, he casually mentioned to Bob that Marsha had been in to see him.

Although the minister didn't reveal anything confidential, Bob's growing paranoia was triggered. This, of course, made Marsha's home life almost impossible, as Bob was becoming physically as well as emotionally abusive when he drank.

Marsha thought, "Is this the meaning of marriage?" She felt they could save their marriage—if they went into counseling. She asked

We did go to counseling for a while. Well, he only went once. But I kept going. The counselor said, "Louise, you have two choices. If he's not going to admit he's seeing anybody, you can either live with it, which a lot of women do, or you can get out. That's your choice. But you can't live in limbo like this."

I learned from being divorced that no one makes your life but you. A lot of people, even at my age, think they need that right person to finish them up. That other person is only the icing. That other person is just something extra.

Bob if he would go with her to a counselor to try to resolve their problems. Although Bob wasn't happy with the idea, he agreed. At the first session, he didn't show up. That evening he explained that work was more important than "that stupid meeting." At the second scheduled session, Bob came but rarely spoke. Afterwards, he told Marsha, "If you have problems, then continue. But I don't think I'm the one at fault." That dark voice in Marsha's head whispered, "If you'll just figure out how to change, Bob will quit drinking and that will solve a lot of the problems." She kept going to Susan, her counselor, hoping to gain the insight to fix their marriage. After many months, Susan was able to help Marsha see the alternatives more clearly. She could accept Bob the way he was and continue in the marriage. She could tell Bob what she needed from the marriage and their relationship and offer to work with him to create the changes they both would have to make. Or, she could leave and start a new life beyond the marriage. Marsha agonized for a long time. Finally, as Bob became more abusive, she finally took the most difficult step. Bob refused to leave, so she moved out with the children and filed for (no-fault) divorce.

Ginger Hawthorne, accepting his affair but with conditions

His first affair was when my parents became ill, and I flew back to the west coast to spend time with them. I said, "Once I will forgive. But not twice." I suggested counseling, but he refused.

When we moved back to California, he traveled to New York for two weeks each month to keep up his clientele. This put a terrific strain on him. He needed somebody. I wasn't in a position to travel with him because I had the children to take care of. About this time, my father died. My husband was resentful when I spent time with my mother, getting her house ready to sell and helping her move. That's when he started his second affair. He found someone, a young lawyer who was brilliant but manipulative.

I told him to get out. He did leave the bedroom, but he lived in the house, not speaking to me for the next 2½ years. He never wanted to talk about it. I would ask him, and he would say, "No, I like things this way." Finally, I said, "If you're not willing to talk about this and you're not willing to work it out, then get out." He left the house in 1986, and we divorced in 1990.

Marsha's story is a composite of several interviews I conducted. We are taught to think of heroic archetypes as male. However, women often need to evoke the female hero within; otherwise oppression or conflict would overwhelm them. FW2 Carol Pearson, a well-known researcher of archetypes, describes the most salient characteristic of the hero: "the ability to ride out and face the unknown..." This is the extremely hard and fateful step taken by every woman I interviewed whose story of irreclaimable marriage and eventual divorce weaves into Marsha's composite story.

Assassination attempt on President Reagan, Washington Hilton

The FW2 Generation were the first, in large numbers, to evoke *the hero within* and accept the consequences. They paid a high psychological price whatever the outcome. If they divorced, some even

Reagan & Press Secretary James Brady shot • American Airlines introduces 1st frequent flyer awards program

I had some money coming from my father's estate, but there wasn't enough to live on. That was one of the reasons that I got divorced. I finally realized that my children and I would be in a better position financially if there was a court-ordered settlement.

now view themselves as failures. They still hear that dark voice whispering, "Why didn't you work harder, longer, or smarter to save your marriage? Why weren't you prettier, skinnier, sexier? What did you do to make him drink, find other women, abuse you?"

The Road to Divorce

Among those I interviewed, only one woman had never married. Many had married two times and a few had three or more marriages. As many as half of those who travel on the marriage road eventually learn about the road to divorce.

Prior to 1969, divorce was hard to obtain. Depending on the state where you lived, you might obtain a divorce once you proved fault such as: adultery, drug/alcohol abuse, imprisonment, physical/mental abuse, incest, insanity, desertion, fraud, or impotence. Many of these faults had been enacted into law as far back as the beginning of this nation. For example, in the 1780s Connecticut passed legislation that allowed a divorce to

**Robin Morgan,
Author, spokesperson
for women's movement**

"Finally realizing that you must get out is crucial. Finally feeling that you must save yourself and your child is crucial—as is finally understanding that you need to do the first so that you can do the second, like the order in which adults with children should strap on oxygen masks in a depressurized airplane. Material goods? Less critical. Besides, there are times simply to cut your losses and get on with living. For all these reasons, I walked away from another home I'd supported, taking with me little but the clothes on my back."

Iranian embassy hostages freed after 444 days • National debt tops $1 trillion • Microsoft releases MS-DOS

Shirley Olson, a defining moment

My husband was having an affair at work. I confronted him, and he said he'd stop. When I found out the second time, I said, "That's it. I don't need this and I don't need you." I was doing pretty well in my job and thought, "I can do this. I can take care of myself and my kids."

Before I knew he was still seeing her, I was raped. My husband was on a trip, and my daughter needed a present for a birthday party the next day. I worked at a clinic and still had on my uniform and lab coat. It was 8:00 P.M. so I left the kids at home saying, "I'm going to the shopping center and I'll be right back." As I walked to my car from the store, this guy grabbed me, pushed me into my car, and made me drive out to the trees behind the shopping center. I remember thinking that it was really ironic because that's where we used to go park and make out in high school. Your mind goes to strange things. About three months later a woman was abducted from the same shopping center and murdered. That really scared me. I wondered, "What if it was the same guy. Could I have prevented this?" I didn't go to the police because back then they never did anything.

be granted for "adultery, fraudulent contract, desertion for three years, or prolonged absence with a presumption of death." But gathering evidence of fault was difficult and expensive, an almost impossible undertaking for women with little access to money for private investigators and lawyers. Only the wealthy could afford to go to Nevada for six weeks in order to qualify for the brief residency requirement that facilitated a quick divorce. In the vast majority of cases in which both partners agreed to divorce, there would be a tawdry and tearful collusion to establish that one of the faults—in different states it was usually adultery or mental cruelty—was making the marriage impossible.

In 1969 Governor Ronald Reagan signed California's no-fault divorce law. By 1985, all states offered the no-fault option. Although specific grounds vary by state, no-fault is considered to be one or more of the following: separation, irretrievable breakdown, and irreconcilable differences.

On Ramps to Divorce

Among the women I interviewed, more than half were divorced at least once yet few of their parents had divorced. Some of the reasons for di-

As a result of the rape, I got pregnant and had an abortion. It was not something that I ever wanted to have to do. I can remember thinking, "Thank God this is available to me." Roe *v.* Wade had made abortion possible not long before this happened. I only told one person about the rape, my friend from the age of three years. She took me to have the abortion and brought me home. I got up the next day and went to work because you just can't let it get to you.

Later I found out that when I was raped, my husband was on a *business* trip with his lover. That was the defining moment. It was when I decided to divorce him.

vorce would have been familiar in any period of American history. Others were modern and are best understood by the terms irreconcilable differences and irretrievable breakdown.

Fault Ramps

Although the divorces were granted under no-fault laws, most divorces sought by FW2 women were due to one of three faults: adultery, alcohol or drug abuse, or physical or mental abuse.

President Reagan & Supreme Court Nominee Sandra Day O'Connor

Adultery: Fault On-Ramp #1. Having an affair was the factor that most frequently lead to divorce among the women interviewed.

Joan Reed, sometimes you just have to throw him out

In 1978, I found out that my husband had a girlfriend. I couldn't handle that. She would call the house. I knew who she was from the bowling alley. Everybody bowled a bit. I walked into a restaurant one time and they were sitting across from each other at a table for two. I thought, "Wait a minute." Then you start putting things together and you start feeling lost. I thought, "This is shit, and I'm not going to live like this."

After I said I wouldn't let him stay, he moved out and was gone for about two months. Finally, I went down to his office and said, "George, this is ridiculous. Either we try to put this back together or let's just call it quits. I'm not going to live like this. It's too hard on the kids and me too." I had three kids and only two years of college. I knew what it would be like trying to find a job.

We divorced, and it was hard. I raised my three daughters, working two jobs for nine years. But, you know, I look ahead and I don't look behind. I'm now remarried and happy with what I have, my husband, and my life.

Annette Funicello, Mouseketeer, Top-40 singer, film star

"Going straight from my parents' home to a husband's felt natural back in 1965. Practically everyone else I knew did it; my mother had done it. Wasn't that the way it was supposed to be? But as I matured, I began to see that marriage wasn't as easy as cutting the wedding cake."

"He's untrue, but what can I do?" This question, from 1964 lyrics sung by Lesley Gore, could be answered in five ways along the passive-assertive continuum: pretend nothing happened; decide that it wasn't really an affair through redefinition; seek joint marriage counseling; counter by also having an affair; separate.

Most FW2 women had imagined perfect marriages without a glimmer of adultery or divorce. As one woman said, "In high school, divorce was a four-letter word." Another mentioned that, in the 1950s, you whispered the words "her parents are divorced." Since divorce was rarely talked about, it is not surprising that women of the FW2 Generation were devastated when it happened to them.

Some women didn't want to confront a possible affair because they didn't know what they would do if the confrontation led to divorce. Women with children and without a career were the most likely to try this strategy. These women pretended that "nothing happened."

Other women redefined the affair by saying, "It was a one-night stand," or "It didn't mean anything." Some accepted the affair but with

conditions saying, "One affair can be forgiven, but not two." Margaret Thompson's story is typical of this reaction.

"I trusted him," says Margaret. "He was a businessman and would say, 'I need to entertain.' I believed him. I found out about one woman and he tried to convince me the affair didn't mean anything. We were separated for several months. Then he came back, and the marriage lasted for about another year. But he didn't quit seeing the other woman although he'd agreed he would. One day I walked into the bedroom, and he was talking to her on the telephone. I said, 'Okay, it's me or her.' He couldn't seem to make the decision, so I made it. I think it really flabbergasted him that I stood up for myself—I wouldn't go along with being a 40-year-old wife and letting him have a 20-year-old girlfriend. After the divorce in 1982, I found out he'd had several long-term affairs while we were married."

Most of the women I interviewed wanted to stay married. When the husband breached the marriage contract by having an affair, they often sought counseling with the hope of reestablishing the relationship. But if the husband wouldn't seek help, there was little to do other than divorce. Edith Andrews told me, "In the early 1970s, my husband was having an affair. I didn't know about it although everybody else in town had figured

Helen Young, ambivalent about affairs that shaped her life

I had several serious affairs over the years. I am where I am today because of them. They were bad choices because they could have destroyed my marriage, my family. They really were bad choices but I can't look back and say I'm sorry. I do regret that the affairs caused me to not give enough of myself to my family. It's not something I'm really proud of but it was fun at the time.

A group of us lived, ate, breathed, and drank together from morning 'til night. There was a lot of social activity and through that I attained a level of success in business. My husband didn't find out about the affairs. He may have but it is part of the old cliché—if you deny it then you can always forget it. But once something is said, there's no going back. He's not a fool. He had to have known. Maybe there was a time when I thought that when the kids were gone, I'd leave. I remember my best friend counting the days until her last child graduated from high school as that was the day she was leaving. And she did. I used to think about that but financially I wasn't able to walk out of my marriage and financially he wasn't able to either. We

Joan Baez,
Folk singer and activist
for non-violence

"We split up, when we did, because I couldn't breathe, and I couldn't try anymore to be a wife, and because I belonged alone.... What I knew in my bones at the crumbling finale to our erratic three years together I could express consciously to myself ten years later. I am made to live alone."

it out. I'm sure I just didn't want to believe it. He traveled all the time and really shouldn't have. There was no reason for it. I unpacked his suitcase one Christmas and found the note, the inevitable letter. Of course, I read it and everything went down hill from there. We fought about it; he didn't want to go to a counselor. Obviously he'd made up his mind about what he was going to do. One person can't rescue a marriage. I was absolutely devastated for years."

Some women, when they found out their husbands were having an affair, countered by having an affair. I recently saw the 1930 movie *The Divorcee* starring Norma Shearer. When I heard the lines in which Ned's affair was considered acceptable but Jerry's (Norma Shearer) retaliatory affair made her a fallen woman, I immediately thought of Patricia Fisher's story. "In the 1970s, my husband started a real-estate partnership with several friends and I was the only wife that got involved. I really liked my part in the business and was feeling so wonderful. I was a stay-at-home mom until then. One of his business partners just saw this blooming person and decided to make approaches for an affair, which I resisted for quite a while. However,

needed both incomes. But I don't know whether he thought, "When the kids are gone maybe I'm not going to put up with this anymore." I don't know. But fortunately we got past that. It's a wonderful relationship now. One of these days we can both retire.

I can't stress enough the fact my husband let me do everything in business. That sounds like an old-fashioned remark, but I do know people whose husbands would not have given them the freedom and the support that I had. I was living in two different worlds; he knew that, and yet he was always here. He was a tremendous father. When I wasn't around to do a lot of nurturing, he was a saint. He is a saint. Because of him, we have two wonderful daughters.

I did succumb after he told me my husband had several affairs. My affair went on for about three years. It ended when I discovered that my husband, quite blatantly, had started still another affair. When I confronted him, he began to talk about how sorry he was and he didn't know how this could have happened. He was being very dramatic. At a certain point, I said, 'Well obviously something is wrong in our marriage because I'm also having an affair.' Suddenly, I became the terrible woman, the terrible mother."

The final reaction to a husband's affair was to separate and initiate the divorce. For some of these women, there was no pretending all was fine, no redefining the situation or con-

Lynn Sullivan, her undisclosed affair leads to a divorce

I felt my husband pulling away from me emotionally. He would come home, turn on the television, and just sit there. That broke my heart. As a result, I eventually had an affair. I had never, ever messed around, even when he was away for months at a time. Unfortunately, the affair ruined my relationship with my husband because I never felt I could tell him and I never did. I only saw the other person about six months, but that was the end of my marriage because I couldn't deal with it.

For the next five years, my husband and I tried to work things out. He kept saying, "I can change. I don't know what it is that you want but I can change." One evening, he kept pushing me, "What do you want? What do you want?" I finally said, "I want out." So we separated.

I felt guilty about the affair and didn't want to ruin his relationship with our children so I suggested that I move out. I wanted some space too. One of the problems was that my father, even though he was a lousy father, had been an incredible husband. I thought when you mar-

ditional acceptance, no reliance on counseling, no countering with their own affair. They looked at their options and moved to end the marriage. Ruth Spiro knew that the divorce would bring her enough money to live so it was a difficult but unencumbered decision. "In 1987 my marriage broke up. That was a shock. There was somebody else involved. We were considered the perfect couple. On the outside, we had everything and we were very lucky. We traveled an enormous amount with the kids to many countries. We water-skied with them every weekend during the summer at our place on a lake. But those years of our relationship were pretty bleak emotionally. When he told me about the other person, I kicked him out."

When asked to name the best things in her life, Ruth replies, "My marriage and divorce are the best two things. I don't have any regrets about the marriage. For that time it worked. It certainly stretched me, but the growth came from the divorce."

Alcohol and Drug Abuse: Fault On-Ramp #2. Substance abuse causes many strains in a family, spilling into multiple areas of the relationship. Jobs may be lost, mental or physical abuse of the spouse or children may occur, money may be gambled or spent on alcohol and drugs, affairs may take place. Alcohol and drug abuse was the second

ried, you got treated like a queen on a pedestal, not like a scullery maid. I was wounded and I just wanted to crawl into a tiny apartment and nurse my wounds.

There had been another hurt, as well. I asked my husband to help me get started in a career. He had the education, knowledge, and skills and could have helped. But he kept saying, "No, this is your thing." I know now he wanted me to fail because he wanted me to be at home. I think I even knew that at the time. It really bothered me. I had followed him all over the country, all over the world. I had always been there for him, but when I really needed him he wasn't there for me.

most frequent cause of divorce among the FW2 women I interviewed. Just as the women had indicated their naïveté in dating, so they spoke of their naïveté in understanding or even recognizing alcoholism.

Parents of the FW2 Generation rarely discussed or even acknowledged alcoholism in the family. It was kept as quiet as possible in an effort to maintain an outside appearance of normalness and happiness. FW2 women who had alcoholic fathers or mothers only knew that drinking was not to be mentioned. So, without any real understanding of the problem or what to do, FW2 women were often overwhelmed by the problems posed by an alcoholic husband.

Carol Lampton's divorce resulted from her husband's alcoholism. She says, "During the '70s, his drinking became an increasing problem, not that anybody was prepared to admit that it was alcoholism. He began to have problems at work. His boss came to me in the early '80s and said, 'This problem needs to be addressed.' One of the bravest things I ever did was attend my first Al-Anon meeting. I felt I was taking positive steps to learn, to change, and to cope with the situation. I got him into treatment in 1981. For most of the 1980s he was sober. I felt good about the marriage, good about my work, and good about my family and home

Charlyne Tucker, naïve about alcoholism

I was 25, hadn't dated much, and knew my goal was to get married and have a family. So I was extremely receptive when my boyfriend started talking marriage after a month of dating. It was November, and he wanted to marry in July, but I convinced him February was better. I'm not sure whether a longer engagement would have changed our decision. By the early 1970s, I realized he was no longer a social drinker. He would have several drinks before and after dinner and often fall asleep on the couch. I was so naïve I never thought of him as an alcoholic because he always went to work the next day.

In 1975, a month before I was due with our third child, he lost his job again. He had been with this company five years. I assumed his job was safe because his manager was a relative. I spent the next two years unsuccessfully trying to convince him to get counseling. He got angry in public and even told off his stepmother in a restaurant. He was so loud that everyone turned to look just as she slapped him.

In late 1977, he left on a business trip. When he called, I told him not to come back. I said

Wilma Mankiller,
Chief of the
Cherokee Nation

"Hugo [her husband] informed me that I could not have a car…. I went straight to the bank, withdrew some money, and bought an inexpensive Mazda. Buying that little red car without my husband's consent or knowledge was my first act of rebellion against a lifestyle that I had come to believe was too narrow and confining for me."

life. In 1989 he relapsed and started drinking again, which totally blindsided me.

"In 1990 he had an automobile accident and was charged with drunk driving. I didn't know this at the time but he was having an affair. I was focusing totally on the drinking. In the spring of 1991 I said, 'I can't live with the drinking so get out.' In December of that year, his company fired him. After months of separation, I finally acknowledged the divorce had to happen."

Drugs, like alcohol, can also wreck havoc in a marriage. A person living with a drug addict may eventually leave because she fears for her personal safety and for the safety of her children.

Physical and Mental Abuse: Fault On-Ramp #3. Not all stories of abuse result in divorce. Some women are unable to leave the relationship, which has undermined their self-confidence. Abbey Goldman's story, however, is one that led to divorce.

She married her high-school boyfriend in 1965 and was initially happy. She worked and attended three years of college before marriage and continued working until her son was born in 1968. After that, her

I was going to get a job, which he had forbidden, and a divorce. He called the next night to say he had been 'born again' and would go to counseling. When he returned, we went to a church counselor. He told her, "My wife has so little self-esteem, she couldn't keep her own checkbook." For the kids, I tried to make the marriage work for two more years. We finally divorced.

During those later years of the marriage, my physical health suffered but my mental health suffered much more. I remember taking the children to visit my parents. My sisters were there with their children. Until then I never realized how tense I was at home and how hard I worked at keeping everything on an even keel. I later learned how alcoholics' wives act and I was classic. Unfortunately, I still was too naïve to think alcoholism.

husband didn't want her to go back to work. By the 1970s, her marriage was slowly deteriorating as her husband began to mentally and physically abuse her. By the 1980s the situation turned worse. She explains, "My husband traveled a lot and became more mentally and physically abusive. There was no drinking or drugs involved. Mostly it was directed at me, not the children. It seemed that when he was traveling things were okay, but when he came home he was just not happy and took it out on me. He was like a ticking time bomb. You never knew if he would be in a good mood or a bad mood. He would come home and just blow up. I thought this was normal behavior. I didn't know better. I didn't discuss this much with my friends. I just more or less kept it to myself. It wasn't a very happy time. I couldn't say anything to my parents. They never liked him from the beginning. That would have been just more fuel to the fire.

"In 1986 we moved to California. For a while things seemed to be okay. Then the abuse began again, and I was afraid he was going to hurt my daughter and me. I feared for my life. In 1988, I filed for divorce. That was a very big decision, but I was living in fear."

Wilma Mankiller

"Once I began to become more independent, more active with school and in the community, it became increasingly difficult to keep my marriage together. ... I began to have dreams about more freedom and independence, and I finally came to understand that I did not have to live a life based on someone else's dreams."

FW2 Isabel Allende publishes *The House of the Spirits* • AT&T sells 22 "Baby Bells" • Princess Grace dies in car crash

Canda Mitans, alcoholism and abuse lead to divorce

My husband was an alcoholic and emotionally abusive. Towards the end, he became physically abusive. It was hard living with an alcoholic, with a person who considered me an idiot and missed no opportunity to pound that in. Even though we saw my parents often, I felt that I had gotten myself into this scrape and didn't want to involve them.

I didn't have many resources as far as gathering strength or getting any kind of input so I had no positive feelings about myself. I stayed in that relationship much longer than I should have because I didn't have any confidence. After nine years, I told him I was leaving. Suddenly, he agreed to go to a marriage counselor, something I'd asked him to do for years. After twelve months of counseling, I finally had the strength to know that I could manage on my own. I wasn't sure *how* but it was the beginning of my getting to know *who* I was.

For nine years I was single and made great strides. I was proud of the life I'd made, proud of myself. I was becoming a person I liked. Then I met this guy and we married. He was an alcoholic and abusive. I lost all the ground I'd gained. I went back to being under someone's

Mental and physical abuses are especially cruel because the recipient feels it is her fault and that the abuse would stop if she would just behave differently. Eventually, her self-esteem is so depleted that she may be unable to take the actions needed to remove herself from the destructive situation. Fortunately, Abbey was able to take that step.

No-Fault Ramps

The introduction of no-fault divorces removed the legal assignment of blame. The underlying reasons why women and men seek divorce are now more readily discussed. Although in each case a marriage crisis is by definition serious, sometimes the divorce step is more of an adjustment rather than a breach of normal life. Gage Worth told me, "My husband and I just went our separate ways. There were no major problems. In my case, I suppose there were cultural differences, immaturity, and an inability to make a real commitment. He wanted to go one way and I wanted to go another. We didn't have kids and we didn't have property, so it was easy to do. As a matter of fact, other women I've met who divorced during the 1970s now say they gave up a husband without serious cause. It would be interesting if someone wrote a book titled

thumb, unable to think for myself. I still don't really understand how that could happen, but it did. That went on for five years until I divorced him.

Finally, I met the right guy but was hesitant to remarry. We lived together for seven years. A third marriage? Why would I want to do that? We were going to a counselor who kept asking why we didn't marry. Finally, she told us to make two lists, one with all the reasons to marry and the other with all the reasons to not marry. We realized we had some old ideas that weren't valid and we married. You see, he's twelve years younger than I am. We work through our problems. We're not afraid to talk about them and examine them. We work really well together.

I Gave up a Perfectly Good Husband: Now I Have to Search for Another One."

Separation / Irreconcilable Differences / Irretrievable Breakdown: No-Fault On-Ramp. For Joy Allyson, the irreconcilable difference was her growing desire to have a child combined with her husband's unwillingness to even discuss the matter. "When my husband and I dated," Joy says, "we talked about his unwillingness to have more children and that was okay with me. He was divorced and had two children. When we married, his 15-year-old son moved in with us. The biggest change was that after having his son live with us for several years, I wanted children. He wasn't the perfect kid but it was a good arrangement—the three of us together—we were a good little family.

"I knew we had decided to not have children, but my husband wouldn't even discuss it with me. Not talking about it was hard on me. Probably he could have talked me into or out of anything, but he wouldn't even talk about it so we actually broke up over that. That was a very difficult time for me."

Susan Cheever,
Author

"Looking backward, I can see that I could have stayed married to any of the men I married. I chose them, and I chose well; they were all good, kind, intelligent men. The things that loomed so large when I was younger…no longer seem as relevant or as earth-shaking as they once did."

Cal Ripkin plays game 1 of 2,632 consecutive game record • *Cagney & Lacey* premiers • Movie: *Victor/Victoria*

Nancy Scott, losing and finally finding herself again

I met a police officer while I was working. I think I was just ready to get married and have a child. He was also a Scoutmaster, and I thought this would work. They say love is a sickness, an obsession. That's the way it was for me. I fell madly in love. Within the year, we were married and three years later my son was born.

Early in the marriage I found out that my husband was a drug addict. I married this guy before I realized what was going on. I was so naïve. I wasn't prepared for something like this. He swore he would never do drugs again so I stayed with him for six years. My son was 2½ when I realized that he was back on drugs. I had given up a tremendous amount of my own ego, lifestyle, and psyche for this marriage. I changed my own personality in order to accommodate his needs, lifestyle, and behavior. We were very, very different. I was raised with the idea that love conquers all so I changed a lot of what I did, of who I was. I finally left him when I realized I was really frightened and scared. I just took my child and left.

President Reagan signs Martin Luther King, Jr. Holiday Legislation

The Road Less Traveled

Sexual orientation is another factor that resulted in no-fault divorces. Although ancient practices differed, in the modern past neither men nor women were allowed to reveal their homosexual orientation without consequences. Therefore, some women as well as men entered into heterosexual relationships and hid their stronger attraction to persons of their own gender. As we now know from coming-out stories, gay women and men are both able to play straight roles for long periods in their lives. Certainly many women had children and lovingly raised

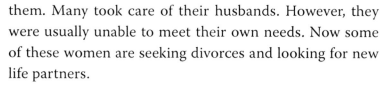

There were debts that fell on me after the divorce. He had not covered any of my maternity hospitalization. He didn't even have me registered as his wife on his benefit package. There were taxes that the IRS couldn't collect from him and came to me to pay. He went on disability from the police force but he got arrested for drugs.

I was really devastated by the divorce. I had given up so much of myself. I really had to get myself back together. Soon I was so happy to be me again. I had stopped being me. I didn't realize the extent to which I had become subservient, changed my style, and become second fiddle to someone. I don't know why I felt I had to do those things but I did until I started being me again.

them. Many took care of their husbands. However, they were usually unable to meet their own needs. Now some of these women are seeking divorces and looking for new life partners.

One woman, we'll call her Jane, told me that in high school she passed a note to a girlfriend describing her interest in her. The girl gave her mother the note, and the next day Jane's father picked her up after school, an unusual event. On the way home, he told her that she would finish high school, go to college, get married and have children and that she was never to send a note like that again. She followed the directive for many years. At one point, after her first divorce, she tried living with another woman. But they feared for their jobs if anyone found out. Eventually, she married "a wonderful man" who knew she was gay but was willing to give her the heterosexual relationship that society demanded. Recently she has divorced again, and has finally told her grown children.

Deborah Tannen,
Researcher, author

Deborah invited her mother to see her new office after she became a professor at Georgetown University. Her mother had disapproved of her younger years and had been unhappy when she divorced six years previously. Her mother seemed pleased and then asked: "Do you think you would have accomplished all this if you had stayed married?" "Absolutely not," Deborah replied. "If I'd stayed married, I wouldn't have gone to grad school to get my Ph.D." "Well," her mother replied, "if you'd stayed married you wouldn't have had to."

Trivial Pursuit, PCP/angel dust, CDs, Cabbage Patch dolls • FW2 Barbra Streisand wins Best Director Golden Globe

Diane Boxwood, just getting by but not knowing why

My husband was in the Army when we met in 1961. We hit it off right away and corresponded for about five years, but rarely saw each other during that time. In 1966, in one of his letters, he suggested I come and visit him in Idaho for vacation. I went and we really hit it off. He proposed to me and we married soon afterwards. In 1971, I had a son. By 1977, I knew my marriage was unraveling. I did a number of things to save our marriage, but nothing seemed to make it better.

Twenty years later, we were having our carpet replaced, and I went down to the basement to get out of the workers' hair. My husband had his study as well as a television down there. I was watching TV when I put my hand down in the cushion and felt a magazine. I pulled it out and saw it was a magazine for gays. I couldn't believe it. I could not believe that he was gay. About a month later, I was in the basement again when the phone rang. I answered it and sat down at his computer desk to talk. I happened to look over at his printer and saw pages in the tray. It looked like a conversation so I read it. Oh, my God. He had been on the Internet

Astronaut Sally Ride on flight deck during Challenger mission

No Money for Gas: Financial Impact of Divorce

In Nancy Atherton's novel *Aunt Dimity's Death*, the amateur sleuth, Lori Shepherd, reflects on her financial difficulties: "It started when my marriage dissolved, not messily, but painfully nonetheless. By the time we sat down to draw up papers, all I wanted was a quick, clean break—and that was all I got. I could have stuck around to fight for property settlements or alimony, but by then I was tired of fighting, tired of sticking around, and, above all, I despised the thought of living *off* a man I no longer lived *with*."

Some women received adequate, even generous, divorce settlements. A second group had adequate court awards that were rarely received.

with other gay men. I was absolutely devastated. I remember thinking, "How could he marry me knowing he was gay?" I realized that was why we hadn't had sex all these years. I thought for years and years—and this is why my self-esteem went down to nothing—that he wasn't attracted to me. I always tended to internalize everything. [*continued*]

A third group, like Lori, just wanted out, let the financial consequences be dammed. Usually women in this last group were already emotionally bankrupt, and the divorce left them financially bankrupt as well. Mary Jackson sums it up: "My husband and I came to an early financial settlement. I gave up a whole lot. I just wanted to make it as easy on him as I could. I didn't want to fight over money. A lot of people thought I was really stupid to do that. Financially, I was. Psychologically it was just better for me."

Uniqueness of Divorce for FW2 Generation Women

We FW2 women now feel smarter and more aware of the ways of the world than we did several decades ago when we first became involved with love, marriage, and divorce. In our early adulthood we were probably more naïve (from Old French naïf—natural, instinctive, rustic) than either our mothers' or daughters' generations. As a person who has lived many places in the United States, I find an analogy between these temporal differences and the spatial

Erica Jong

"When Ken and I met, each of us had been married—twice in his case, three times in mine. We stamped the phrase *A Triumph of Hope Over Experience* in red on our wedding announcements right over the line 'Erica and Ken are astonished to announce their marriage.' ...at our wedding celebration in 1989 people were taking bets on how long it would last. Sixteen years later, they've thrown in the towel."

Diane Boxwood's story concludes, finally finding happiness

My husband was out of town when I found the Internet message. I put a note on the kitchen table saying I knew he was gay, I'd flown home, and we'd talk after I got back. When I returned, he told me he went berserk and considered suicide when he read my note. I said, "I had no idea that you cared how I felt. I thought you'd be glad to get rid of me." He felt that by getting married and having a child, he was solving the problem because in the '60s you didn't come out. His family only learned he was gay when we divorced. He was just living a lie.

He gave me a month to get used to the fact that he was leaving. He told me I would have to make friends and go out with them. He knew I couldn't stay in the house by myself and not have any outlet. I'd spent all those years with just my family. After he left, I felt like I'd been put on a desert island all by myself. I cried and cried and cried.

I had asked him to stay but he refused. I said, "You can continue your lifestyle. I just don't want to know about it." Now I see that it wouldn't

differences I've observed in this vast country. To put a sharp point on the analogy, you would probably agree with me that citizens of Springdale Falls, Oregon can live in a more unguarded fashion than citizens of New York City. My New York friends have tried to teach me the art of street surveillance when turning any corner and starting down a new street—when to change sides of the street, when to back off and try another block. But street sense is ingrained through some unpleasant experiences and even more unpleasant possibilities. I grew up in Oklahoma City, and I never had occasion to learn street sense.

Similarly, generations of women are probably as wary as they need to be, living in their times. My parents' generation and my children's generation both grew up in a tougher America than I did. In no part of our lives has this been more true than in love, marriage, and divorce.

We were probably the first (and last?) generation to believe implicitly that marriage was held in place by emotional rather than pragmatic ties. The prosperity of that era assured us that we would never lack the material necessities. Our parents must have struggled financially, but they didn't burden us with those memories. Living hundreds and even thousands of miles away from our parents was an unexpected consequence of college

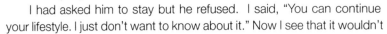

have worked but at the time he was my security blanket.

After he left, I was very angry, but then I forgave him because what else are you going to do? He is a very kind man and a good father. Everybody tells me I'm so wonderful and asks, "How could you forgive him?" I say, "He didn't ask to be born that way. He wasn't bad to me." I've since learned that there are thousands of us out there who had husbands that kept their homosexuality a secret. I had no idea.

Now I've developed a wonderful friendship circle and I have a very satisfying social life. I have great friends and go out almost every weekend with someone. I didn't think that I could ever be happy again, but I am.

attendance, the Vietnam War, our husband's job mobility, and—sooner or later—our own employment needs. Distance from our parents and early friends made divorce somewhat easier since our "failures" weren't constant reminders to our parents and their friends.

Divorce and remarriage occurred so often that blended families were commonplace. I remember one night in the early 1980s when very young Will began to cry at the dinner table. We asked what was upsetting him. He said haltingly, "I don't have a stepmother or stepdad like all my friends." It occurred to me to say that his childcare family at Stanford, Ana Maria and Eduardo, dearly loved him, and he could think of them as his stepparents. He was OK with that.

Many FW2 Generation women were the first but not the last in our families to divorce. Sometimes older sisters divorced after we did. By then, we'd learned how hard divorce is on everyone involved—spouse, children, parents, siblings, and ourselves. Yet sometimes divorce is a courageous act that overcomes a destructive impasse in a marriage. Ex-partners and children are often happier once life begins again without daily strife. Unfortunately, interviews revealed that some FW2 women have plain old-fashioned broken hearts over what happened. Healing will take still more time.

Geraldine Ferraro 1st woman vice presidential candidate for major party • "Where's the beef?" • Reagan re-elected

Amazing Grace:
Spiritual Lives of the FW2 Generation

Religion in the Context of the Time

On each Sunday morning when I was young, my sister and I donned our freshly washed, starched, and ironed dresses, added our white gloves, and rode with our parents to the First Baptist Church in downtown Oklahoma City. All the Butlers belonged to the same church, a family affair. I talked with cousins and aunts and uncles there each week. Some of my school friends attended Jewish services on Saturday, but almost all of the others attended Christian services on Sunday morning at the Baptist, Methodist, Episcopal, Lutheran, Presbyterian, and Catholic churches that were visible everywhere in town.

The Sundays of my childhood weren't times for playing out and about. Sunday mornings were for church. After the service we sometimes went to a restaurant, a treat in itself since we rarely ate meals out. I wasn't prohibited from playing with friends in the afternoon, but the play was to be quiet and respectful of the day. Sometimes I listened to music on my little 45 RPM record player. As I got older, I did homework as I listened. Around 4 o'clock I tuned the radio to *The Shadow*, a program that held me enthralled from its opening line, "Who knows what evil lurks in the

Annalee Draper, fire becomes a transformative event

Spiritually, I got a big, giant kick in the butt from God. A wildfire burned 50 acres surrounding me one windy day, at the end of a long dry summer. Fortunately, I was home at the time, and as the fire approached nearer, I quickly closed the heavy wooden interior shutters with iron bars. I jumped in my car, drove as far as the end of the driveway, got out and was trying to open the gate when the flame came roaring down and leaped, like a huge burning sheet, right over my head. It was traumatizing but I got out of there in my car. When I turned and looked back up the hill all I could see was a huge tower of flames. I felt I was losing everything. The fire marshal came up in his jeep and I shouted, "My house! My house!" and he said, "Sorry." I thought everything was gone.

At that moment, I just felt God's presence. I had never been religious before. I suddenly felt, "Everything is okay, it doesn't matter. I'm here, you're here and this is just material possessions." I was so at peace.

After it was safe to return, I went back up the hill and found the house was fine. The ivy had burned off the walls. The bougainvillea had burned off the walls. Some of the windows

hearts of men?—*The Shadow* knows." Then came the best time of all. On Sunday evenings, my sister and I alternated fixing dinner with our father. On my week, we always prepared open-faced sandwiches of sardines and mustard. Occasionally, we substituted smoked oysters. Even though we just opened cans, I thought I was cooking. But, most of all, I loved the time alone with my father. In the late 1940s and 1950s, Sundays were about religion and family.

The Decades Bring Changes to Religion in America

Mainstream forms of Christianity and Judaism were the religions of my generation's collective childhood. Other religions were undoubtedly practiced around us, but they were invisible to me as a child. As we entered adulthood, other religious and spiritual movements were not only visible but much discussed.

The foregrounding of religion in mass culture actually began in the 1950s. Most notably, a Baptist minister from North Carolina, Rev. Billy Graham, brought revivals of traditional Protestantism to cities like mine across America. Religious audiences unseen since the religious revivals of the 1920s filled football stadiums. Graham, refreshingly different from

had shattered. But apart from that there was no damage. Of course, I lost over thirty big trees on my wooded acre. They were mostly pine and just exploded.

Then the neighbors came up and said, "Oh, it's a miracle." Soon afterwards, I found a small Christian group and started going to church and studying the Bible. [*continued*]

.

the huckster evangelists of the prewar era, took religious news off the Saturday church page and placed it on the front page.

Change Brings Social Justice to the Foreground of Religion. Two things were clear to my wartime generation as we stood on the threshold of the 1960s and our own adulthood at the same moment. First, the

future belonged to us in many different senses—as young people, as Americans, as survivors or at least spectators of recent devastating events. Second, initiative for changing the world was shifting from the Gray Old Men to much younger people. The decade of the 1960s was only 31 days old when four black freshmen at a segregated North Carolina college entered the Woolworth's store in Greensboro, bought

The Reagans presenting Mother Teresa the Medal of Freedom

Annalee Draper's story concludes, joining the Christian group leads to other life changes

In my mid-to-late thirties, I had wanted to get married and settle down, but I never really found the right person. Then, after the fire when I started going to church, I got angry and wondered what was wrong with me. I became really angry with God and finally I had a lot of conversations with Him over this.

Then I just realized, "OK. If it's your will that I remain single and alone in life, then I accept it." I became very much at peace with myself, and three weeks later my friends introduced me to the man who became my husband. After that first date, I turned to God again because I was kind of afraid. I said, "Please, if it is your will that I have a companion in life, then I'll let you decide because up until now I have chosen one wrong person after another."

I was strong willed, and each man I had chosen over the years was always the wrong person. I have to say that if I'd been left to my own devices I never would have looked at this man twice. I never in a million years would have envisioned myself with him much less have married him. The first year was really rocky because both of us had been single for a long time.

Jaune Quick-to-See Smith,

Painter and printmaker

"The Sacred isn't housed in a building or worn around your neck or something in the sky. The Sacred is the here and now we reside in, all breathing the same air, all imbibing the same water and made of the same earth with 'the life force' flowing through all living things."

some school supplies, and then sat at the lunch counter and asked to order food. When they were refused service, they continued to sit at the counter. The civil rights sit-in was born; it soon spread to ten other cities. A month later *Time* magazine summarized civil rights news: "The young Negro, particularly the young college Negro, is now leading the battle for equal rights. And unless he is tossed into jail and onto a road gang, he is going to lead the battle for a long time to come."

The 1960s were the decade of youth. This was evident not only in music and lifestyles but also in politics and religion. The Southern Christian Leadership Conference, founded three years before by Rev. Martin Luther King Jr. and other ministers, began to organize student sit-ins in 1960. White as well as black youth headed south from other parts of the United States, often coordinated by churches, synagogues, and campus ministries. Mario Savio, the 22-year-old founder of Berkeley's Free Speech Movement, who had earlier traveled to the South to help in voter registration campaigns, said, "I am not a political person. My involvement in the Free Speech Movement is religious and moral."

We rubbed each other the wrong way. There was a lot of tension and I would just pray every night in bed. I would just lie there and say, "God, help me get through tomorrow. Help me get through one more day with this man. Help me do it."

But I tell you, we've been very happy. It's the best thing as far as a marriage that I could ever have expected. We've been married for nine years now.

In this photograph [*right*] treasured by a classmate of mine, her future husband, Rev. John Claypool, meets with Rev. Martin Luther King Jr. in Louisville, Kentucky in April 1961 to plan civil rights campaign strategy. During the years Claypool served as its minister, Crescent Hill Baptist Church was one of the first congregations in Louisville to integrate. Like many other young ministers, priests, and rabbis of the 1960s, Claypool continued to work for social justice until he died in 2005.

Change Reveals and Merges the Many Faces of Religion. Youth in the 1960s were more aware of global cultures and traditions than their parents had been. The number of religious and spiritual options they discussed and sometimes espoused increased greatly during this period. Newspapers, magazines, television, and college classes brought information on Buddhism, Hinduism, Taoism, Shintoism, and Confucianism as well as movements such as Transcendental Meditation. Young members

Charlyne Tucker, seeking a spiritual life

In my 30s, I turned back to religion and tried to find comfort and answers. Unfortunately, we had joined a fundamentalist church, and they told me I had to do everything for my husband and make him head of the household in all things, no matter what he did. I could not even wear my hair shorter than his. I rebelled. I did not know what I needed spiritually, but I knew this was not it.

I've been searching and wanting to grow spiritually all through my life. It goes in spurts. Sometimes I emphasize it a lot and other times I don't. I've found that over the years, I've become much more practical than I ever was before about that. I'm not drawn in by fundamentalism. I look more for what is in me that is spiritual rather than for a God in heaven and a devil in hell.

I am seeking to find my place in the world.

of the Hare Krishna sect, in saffron robes, handed out literature at the airport. It registered with college youth when a newsmagazine in 1961 stated about the most famous historian of the day, "Arnold Toynbee is an apostle of an amalgam of Christianity and Mahayanian Buddhism." An unprecedented fusion of Western and Eastern beliefs gained momentum during the 1960s.

Change Looks Inward, As Well. As many churches and Reform Jewish synagogues turned to social action in support of civil rights, they also embraced new forms of music, tentatively accepted gays, and even ordained a few women as ministers and rabbis. Clearly change was afoot, and nowhere more so than in the Catholic Church in the aftermath of Vatican II. On March 12, 1965, for the first time, altars in Catholic churches across America were turned to face the congregation. Priests said Mass in a mixture of Latin and English, then entirely in English.

As if this change in liturgy were not enough, Vatican II also changed the church's view on ecumenism and encouraged its members to understand other religions. No longer did the Catholic Church state that it was the sole avenue to salvation. This was an important change for my Catholic friends who previously had to wait outside any non-Catholic church

Iran-Contra Affair disclosed (sell arms to Iran at inflated prices to fund anti-communist Contras in Nicaragua)

when the rest of the class went inside on a field trip. Now, they too were able to visit other places of worship. As a teenager, if I ate Friday dinner out, I always knew who was Catholic. She was the only one ordering fish. After Vatican II, the American bishops authorized meat on Friday. Many ways in which Catholics differed from other Christians were eliminated by these changes; sharp boundaries became blurred.

A Kaleidoscope of Changes in Perspective. I can't write about the 1960s and 1970s without recalling "the Age of Aquarius" as captured in haunting melodies and memorable lyrics of the "American tribal love rock musical" *Hair,* which ran on Broadway from 1968 to 1972 and has been revived ever since: "peace will guide the planets and love will steer the stars." This was definitely not the perspective of my childhood religion.

In addition to dramatic changes in religious social activism, religious inclusiveness, and internal religious modifications, other events altered our worldviews. Revelations about the war in Vietnam during that period made us question the piety of politicians. The sexual revolution enabled us to embrace and enjoy the physicality of sex, which in generations leading up to ours was often described as a "woman's duty."

Emily Cappis, leaving the church

I have a brother who is 15 months younger than I am. As a baby, he had severe colic that took all my mother's time for many months. During that period, I think the message to me was that he was favored. I felt that way all through childhood. I had to wear glasses when I was five. I was overweight. I would always look down and not look up at people. Meanwhile, my brother was this cute little effervescent kid that talked to anybody. As a result, I felt awkward, inferior, and unattractive.

I had very low self-esteem and a lot of anger inside due to a lack of bonding with my parents and their lack of guidance. It showed its ugly face most vividly in my college years when I became a real recluse. However, it was the 70s that were my rebellious years. I broke away from my traditional Christian upbringing, stopped going to church, stopped praying, stopped all of the spiritual activities that I had been brought up in. I got out into the world a bit and drank alcohol. I even tried pot two or three times, but I never got into hard drugs. I was the black sheep of the family.

Homosexual relationships, undiscussed in our childhood, became more open. New laws and medical technologies enabled us to think about the future course of our lives in ways that were never before possible. All these disparate developments, plus many more, created a changing kaleidoscope of new attitudes and beliefs that altered the fixed religious perceptions of our childhoods.

Each Succeeding Decade Brings More Changes. While changes in the religious landscape of the 1960s were probably the most influential for FW2 women because they occurred in our formative early adult years, changes in later decades also affected our lives. The 1970s saw a revival and significant growth in evangelical and charismatic religions—it was newsworthy but not puzzling in 1976 when presidential candidate Jimmy Carter said that he was a "born-again Christian." The 1980s heralded the rise of New Age spiritualities that became popular culture phenomena in the 1990s. Multiculturalism was also transforming America. Dr. Diana Eck, professor of comparative religion at Harvard University, reported that at the turn of the millennium, there were six million Muslim Americans. That number was greater than the number of Episcopalians or Presbyterians and as large as the number of

What started the rebellious stage? It was rather a superficial thing. Whenever I would go to church I would just feel like this awful sinner and come out crying and just feeling worse about myself. I stopped going to church because I would feel so bad after each service. From there it got worse.

What I know now and didn't know then was that I think the Lord was trying to make me aware of dependence on Him and how He is the one that could change my life and make me a stronger person internally. He could keep me on track, living the good life that was my goal. He knew that I was still the good little girl I was brought up to be. It was after I stopped going to church when I had no Christian support system that I got into the world. [*continued*]

Jews in America. Moreover, Eck noted there were another four million nontheistic American Buddhists and one million multitheistic Hindus.

If I were a child today, I might talk about friends attending not only churches and synagogues but also mosques and temples. I'd mention unchurched friends, some of whom have a lapsed faith, as well as agnostic and atheistic friends. And I wouldn't be able to conclude my list without noting friends who take strong humanistic and ethical stands although their theistic beliefs are private. In other words, it would be unrealistic to talk about religion in America today without acknowledging the wide diversity of beliefs brought about both by multiculturalism and by a unique fusion of precepts (particularly those of Buddha and Jesus) from Eastern and Western religions.

Practical Impact of Religious Change on FW2 Women

Later in our lives, changes in the religious and spiritual climate altered our perspective. But our formative adolescence was spent in the pre-change era. This affected us in at least two ways. First, although we didn't

Virginia Wade,
Tennis star

"Regardless of setting or obvious available means, one has the right, which need never be surrendered, to graduate, to ascend. Within whatever context one exists, to focus on a realistic ambition and use every possible source of inspiration to confront the issues that separate you from what you want, is the spiritual inheritance of each of us."

Challenger explosion kills seven • Surgeon General calls for end to silence about AIDS • Marcos flees Philippines

Emily Cappis's story continues, finding Jesus and the Human Potential Movement

Fortunately I changed in 1978. That was the pivotal year. That was when I decided to follow Jesus. I made a strong commitment to Him and got out of my rebellious stage. I came back to the values that I'd grown up with. That decision firmly shaped all the rest of my life. I started going back to church, reading the scriptures, and praying. That was a pivotal year for me, a pivotal decision.

I joined the Human Potential Movement. That helped me examine and resolve issues with my parents as well as a lot of the internal unhappiness that was going on inside of me.

I became active in the Human Potential Movement because my best friend had gone through one of their seminars and I could just see the light in her eyes. I could see that she had gotten a lot out of it. There are many in my Christian circles who would have looked down upon this step. After I got out of it what I wanted to get out of it, I never went back. But at least for those years, it was a beneficial decision to work on some of the anger and the low self-esteem that I had inside of me because it was affecting my relationships. Your self-esteem affects everything you do.

Patti LaBelle,
R&B/soul legend

"I'm a Jesus girl. Always have been, always will be. From the time I was a little girl singing in the choir…some high-ranking church officials made me feel unwelcome because, they said I was singing the devil's music. Their comments hurt, and hurt badly. But, as with most painful experiences, it taught me something important. I don't need to be IN church for God to be in me. And I don't need to go to church in order to strive to live my life as He would want me to."

always marry someone with the same religious heritage as ours, the religion of a future spouse was openly discussed between parents and daughters. Catholics were instructed to marry within the faith. A non-Catholic woman was warned to not get serious about a Catholic boyfriend because she would "have to convert." That phrase, "have to convert," had a strong negative connotation in the non-Catholic households of our youth. Jews were told to date anyone but to marry a Jew. Cross-faith marriages did happen, but they often entailed difficult decisions about which religious observances to attend or even whether to attend.

Second, FW2 Generation women were likely to move away from our hometown for a husband's education, job opportunity, or military service. This meant that we had to find a new church fellowship even if we had married someone of our own faith. Education increased the challenge of finding just the right church for ourselves and our children. Churches now had to be vetted not only for their doctrines but also for their involvement in community life and commitment to social justice.

I came out for the better but after I finished the seminars, I turned to my church and to my religion for inner strength. I probably wouldn't join the Human Potential Movement now but I learned to be open and honest from then on. [*continued*]

The uprooted character of the 1960s, when we were marrying, moving, having children, and coping with massive changes in American society and politics, left the door open for many later changes in our religious and spiritual convictions.

Religious Versus Spiritual

I grew up in the era of "Give me that old time religion and it's good enough for me." *Religion* was the word we used; I don't remember any discussions involving the word *spiritual*. Somewhere along the way, many FW2 women started to speak of their spiritual lives. Distinctions between the adjectives *religious* and *spiritual* are more complicated than they initially appear. We tend to think that a religious person subscribes to doctrines that are quite old, within a religious institution that changes slowly and centrally. When we think of a religious person, we imagine her attending services in fellowship with others at a place of worship.

Reagan & Gorbachev discuss Intermediate-Range Nuclear Forces treaty, Iceland

Reagan & Gorbechev meet in Iceland on missile reduction plan • Chernobyl nuclear power plant explosion

Emily Cappis's story continues, entering the Catholic seminary

Although my father became a Buddhist in the late 1960s, the values I learned as a Catholic have always influenced me. By the mid 1980s, I was quite sure that God wanted me to enter a convent. I was devastated when I wasn't accepted by the convent. That threw me for a loop. I was sure that was where He wanted me. When I wasn't accepted I had to rethink what His purpose was for me. That's when I entered the Catholic seminary to go on this journey of really finding what He wanted me to do. I thought I could find my life's purpose in Catholic seminary but what happened was entirely different from what I set out to do.

I began questioning a lot of things that the Catholic Church was teaching. I questioned the rosary, statues, medals, holy water, even the office of the Pope. Many things didn't make much sense to me from what I read in the scriptures so I began questioning what they were teaching. I never finished Catholic seminary. I went about three-fourths of the way and then left.

Spiritual is a more ambiguous adjective. A spiritual person may not subscribe to well-defined doctrines. The beliefs that a spiritual person espouses are likely to be personal and evolving rather than collective and fixed. The context of spiritual insights may be mystical and therefore difficult to communicate in conventional terms to others. We imagine that a spiritual person is asking fundamental questions about the nature of life and the nature of God.

Researchers have investigated how different generations view issues that can be defined religiously versus spiritually. Wade Clark Roof, in his study of the Baby Boom generation, writes: "*Spirit* is the inner, experiential aspect of religion while *institution* is the outer, established form of religion." Roof's analysis links spirituality to religiosity via an inward/outward, informal/formal distinction.

Joanne Beckman, a Duke University scholar on religion, writes: "Spirituality is a means of individual expression, self-discovery, inner healing, and personal growth." Beckman's statement doesn't controvert Roof's but puts more explicit emphasis on the self and breaks the direct connection between spirituality and religion. We can trace this idea at least back to the early 1970s when The White House Conference on

By 1987 I knew I wasn't really in doctrine with the Catholic faith. That's when a friend of mine introduced me to a Pentecostal camp. What they were teaching there resonated with what I was reading in the scriptures. Eventually I did work for that camp from 1989 to 1992.

My family was totally shocked. Here was this little girl who wanted to go to the convent and now she is a Protestant. Nobody refused to talk to me or chided me for my decision. But they were totally shocked. [*continued*]

Aging issued its report stating "all persons are spiritual, even if they have no use for religious institutions and practice no personal pieties."

But today, in a Red vs. Blue America where intolerant voices at both extremes dominate national as well as interpersonal discussion, the gentle statement of the '70s seems quaint. Although a recent *Boston Globe* article reported that "a new generation of evangelical leaders are rediscovering their progressive roots," too often *religion* is used to divide us while only the optimistic hope that *spiritual* might connect us. In the final analysis, the individual's own perspective will determine her use of the words *religious* and *spiritual*. While these words are not interchangeable, elements of both are invoked when we talk about aspects of our consciousness that look outside ourselves, bring God or transcendent forces of nature into our thoughts, join our faith with others, and help us better understand what we can do to live meaningful lives.

How Much Do Religion and Spirituality Matter?

In the aftermath of World War II, Americans sought stability and an idealized way of life that would help them move beyond the tragedies of war. Regular church attendance mattered because it symbolized

Emily Cappis's story concludes, finding God's will

In March of 1995, I took a train across the country to visit my brother. There was a mission agency nearby, and I decided to explore it. Their open house lasted about a week and by the end of that time I knew that this is where God was calling me. At the age of 53, I finally figured out God's will for me. I finally figured it out. I moved here in January of 1996, and that's where I'm still working.

This is a non-denominational Christian agency where we do training, educating, and research. We are a home base for missionaries who want preparation for field work. This was definitely a big change in my life. I was always salaried until then. Now I live on donations. That was a big step for me—living by faith. I've also gone from a rural area to a big city. I'd always heard so much about the smog and the crime and earthquakes. I definitely had my reservations. But I knew God's perfect will for me was to be a missionary and this was the place He wanted me.

Now I am someone in service to the Lord until the day I die. In other words, I'm building up His kingdom in the way that He has purposed for me. I think the most important thing is

BIBLE

one aspect of that return to normalcy. But sixty years and several wars later, the world is increasingly perceived as a whole and not a very large whole at that. Pluralism in religion and spirituality continues to grow. Religious and spiritual beliefs influence each other, and boundaries between them continue to blur. In old and new ways, religion and spirituality still matter.

"... a little help from my friends." In books we read in college, such as *The Lonely Crowd* and *The Split-Level Trap*, some social scientists derided both religion as fellowship with others and sociability in general. They argued that Americans were conformists; even in worshipping the God of all Creation they sought the company of others as much like themselves as possible. That criticism was undermined in two ways from the 1960s onward.

to follow the will of God for your life. You should do what He has called you to do because He created each one of us for a specific purpose in building up His kingdom. It is for us to discover what that is and to do it.

Many of the societal changes go against my Biblical values. But no matter what societal changes were taking place, except for that brief time when I was rebellious, I've been on a rather singular path that didn't include a lot of options. But that was the way I wanted it. If you serve the Lord then there are choices that are not an option for you as far as ethics or morals. And the best is yet to come.

First, when congregations were called to battle during the civil rights and antiwar protests of that era, they linked arms with others unlike themselves in race, class, education, and age. Second, the next generation of social scientists argued that groups are essential in social progress and individual well being. The Beatles got it right in their song, "I get by with a little help from my friends." Researchers confirmed that social support, whether in the form of natural social networks of family and friends or *ad hoc* "support groups" extends life itself, even among the grievously ill. For many Americans, religion is a major source of social support.

FW2 Women Speak of Their Religious and Spiritual Lives

As you'll read in their stories, some FW2 women maintained the faith of their childhood while others began to explore new approaches, thinking about a spiritual rather than a religious life, a choice between enlightenment and redemption, a distinction between personal faith and the institution of religion. Religion, faith, and spiritual experience have been significant across our adult years in different ways for different FW2 women.

Lois Cameron, spirituality is a process

I remember one day walking outside and holding the hands of my kids and just looking at the trees and the leaves and saying, "I do believe there is a God. I do believe there is a God." It was a time when I felt like an emotional yo-yo. I felt like I was going nuts. God was really good. He really did meet me. We were around a lot of believers, a lot of Christians that were encouraging, that were a support system.

When my husband and I moved again, I realized that my support, my spiritual strength, came from friends rather than from the Lord Himself. It was almost like it came to my mind that God said, "It's just between you and me kid." It was life changing again.
Again I knew where I needed to go for my strength. I knew then that when things were falling apart around me, there still was a source of strength that I had, that I could pull from.

Later, when life gave me a large share of suffering, I knew I could not be here apart from my relationship with Christ. I could not

The women telling their stories in this chapter reflect the constancy-change continuum mentioned above. Their words categorize them into one of three groups—those who experience their spirituality as a process, those who were significantly influenced by specific events that altered their relationship to God, and those who link their personal philosophy of life to the expression of their understanding of spirituality.

Spirituality as a Process

Women who spoke about seeking their spiritual selves or growing spiritually or searching for a way to heal through spiritual means can be described as viewing spirituality as a process. For example, Lois Cameron described herself as a person who is "in the process of still growing into who I think the Lord would want me to be. I am a very spiritual person because of my relationship with Christ." After many moves early in her marriage, she and her husband in the 1970s found themselves once again in a new community where they knew no one. They accepted an invitation to join a Bible study group. Lois says, "I think I was spiritually fairly keen as a young person, but as we started going to the Bible

live without that spiritual part of my being. I have to give Him the honor and glory for what He has done. I realize my need to be what He has made me to be. My question and my quest is "Who is that?"

study class, I realized more fully what Christ had done for me. Even if nobody else had been alive, He would have done it for me."

Ann Baxter also explains her spiritual quest in terms of a process. She says that at the end of the 1990s, "I finally decided to begin my spiritual seeking....I hadn't gone to church for a long time. Then I started doing some things. Locally we have Discover U, which offers courses. I took one called Introduction to Buddhism and another one called Primordial Sound Meditation. I joined a group where we read *The Seven Spiritual Laws of Success*. I was really fascinated by it. Then I joined a meditation group."

The process of becoming more spiritual occurs within mainstream religion as well as nontraditional spiritual experiences. Georgia Lafferty, for example, says that the "deepening of spirituality" has been one of the best aspects of her life. "As I've grown older, I have remained a Presbyterian and so has my brother. Both of us are very active in our church work. I've gotten more involved, and as we speak I'm in the process of launching an Internet Bible study for my church. It's been wonderful and rewarding." Roberta Katz, on the other hand, has charted most of her spiritual journey outside her Jewish faith. As she explains, "I've gone beyond organized religion." In the 1970s, she began to read the works

Roslyn Galvin, loss leads to seek a better understanding of her spiritual self

My father died in the early 1970s. He wasn't sick. He just had a heart attack and died. At the time, I was agnostic although casually interested in meditation and paranormal events.

When he died, I joined a meditation group and the very first time we met I had an out of body experience. This sounds weird to people but it happened. I had never thought of the self as being separate from the spirit. I just thought of our physical bodies. When I had that experience, it showed me there was a spiritual self that lived on beyond the body. It just changed my whole philosophy and belief system. It was kind of frightening because I didn't know what to do with it.

The next time we met, it happened to me again. At that point, I became interested in studying the Bible and going to church. I'm not really an avid churchgoer or a student of the Bible but it just opened up that whole possibility. I didn't continue with the meditation group. I feel that everybody has her path or way of becoming a believer and that was mine.

of Edgar Cayce and Paramahansa Yogananda. Both of these individuals left teachings that are used for spiritual growth. Roberta says that these works "...explained a lot of things that I had been thinking about for a long time." When asked about the three best things in her life, Roberta says, "My spiritual growth is probably the most important thing to me. It has gotten me through a lot of dark days."

Event/Experience-Based Religion or Spirituality

Many FW2 women think of the development of their religious or spiritual life as a process because steps toward an ill-defined goal extend across many years. For others, specific experiences cause a more rapid shift in their religious or spiritual perspective. Suzanne Fielding, for example, devoted no time to this dimension of her life until her husband died in an accident in the early 1980s. They had been married only a few years. "It was like hitting a brick wall." She began to focus on the spiritual questions raised by this tragedy in an effort both to deal with her grief and to try to find herself. She recalls that time as a "real growing period." For the 1980s onward, she estimates that her spiritual journey has represented almost a quarter of her life.

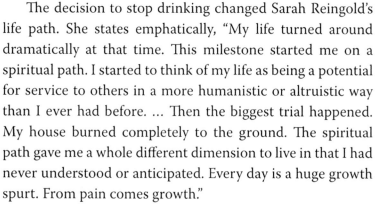

The decision to stop drinking changed Sarah Reingold's life path. She states emphatically, "My life turned around dramatically at that time. This milestone started me on a spiritual path. I started to think of my life as being a potential for service to others in a more humanistic or altruistic way than I ever had before. ... Then the biggest trial happened. My house burned completely to the ground. The spiritual path gave me a whole different dimension to live in that I had never understood or anticipated. Every day is a huge growth spurt. From pain comes growth."

Traumatic events don't always move a person toward religious faith or spirituality. Mary Jackson exemplifies those women who felt they had lost their faith but who still turned to the church for other needs in their lives. You may remember from Chapter 2 that Mary's parents were divorced and her mother died just before Mary graduated from high school. College was an exceedingly difficult time for her as she sought to make sense of the world. When she married, at the end of her senior year, she and her husband chose to participate in a church that enriched her life but not

Wilma Mankiller, Chief of the Cherokee Nation

"That [automobile] accident in 1979 changed my life. ... I came very close to death, felt its presence and the alluring call to complete the circle of life. I always think of myself as the woman who lived before and the woman who lives afterward. ... it proved to be a deep spiritual awakening ...a very Cherokee approach to life—what our tribal elders call being of good mind."

Virginia Garfield, religious fanaticism leads to divorce.

I had my third child in 1975. At the time, I was somewhat involved in the local church, a small, old country Methodist church. Once the girls got a little older we decided we'd better start being regular church goers because we wanted to set a good example for them. The church always needed money and they always needed help. There was no youth group so we started one. We did fundraisers and Christmas bazaars and summer camp projects.

But then the situation changed. My husband had never been particularly religious. In fact, he was a real hell-raiser in college. He became a religious zealot in the late 1970s and decided I wasn't doing as I was told. I remember saying to him, "I never have, why should that surprise you now?" He went off the deep end. He stayed in the Methodist church until our pastor left and then decided that the church wasn't filling his needs. So he dragged us all, literally dragged us, to this evangelical, charismatic non-denominational church. He said, "You don't have to come if you don't want to, but my kids are coming."

from a spiritual or faith perspective. She explains: "I lost my faith in college and really never got it back. But we were in a church that was on the forefront of artistic expression and civil rights. I became good friends with the minister, and he was very encouraging to me. But spiritually, I sort of got nowhere."

Philosophy and Spirituality

Sometimes the concepts gleaned from childhood religious experiences continue as cornerstones of a personal philosophy long after the person has moved away from formal religion. For example, Harriet Magill places no emphasis on spiritual matters across her adult life, not even when she looks into the future. She says, "I don't go to church. I just try to live by the Golden Rule and believe in a higher power and hope it will all work out. I trust that it will. I don't put a lot of inner effort into that. I just try to live the best way I know how." Deanna Greenlaw's words echo those of Harriet. "I'm not religious but I sure do believe in the power of goodness, in the importance of practicing compassion, and have a strong sense of something greater than myself, spirituality if you will. Everything else is impermanent." Other women also mention that if you "do unto others as

The people there were wonderful, but I just shook my head a lot. They taught that the earth is not several billion years old, but is 3,000 years old because that's what the Bible says. That's it. Case closed. Women were to wear dresses and to have teas. There were no women on the boards. I had always been a leader, a take-charge kind of person. I had been chairman of the board of directors in our Methodist church for three years. Not that I needed to do that again but it annoyed me that I couldn't be on the board even if I wanted to. Then one day at church they introduced the high-school class after they sang a song. The man announced, "Ladies and Gentlemen, I introduce you to the future businessmen and housewives of America." My girls were just mortified.

Eventually all of this led to our divorce.

you would have them do unto you" you are leading the best life that you can.

Religious scholar and FW2 Karen Armstrong points to the universality of the Golden Rule when she observes, "...all the great world faiths—including Confucianism, Hinduism, Buddhism, Judaism, Christianity, and Islam—agree on the supreme importance of compassion." In highlighting the commonness across these religions, she explains, "The essential dynamic of compassion is summed up in the Golden Rule, first enunciated by Confucius in about 500 BCE: 'Do not do to others as you would not have done to you.' ...Buddha also taught a version of the Golden Rule. He taught his followers to...send out positive thoughts of compassion, benevolence, and sympathy to the four corners of the earth, not omitting a single creature from this radius of concern. ...Rabbi Hillel, the older contemporary of Jesus, taught the Golden Rule [when he said] 'That which is hateful to you, do not do to your neighbor.' ...Jesus...told his followers to love even their enemies and never to judge or retaliate. ...Islam is also committed to the compassionate ethic. ...On the Last Day the one question that

Bernadine Healy,
Cardiologist and first woman to head the National Institutes of Health

"You sometimes get a few scratches when you grow up on the concrete pavements of New York, but with the spiritual and emotional support that came from our tight-knit families, we learned a lot about hard work, courage, and faith in tomorrow."

Students killed in Tiananmen Square • Exxon Valdez leaks 11 million gallons of crude oil • *Seinfeld* premiers

Kate Shapiro Chen, spirituality in all aspects of life

Spirituality is in everything that I do. I am an extremely spiritual person in a non-traditional way. That spirituality has been expressed in my interest in philosophy back in college, in my marrying a Buddhist, and in my getting an adult bat mitzvah.

Like most Jewish women my age, I never had a bat mitzvah as a kid. So I went back in the early 80s as an adult, studied, and participated in the formal ceremony.

Furthermore, all the things that I write are explorations of moral and ethical issues but not in any traditional sense. For me, development of the self, the expressive elements of my life that allow me to write, and my spirituality are all lumped together.

God will ask Muslims is whether they have looked after the widows, the orphans, and the oppressed, and if they have not, they cannot enter Paradise." Armstrong concludes by calling on all people to be "educated in the simplest of all principles, the Golden Rule." And, not surprisingly, many of the women I interviewed had been educated to believe in the Golden Rule. Even those like Harriet and Deanna who have left formal religion would agree with Edith Andrews who says, "I certainly have a strong belief. That has never been shaken. What was shaken was the implementation." Although she no longer attends church, she continues to feel a strong sense of faith and is guided by the Golden Rule.

Buddhism's teachings of expressing compassion and seeking enlightenment have influenced many in the FW2 Generation, at least many more than in their parents' generation. For example, during a time of crisis in her own life, Maureen Devlin learned about Zen Buddhism through a friend. Soon afterwards, she went to a Zen Monastery where she had a mystical experience, a revelation that changed her life by putting her in touch with her spiritual self in a way that the Episcopalian religion of her childhood had not. She says that she had often felt "the words get in the way. But in zazen, the meditation practice of Zen Buddhism, it is

just prayer without words. So I don't find there is any conflict between Christianity and Zen Buddhism at all." Although she left the monastery after a few months to return to her marriage, she recalls that time as a "critical turning point in my life." The spiritual tradition she tapped into helped her look deep into herself to understand her inherent wisdom and compassion and to find her own sense of well-being. She considers Zen Buddhism to have been responsible for the most transformative experience in her life.

Spiritual Quest Changes Over the Lifetime

How much effort does a person give to religious or spiritual thoughts and activities? Each decade of life is likely to have its own proportion. To better understand the attention given to religious or spiritual matters, I set up the following task for the FW2 women I interviewed: *Let's say that each decade of your adult life thus far equals the number 100. Estimate what percent of your effort you have given to Family, Education, Employment & Service, Health, Expressive, Self, and Spiritual journeys in these decades.* I then

Alice Walker,
Author

"Although I am constantly involved, internally, with religious questions—and I seem to have spent all my life rebelling against the church and other people's interpretations of what religion is—the truth is probably that I don't believe there is a God, although I would like to believe it…. Like many, I waver in my convictions about God, from time to time. In my poetry I seem to be for; in my fiction, against."

Soviet-Afghanistan war ends after 9 years • Barbara Clementine Harris is 1st female bishop of US Episcopal Church

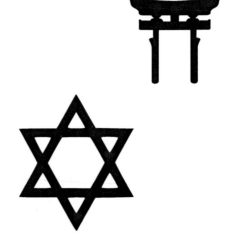

asked the same question with "the future/the rest of your life" as the time frame.

Because the decades of the 1960s and 1970s were dominated by education, family, and employment or volunteer service, demands on their time left little for spiritual matters. In the 1980s, many women who had not already entered the workforce sought employment. As family demands diminished, emphasis on the self (defined as "the journey to become the person you are today, including early pulling away from family, emotional development, self-esteem, and what is called self-actualization") increased.

Among the women I interviewed, spiritual emphasis was low and relatively unchanging from the 1960s until the 2000s. Only when asked about the future was there significant change, with more than half stating that they anticipated greater emphasis on their spiritual journey. They finally have time to reflect on the life they have lived so far, question the meaning of it, and seek to create the life they want to live from this point forward.

This increased emphasis on religious or spiritual issues coincides with other research literature documenting another aspect of an in-

creased attention to spirituality as we age. The nonmedical literature on menopause emphasizes how emotional and physical changes associated with this life change mark the beginning of a time when many women reflect on the purposes of their lives and connect with their spiritual selves.

I wonder how the responses of FW2 women about their spirituality would compare with those of their mothers and daughters. Would the trend of religious and spiritual beliefs be from narrow to wide and wider? I think that is probably the case. However, it is also evident that many Americans are returning to more orthodox beliefs and observances. In noticeable numbers, American Protestants, Catholics, Jews, and Muslims have pulled back from assimilation. Were we, the college students and young marrieds of the 1960s, the wayward generation?

Whether wayward or not in the past, our spiritual quest is a very private enterprise that changes over our decades. As the FW2 Generation looks forward, it is useful to see how researcher Jane Marie Thibault analyzed the importance of spiritual matters and aging. Here are two statements describing her perspective that spiritual journeys are searches for meaning in life:

"The spiritual component of a personality is the dimension or function that integrates all other aspects of personhood ... and is often seen as a search for meaning in life.

"...spirituality is the way [a person] ... seeks, finds or creates, uses, and expands personal meaning in the context of place in the entire universe."

Perhaps spirituality is a part of every personality, the warp on which people weave the threads of their lives into one fabric. Perhaps it is the outer sphere of personal meaning, the farthest point from which our questions can bring back responses we understand.

Diamonds *Were* a Girl's Best Friend: Seven Life Capitals

Investing in Diamonds or Dreams

When I was growing up in the 1950s, my mother turned song titles into often-repeated words of wisdom, such as "diamonds are a girl's best friend." The message of women, men, and money was clear. Most of us in the FW2 Generation were brought up to believe that a man would provide for us. We didn't think about building our own financial assets and we certainly didn't think about investing in our dreams or acquiring "assets of independence."

In our early 20s in the early 1960s, we saw life as infinitely long. If we had dreams beyond marriage and children, we thought there was plenty of time to fulfill them. Dreams were for *later*. We didn't realize that every dream requires an investment plan. Every dream requires investing in ourselves.

Investing, whether in diamonds or dreams, wasn't talked about much in our homes. Saving, yes, but not investing. Our parents didn't think about investing in a positive way. They had seen investments become worthless during the Depression.

About fifty years after the bank failures of the Depression, not long after I turned 40 in 1982, my parents learned that Oklahoma City's Penn

Square Bank was failing. My 73-year-old father stood in a long line for six hours in the hot July sun outside Penn Square Bank to claim his money if he could. While standing there he thought that Yogi Berra was right, "It's déjà vu all over again!"

Today it is almost impossible to not follow the stock market's ups and downs. Yet when our generation was born, the Dow Jones Industrial Average wasn't a big deal. For example, it ranged from a low of 92 to a high of 119 in 1942, my birth year. In 1972 when I turned 30, the Dow crossed 1,000. When I turned 50 in 1992, the Dow hovered in the low 3,000s. Then, in a fit of "irrational exuberance," the Dow flew to over 11,000 in 2001.

During the lofty 1990s, even those of us who hadn't paid much attention to managing our financial retirement assets began to think and to talk about investment strategies—stocks versus bonds, individual investments versus mutual funds, government treasuries versus savings accounts, 401K plans versus Individual Retirement Accounts. We filled out worksheets to project how much money we would need upon retirement. Then, in a mini-echo of the experiences of our Depression Era parents and grandparents, we suffered from the bust in stock prices. Some women I interviewed said they would be working longer than planned in order to rebuild their retirement fund. Others said they were scaling back their retirement goals.

The Seven Life Capitals

Learning how to invest our financial capital is one important life lesson that we all have finally acknowledged. We're learning we have to make decisions *now* rather than *later*. But in spite of my mother's mantra, there is more to a rich, fulfilling life than just dollars. And diamonds are far down the list of a "girl's best friends."

Based on hundreds of hours talking with FW2 women and hundreds of more hours pouring over their transcribed words, I submit that there are seven aspects to a fulfilling life. To emphasize their mutual equivalence and complementary roles, I call them the Seven Life Capitals:

- *Emotional Capital;*
- *Physical Capital;*
- *Cognitive Capital;*
- *Spiritual Capital;*
- *Social Capital;*
- *Financial Capital;*
- *Temporal Capital.*

While not everyone will want to invest in or spend these capitals in the same proportion, they are the elements of our life, what we might call our *Life Capital portfolio.*

Emotional Capital

Perhaps the most basic of all the elements in our life portfolio is this first one—Emotional Capital. We are born with the capacity to experience mysterious self-generated feelings, moods, and passions that range from joy and love to rage and hatred, from optimism to pessimism, from euphoria to depression, from self-esteem to self-abasement, from generosity to selfishness, from pleasure in others' good fortune to envy and *schadenfreude*, etc.

- *Emotional Capital is the collection of affective or feeling resources of conscious lives.*

What Does This Definition Mean? The source, number, and role of *emotions* has been defined and debated by philosophers and scientists for centuries. Perhaps

Operation Desert Storm liberates Kuwait from Iraqi invasion • Amateur video records police beating of Rodney King

earlier, but certainly by 1649 when René Descartes published *The Passions of the Soul*, emotions were examined and distinguished from cognitions on the one hand and physiological states on the other. Descartes thought there were six basic emotions, four positive and two negative, with all others derivative of these: wonder, love, desire, joy, hatred, and sadness. Within our lifetime, emotions have primarily been the domain of psychologists who are less interested in how emotions originate and where they reside than in the influence of emotions on our motivation and ability to carry out plans and actions. However, in 1997, neuroscientist Candace Pert published *Molecules of Emotion*, a landmark book in which she summarized her research on neuropeptides, delineating the biochemical foundation of emotions and their body-mind connection, "going back and forth between the two and influencing both."

Linda Ellerbee,
Television journalist and author
"Emotional ties connect women. They are the ties that bind us, move us—and often make us double over with laughter."

How Women Manage Their Emotional Capital. Emotions become a capital for us when we recognize that they are our resource of feelings, empathy, and authentic responses that we accumulate and spend. Gail Henshaw told me a classic story of overspending Emotional Capital. Gail was married with two children. Her husband supported the family financially but traveled frequently and didn't participate much in the activities of the household. He did not spend time with the children or provide emotional support to Gail. Since he bore the burden of providing for the family, he expected her to make all necessary adjustments to his needs and never thought to thank her for her efforts. The children were truculent teenagers who certainly didn't appear to appreciate all that Gail did for them. Gail was a member of a church board that was acrimoniously divided over hiring a new minister. Gail sided with neither faction and therefore was often caught in the middle of arguments. No one valued, or at least no one expressed to Gail that they valued, all the work she was doing for the church. At the same time, Gloria, director of volunteers at the local hospital where Gail gave still more of her time, was going through a difficult divorce but didn't want

Clinton elected president • Concern about women and AIDS • Navy Tailhook sex scandal • Nat'l debt: $4 trillion

to give up her position even though she was neglecting it. She shifted most of her responsibilities to Gail but didn't give her any credit for the additional work because she was so wrapped up in her own problems.

Gail gave and gave of her energy, her love, her joy, her courage, and her sense of hope. She said that one day she confided to her best friend Linda, "I feel spent. I'm sad and angry that everyone expects something from me but no one is willing to give me anything in return. I have nothing left to give." Gail had spent more Emotional Capital than her account held. She was emotionally bankrupt until she identified new ways to take care of herself, allow herself time to do activities she enjoyed, let a friend help her, and find people who would express gratitude for her hard efforts.

Overspending. If we overspend our Financial Capital, our bank or our creditors will soon bring the problem to our attention, and we will need to replenish the balance. So it is with Emotional Capital. When we spend more Emotional Capital than we have—everyone may need to do this sometimes to deal with crises—then we must have ways of replenishing the Emotional Capital. Women more than men find themselves in lifestyles that cause them to deplete their balance of Emotional Capital. One woman I interviewed said: "If nothing ever comes back to me, how can I have more to give?"

Sarah Brady,
Chair of Center to Prevent Handgun Violence
"Opponents of the Brady bill argued that a waiting period was 'inconvenient.' In the Brady household, we could tell them something about inconvenience: the pain, the injuries, and the cost—emotional and financial—that can result from a gunshot wound."

Physical Capital

The fundamentals of our Physical Capital are given to us at birth, and much of that inheritance was assembled at the time of conception. Except perhaps for Spiritual Capital, none of the Life Capitals is entirely under our control, and Physical Capital fluctuates more than we wish. Many people unfortunately can't rely on their Physical Capital to be adequate for the active living that the rest of us take for granted. They must nurture and ration what we spend so carelessly.

- *Physical Capital consists of the proceeds from the initial genetic make-up of the body and from lifelong efforts to nourish and exercise the body for strength, agility, endurance, and reliability.*

What Does This Definition Mean? We had absolutely nothing to do with the size of our Physical Capital birthright. Some people acquired an ample inheritance. Others did not. Surprisingly enough, considering the restricted balances of some other Life Capitals that people must contend with, we are collectively a healthy species. Moreover, as the six major causes of good health are better understood by more people (genes, environment, nutrition, exercise, relaxation/rest, and optimistic attitude), we see more examples of *deliberate health*

in which people befriend, so to speak, the five causes they can influence in order to achieve the best health that they are capable of. They avoid unhealthy environments, eat sensibly (less fat, less sugar, less additives, and just plain less), exercise for cardiovascular strength, maintain body flexibility and muscular conditioning, keep stress to a minimum, get enough sleep, and focus on affirmative thoughts, experiences, and relationships.

Many people even challenge their genetic limitations. You may remember the story of Jim Fixx. His father had a heart attack at the age of 35 and died from a second heart attack at the age of 43. His mother also had heart disease at a young age. Fixx began to run in order to strengthen and conserve his Physical Capital. Millions of runners hit the paths after reading Fixx's gospel of fitness, *The Complete Book of Running*. Regrettably, Fixx died while running on a Vermont trail at the age of 52. However, he might have died a decade earlier, as his father did, if he hadn't invested in his Physical Capital.

Quite apart from our genetic inheritance, parents are an early and strong influence on our Physical Capital. Parents' opinions on health, their guidance of our childhood activities, and their own behavior become our models. Unfortunately, parents are not well-informed about nutrition, either their own or their children's. The Standard American Diet, such as it has become in recent generations, depletes Physical Capital through nutritional imbalance, frequently leading to obesity and the resulting loss of muscle tone. Poor diet and lack of exercise contribute to the American disadvantage in life expectancy relative to other countries. Demographic correlates of obesity suggest that stress (from insecurity, noise, crowding, etc.) leads to compulsive eating and lethargy, which in turn trigger other events in a downward spiral of health.

Virginia Wade,
Tennis champion
"You need to harness your energies in order to convert them into an asset."

How Women Manage Their Physical Capital. Some parents heedlessly destroy their children's Physical Capital. You may remember Harriet Magill's story from Chapter 4. She told me more about the result of her mother's abuse. "My spine began to disintegrate in the early 1990s. I began getting shorter and having a lot of pain, a tremendous amount of pain in my legs, my lower back, and my neck as well. Eventually I had seven surgeries on my spine and am now bolted together from my neck to my fanny. My neck was damaged from the cumulative effect of the whiplash that occurred each time my mother slapped me. My lower back was damaged from being hung by one arm and kicked in my back during most of my childhood. You can't get hit that much without something happening to you. Eventually my spine just began to rot. I used to be 5'9" and now I'm 5'3". Four years ago they put in a morphine pump to control the pain."

Harriet wanted me to know that although she was abused, she never abused her children. As a trained nurse, she knew that abused children often become abusing adults, and she was determined to break the cycle. She had learned the hard lesson of the importance of protecting the initial deposit in one's Physical Capital account.

Unless we have been injured like Harriet, adult life is a series of second chances. Cynthia Fletcher was nearing the age of 50 when a chance fall led to unaccountable bleeding. "They did a CAT scan right away. I went into denial about what they saw or didn't see. But I had a wonderful surgeon who took out a totally encapsulated kidney cancer about the size of a grapefruit. It was a huge wake up call. I thought I would live forever. This put some things in perspective. I started running. My husband and I get out there together. Now I run in marathons. I just qualified for the over-60 class which is great because I'll be one of the youngest runners in it. I tell my friends, 'Now is the time to get healthy because otherwise you won't have a later life and you'll spend the whole time in a doctor's office.' It is so important that we take responsibility for our own health at this age. Just to change our diet is horrendously hard, but it's doable and all the information is out there. People say it is selfish [to take time for physical training], but it is not selfish. It is more selfish to die early or be sickly for ten years and not be able to do things." Cynthia ended her remarks by saying, "This is my soapbox: Save the world later. Get healthy first."

Patti LaBelle,
R&B/soul legend
"You preach a better sermon with your life than you do with your lips."

Cognitive Capital

Three hundred years ago the philosopher John Locke said that each baby was born with a "blank slate" on which experience would write knowledge over time. A hundred years ago the psychologist William James said that each baby comes into the world in a state of "blooming, buzzing confusion." More recently it has been argued that linguistic patterns, for example, are somehow prefigured in the brain at birth—an inference based on the fact that infants and toddlers learn language at an incredible rate. By and large, however, we are not born with Cognitive Capital.

It is more accurate to say that we are born with the raw materials of Cognitive Capital: perception and intelligence. But these resources are more than an initial deposit in our Cognitive Capital account. They are the two investment counselors working on a lifelong Cognitive Capital asset management program.

- *Cognitive Capital refers to the analytical, creative, and practical abilities to acquire and use knowledge and skills, as well as factual knowledge that derives from the exercise of knowledge and skills.*

What Does This Definition Mean? Cognitive Capital is related to intelligence, but it is not the same. Intelligence is frequently defined as an innate capacity to learn that does not change significantly throughout the stages of life. For that reason, the results of intelligence tests taken by the same person over time show approximately the same score. Cognitive Capital, however, can be increased over time.

Lifelong learning, a phrase popularized by academic continuing education programs in the 1970s, is the investment half of Cognitive Capital. The account can be cultivated—added to—over the life span through formal education, self study, life experiences such as travel, association with others, and simple daily mindfulness. But Cognitive Capital is to be both accrued and used. Unlike intelligence, Cognitive Capital can be shared with others with mutual gain. Also unlike intelligence, Cognitive Capital has a "use by" date and must be refreshed because memory distorts knowledge and in any event the world changes constantly. We spend Cognitive Capital as we develop and executive successful life plans.

How Women Manage Their Cognitive Capital. One of the most striking stories I have read of education denied, deferred, and eventually fulfilled by a woman born during the war is that of FW2 Joyce Kennard, Associate Justice of the California Supreme Court. She was born in 1941 on the island of Java, and her

Ruth J. Simmons,
First female president of Brown University and first African American president of Smith College
"As president of Smith College, a place of uncommon resources, I urge students to remember that they will benefit from those resources but that they will perhaps learn more from unexpected sources. I admonish them to be watchful and open-minded lest they fail to recognize those moments of learning."

earliest memories are those of living in an internment camp with her mother after the Japanese conquest of the South Pacific. Her father had died in another camp. After the allied liberation, "I attended a tiny school run by Catholic missionaries. ... The school folded when I was 13. The only other school was five day's sailing away, so that's where my mother took me." There was no high school, and eventually her mother was able to move the pair to Holland. Her high school career was short-lived because "A tumor on my leg led to an amputation above the knee." Falling too far behind to catch up in high school, she learned typing and shorthand and became a secretary at sixteen. A special U.S. immigration program for displaced former residents of

Pacific Islands brought Joyce to California in 1961—alone, because her mother remained in Holland as a backstop for her. After six years of working in low-level positions, Joyce was finally able to begin college at UC Berkeley as a 27-year-old freshman. After finishing Phi Beta Kappa at Berkeley, Joyce was encouraged to attend law school at the University of Southern California, where she also earned an MA in public administration. After working as an attorney for a dozen years, she began to climb the ladder of judgeships that led to the high court.

Pamela Ratcliffe, in contrast, did not complete high school but did eventually get her GED. She says of her desire for Cognitive Capital, "I've always been extremely hungry for knowledge and immensely curious. I read constantly." Other women's comments show a continuing desire to invest in Cognitive Capital: "I intend to learn another language." "I plan on traveling to learn about other cultures."

Moving from the acquiring or investing aspect of this capital, we look for examples of how Cognitive Capital is used or spent. Here are a few from the FW2 women I interviewed: "I want to increase my knowledge and skills so that I can be even better at my work." "I want to share what I've learned by volunteering in a nearby elementary school." "I give talks at women's clubs about investment strategies."

In this regard I often think of my father's mantra, "Learn something new each day." For him, it could be as simple as a new fact from the newspaper or as complicated as the mechanics of his new tractor. I remember one phone conversation with my father in which I described the quail family that I watch from my office window each day. The quail parents bracket their chicks, one in the lead moving on to new feeding territory and the other at the rear ensuring that none of the chicks stray. The parent at the rear often hops up on a rock in order to see the chicks better. After listening to my observations, my father responded, "Now I've learned something new today."

Like his fellow Oklahoman, Will Rogers, my father never met a person he didn't like, and it seemed that he never met new knowledge that he didn't like—by which I mean that he did not have a preconceived idea that some things counted as knowledge while others did not. I think his daily encounter with new knowledge assured him that he was still learning and growing. Like so many others at that place and time, my father never had a chance to test his able mind in college, which caused him to value knowledge even more. My father was always adding to and spending from his Cognitive Capital. He frequently used this asset in exchanges with friends and family, and I imagine that within a few hours of telling my father about the quail behavior, he had shared the story.

Ellen DeGeneres comes out as gay • Dolly the sheep is cloned • Dow jumps to 8,000 • Princess Di dies in car crash

I saw a quote recently that my father would have liked. Given the source, it probably refers to a combination of Cognitive and Physical Capital, which is not surprising since Life Capitals often work together. Vernon Law pitched for the Pirates and won the National League Cy Young Award for leading his team to the World Championship in 1960. He said, "When you're through learning, you're through."

Spiritual Capital

Spiritual Capital is the first of the Seven Life Capitals that moves outside of us as individuals. For some, Spiritual Capital and a spiritual life are associated with formal religion. For others, being spiritual and seeking to understand life beyond science and the observed world takes place outside a particular religious doctrine.

- *Spiritual Capital means the resources that accrue from looking beyond the physical and material aspects of life, from a search for understanding of the source of existence, from the quest for meaning and purpose, and are spent through values associated with choice, conscience, and responsibility.*

What Does This Definition Mean? Spiritual Capital looks beyond the known to find other contexts of meaning for our individual lives and all human life. The external source may be God, or the soundless harmonies of the natural world to which we women are so attuned, or the awareness that thousands of years of searching for universal ethics and moral purpose makes us a very peculiar species on this planet—whatever that fact might imply. Mark Twain said that humans are the only animals that blush—or need to. Similarly, let's say that if it occurs to humans to ask questions about the circumstances of existence far beyond their empirical knowledge, then they should honor the mysterious impulse of those questions by asking them mindfully and often.

It is also characteristic of Americans and our generation to ask, "Of what use is spiritual consciousness? If there is a practical side to faith and spiritual consciousness as well as a metaphysical side, please tell

us the practical side first." In the 1950s, many of us were influenced by *The Power of Positive Thinking* by Dr. Norman Vincent Peale. This book was on the bestseller list for an incredible 186 consecutive weeks after its publication in 1952. Throughout the intervening years it has sold more than 20 million copies. Peale's simple message was 'faith in God and faith in yourself.' *The Power of Positive Thinking*'s early impact on my generation may have contributed to our lifelong optimism. Certainly ideas similar to those expressed in Peale's book have convinced many people that they have the power to change their lives.

For most people, Spiritual Capital is a very personal resource, not something we talk about. A sense of being grounded with respect to questions of existence gives us inspiration and fortitude. For some seekers Spiritual Capital resides in the mind-settling quality of the answers, while for others it resides in the mind-unsettling quality of the questions. Spiritual Capital is perhaps the hardest of the Seven Life Capitals to define, and yet most people know when they have it, and they sustain it in different ways—personally through prayer, meditation, nature, literature, music, and art; interpersonally through fellowship with others; and socially through acts of compassion and service.

How Women Manage Their Spiritual Capital. There is a conventional form of Spiritual Capital that is not to be ignored or patronized. Annette Funicello, our FW2 Mouseketeer, learned in 1987 that she has multiple sclerosis. This progressive disease exacts a heavy emotional toll from the sufferer and her family and friends. Annette writes in her memoir, "Through it all the one constant in my life has been faith. My faith in God is such that I believe my illness has a purpose and a meaning, although I would never presume to imagine what that might be. Perhaps I can offer others comfort and hope. The Lord has been good to me throughout my life, He's never let me down."

Conventional belief, by definition, is widely shared. The language of conventional belief enables even strangers to express sympathy and support for a sufferer. Annette writes that strangers come up to her in public places and say, "God bless you, Annette" and "I grew up with you, Annette, and I'm praying for you."

Social Capital

Polly Baca,
First Hispanic woman elected to the Colorado state House of Representatives and state Senate

"At nineteen, I won an internship with the state Democratic party during the 1960 presidential campaign ... which gave me an opportunity to meet many Kennedy operatives. ... One was Carlos McCormick....After I graduated from college, Carlos arranged an interview for me with the director of research and education for an international labor union."
[continued]

Social Capital moves us away from resources that are under our own control and causes us to focus on relationships with others. We have our earliest experiences with Social Capital when we are children engaged in an evolving relationship with our parents, siblings, grandparents, etc.—Social Capital begins at home. Later, Social Capital expands to include friends, schoolmates, and colleagues as well.

• *Social Capital is the network of relationships with family, friends, and acquaintances that is marked by trust, mutual support, and reciprocity and that function in the context of bonding or bridging friendships.*

What Does This Definition Mean? Lyda Judson Hanifan, who wrote about rural school communities in 1916, is sometimes credited with originating the concept of Social Capital. However, it was Jane Jacobs, a defender of community life in large, increasingly "monumentalized" cities, who first made this concept widely known. In her 1961 book, *The Death and Life of Great American Cities*, she described how her neighborhood in Greenwich Village thrived because of a network of interdependencies. A community functions well when bonds of trust and cooperation connect the individuals. She believed that any urban change that diminished connections also diminished the community. Her adversary at the time was Robert Moses, New York City's concrete czar, who wanted to build a cross-town freeway through the heart of Greenwich Village. His political and financial resources versus her book were an unequal match, but New Yorkers had seen enough cherished neighborhoods demolished and paved over. Jane Jacobs won.

Other work examining Social Capital, for example by Pierre Bourdieu and James Coleman, ensued, but in 2000 Robert Putnam, a sociologist at Harvard University, published *Bowling Alone: The Collapse and Revival of American Community*, and the discussion of Social Capital reached television talk shows. Putnam distinguishes two kinds of Social Capital—bonding and bridging. Bonding capital is prominent *within* a group, is one of the elements that keeps a group close, is evidenced in shared values, and leads to reciprocity within the group. For example, at one point in their lives women friends go to each other's children's weddings, sharing in the joy. Later they attend each other's parents' funerals, bringing food and providing comfort. Bridging capital, on the other hand, enables a person to cross into other groups or community networks in order to accomplish something. An informal synonym for bridging capital is schmoozing capital. If you need to line up several community factions to make something beneficial happen, ask a good schmoozer to take care of it. Odds are that she already knows the people to call in each group, as well as the names of their partners and children.

Let's look at Social Capital in terms of building it, preserving it, and using it. If you always need help from a friend but can never reciprocate,

Polly Baca
[continued]

"The director offered me a job in Washington, D.C.,... I knew that such an opportunity did not come along often ... and I felt strongly that I had a responsibility to other women and minorities to accept the job. I learned two new lessons: one, networking pays off; two, be a risk-taker. Taking a risk can lead to some incredibly exciting life adventures."

then your relationship with the friend will probably wane. If you betray the trust of a friend or family member, you will probably find that you have overdrawn your Social Capital and may be insolvent for a long while. On the other hand, if you comfort a friend who is going through a divorce, or if you drop everything to be with a friend in the middle of a health crisis, then you are banking Social Capital for the future when you may need help.

How Women Manage Their Social Capital. Almost every woman I interviewed voluntarily mentioned the importance of friends and friend-ships in their lives. Marian Rosen's comment illustrates the support that comes from *bonding social capital.* "From the early '70s until I went to law school, I belonged to a women's consciousness group. It was the source of really strong friendships that I still have. Four of us meet together every couple of months. We're always there for the important life events in each other's lives such as our children's weddings. My friendships with women have been enormously important and supportive. For example, when I had breast cancer my women friends rallied around and saw to it that I never went to a doctor's appointment alone. The night I was in the hospital, two of my friends replanted my tiny garden. They were still at it at midnight. It was a surprise for me when I came home, and that was great."

In a similar vein, Sarah Reingold points to the fulfilling role that friendships have played in her life. "When I graduated from high school, I thought I would have a life companion. Instead I have lifelong friends. I am so fulfilled by the number and the depth of these friendships."

She went on to tell me how friends made the difference when her home burned in a fire that swept her entire community. With everything lost, she found hope and comfort in what she called the "amazing little acts of heroism from generous people—friends and neighbors." She said, "This didn't happen just for me. I got to see this incredible human spirit at work on every street where every house had burned to the ground." Then she spoke about the importance of relationships, both during times of crisis and throughout a lifetime. "[Losing everything] forced me to realize it is people that matter, not material things, not structure, not security. People are your structure and security. Strangers came out of the woodwork to offer help and comfort.... Relationships are our greatest gold, our food and nourishment. The only thing that we have at the end of our lives is the love of and for other people."

Bridging capital, the second type of Social Capital described by Putnam, has also been important in the lives of these women. Nancy Scott, in the following story, tells how her life was changed through a new friend's help. "I was working at a medical facility for a couple of years and there I met a woman who was very instrumental in getting me into a graduate program. She moved out of state to get her master's degree. She

called me and said, 'You really have to come up here. They're giving out grants, and you just have to apply for one.' I went up there, and she filled out all the papers for me. I was accepted and got into a program where I really excelled. Those are the best years that I can remember in my life."

According to the research literature, trust is an important component in Social Capital, and Martha Corelli's comments corroborate this: "My children have become my best friends, all three of them. They will always be supportive, and I can always trust them. It's extremely important to find people you can trust, people who won't betray you."

But when trust breaks down, it is difficult or sometimes impossible to rebuild a relationship, and Social Capital shrinks. Barbara

Mathias says, "My husband left me after 12 years to return to his ex-wife. She didn't stay around long, and he came back. He said he was sorry, but I just couldn't trust him. I couldn't build our relationship again."

Virginia Garfield, perhaps more than anyone else I interviewed, speaks about friends as assets: "I have great friends and count myself as rich. I may not ever be truly financially rich, but I wouldn't trade my friends for all the money in the world. I pride myself in being a good friend. I just want to continue developing my friendships and relationships with my family."

Financial Capital

Financial Capital is where this discussion of the Seven Life Capitals began. And because it is best understood, it is the easiest to specify here. Like Social Capital, Financial Capital is not entirely under our control since external events can significantly increase or decrease the asset.

- *Financial Capital includes the aggregate of cash, stocks, bonds, mutual funds, insurance and other liquid assets that are available for use.*

What Does This Definition Mean? Years of employment (ours and/or our spouses') combined with saving and investing provide financial resources that are used throughout a lifetime to increase other life capitals and to ensure monetary security in our later years. When we approach retirement years, we realize there are fewer options for increasing our financial resources. Consequently, many women interviewed mentioned financial issues. Probably the best recommendations I heard dealt with the importance of knowledge: "Know all you can about finances. Don't depend on anybody else to do it for you." "Once I retired I became the manager of my own portfolio. I got involved in the stock market and joined an investment club. I became aware of my own financial position." Unfortunately, women frequently give away not only their Emotional Capital resources but also their Financial Capital. A (grown) child needs your help and you give her or him money; a friend gets in a difficult situation and you give her or him money; your sibling makes a few bad investments and you provide some tide-over funds. Woman give, give, give. When women give too much, they jeopardize their own security.

How Women Manage Their Financial Capital. Evelyn Wilson links two of the life capitals—Physical and Financial—and suggests their relationship: "I have some fears about financial and health matters. If your health goes down badly, it can negatively affect your finances."

Ruth Spiro speaks passionately about the importance of understanding financial needs and focuses on these issues in both her personal and current professional life. When she divorced, she found that all the financial matters that her husband previously had managed suddenly required her attention. She lacked the knowledge then, but has since acquired the expertise and routinely speaks to women's groups about this subject. She says: "We're the first well-educated generation of women and we're all scared because money is so isolating that nobody wants to talk to anybody about it. We can talk about anything else. Nobody knows where to go [for financial guidance]. Some women give their money to a nephew or a friend to invest, and they lose it. Stories are just rampant from prominent people who you would assume would know better."

Judge Judy,
Attorney Judith Sheindlin, popular television show host and author

"Who's nurturing the woman; who's tending the tree? You are the trunk of the tree. You need to say to yourself, 'I have to nurture myself.' ... Spending your money on things that give you pleasure once in a while is food for the soul. Don't feel guilty. Consider it a long drink of water for the trunk of the tree."

Research shows HRT raises breast cancer, heart attack, and stroke risks • Terrorist bomb kills hundreds in Bali

Ruth continued, "From the work that I've been doing, it becomes even more apparent what a huge need there is for women to have places to go that don't have an agenda. It is bad enough to get the accountant to talk to the lawyer to talk to the financial planner. Most women I talk with can't even describe what a financial planner does; never mind what the broker does. My advice is, independent of how much or how little you have; understand what you do have and what you need for the future."

Temporal Capital

The last capital, Temporal, is rarely thought about, yet it is the one that determines how long we'll be able to invest in and benefit from use of our other Life Capitals. We can't fully control Temporal Capital and yet, on the average, we can expand it considerably through judicious investments of Physical, Financial, and Cognitive Capital.

Linda Ellerbee

"I am grateful for every day [since her mastectomy]. I know it sounds corny, but I still do a lot of work in this area and a lot of women call me who have just been diagnosed with cancer. I'm very grateful because every year I'm alive is a year I get."

- *Temporal Capital includes the amount of time available in a person's life and has the two dimensions of quantity and quality.*

What Does This Definition Mean? We might think of Temporal Capital as both the first and the last of our life capitals for it is there at the beginning of our life, and our present lives end when it ends. We want a large quantity of Temporal Capital, but we also want the quality of our Temporal Capital to be worth possessing. We are often talking about the quality of Temporal Capital when we discuss "quality of life."

Our mothers in Rosie's generation did not know about the negative effects of the Standard American Diet, the Standard American Exercise Regimen, and the Standard American Lifestyle on vigor and longevity across the life span. Our mothers were hardy, but often their last 10 or 20 years were compromised by heart disease, lung disease, Type II diabetes, osteoporosis, etc.—conditions that could have been prevented or delayed with more awareness of the Devil's bargain (easy decision now, hard payback later). Health research tells us how to prepare for and then live vigorous older lives, preserving quality of life until the last breath.

Perhaps you remember a book from 20 years ago, *Lives of a Cell*, by the physician Lewis Thomas. Based on his knowledge of the inherent ruggedness of our bodies, Thomas projected that we could continue on with high vitality for many years longer than we now do, on the average. Thomas said that our end, when it must come, could be that of the "wonderful one hoss shay" in the poem by Oliver Wendell Holmes. That New England shay was so well constructed that, when the end came, every part of it collapsed at the same instant.

Ten years ago the Palo Alto physician Walter Bortz published *DARE to be 100*, which adds detail to Thomas's picture of vigorous aging ("DARE" stands for Diet, Attitude, Renewal, and Exercise). He makes it clear that the most important investments in quality of life (I would add, like the most important investments in other Life Capitals) are made when we are much younger; their value compounds for our later years. But investments made now will also continue to come to fruition in our coming years.

How Women Manage Their Temporal Capital. In the interviews, women frequently made reference to the different times of their lives—a positive time, a satisfying time, a scary time, a difficult time. Time is sometimes viewed as lost, not spent. One woman, for instance, mentions that she "lost time because of my health situation."

In the second half of life, as we reconcile ourselves to what is becoming a limited rather than limitless resource, we develop different attitudes toward the remaining Temporal Capital. These attitudes range from negative to appreciative to expansive. Edith Andrews' comment illustrates the negative perspective on time: "I don't have enough time left in my life to go back to school and accomplish what I want." Similarly, Ginger Hawthorne says, "The time for many of my dreams has passed. I've always put them on hold, and now there isn't enough time." But she ends her comment differently: "I'm just going to have to shape my life in a new way."

Gage Worth acknowledges the finite time ahead but with a most positive perspective. She believes she can dedicate her Temporal Capital to her life's passion. "Now is the time to rededicate myself to a cause," she says, "and I'm ramping up instead of down. ... I think that when people reach 60, they should give it all they've got. Let it rip because there's nothing holding them back at this point. So I'm really going to take advantage of the fact that I'm still full of energy and I've got a lot of experience now so I can really go for it."

The Bottom Line of Life Capital Investments

From the interviews I distilled seven bottom-line conclusions concerning the Seven Life Capitals:

Emotional Capital requires especially careful balance between spending and replenishing. Women are generous with Emotional Capital. Since in these respects they are doing "what women are supposed to do," their generosity is often not acknowledged or reciprocated. Several women I interviewed had suffered emotional burnout at one time or another. If you look up "thankless" in the dictionary, you will find a list of women's traditional duties.

Physical Capital is an asset that is often ignored when we have it and lamented when it is gone. If we follow a plan of regular investment in Physical Capital through diet, exercise, stress reduction, and rest, there is likely to be an ample balance whenever we need it in life. If we have already lost some Physical Capital, we should invest in what remains, so that we can enjoy its benefits longer.

Cognitive Capital usually receives the heaviest investment in our youth when education and the demands of employment cause us to acquire knowledge and skills. Cognitive Capital, like Physical Capital, has a naturally sinking balance. Left unrefreshed, it slowly disappears. Since Cognitive Capital underwrites so many of our responsibilities and pleasures throughout life, it requires our continual investment to ensure we keep growing.

Spiritual Capital tends to be a closely held asset at the present time because some self-declared spiritual spokespersons have violated the public trust by their behavior. It may be best to keep our private beliefs private, but not to the point of ignoring them. When crisis overtakes us, we don't want to be out of touch with our spiritual resources. Nor is Spiritual Capital an isolated asset. For example, meditation, a form of spiritual investment, reduces stress and increases Physical Capital.

Martha Reeves,
Lead singer of Martha &
Vandellas
"One thing Maxine [Powell, her etiquette coach at Motown] taught us is that you have to have a life outside of music. Invest in yourself some other way, she said, because you can lose the money and the fame, and then where are you?"

Social Capital is a chameleon, sometimes seeming to be Emotional Capital (a feeling of well being in social interaction) or Cognitive Capital (knowledge of who knows what in various social networks). Then it reappears as itself—fungible but perhaps short-lived. "Your recent service to my sister's son-in-law means that I owe you a favor," as someone in Tony Soprano's family might say. This capital grows through a judicious balance of investing and spending. To only invest gives us none of the benefits, and to only spend depletes the asset.

Financial Capital has a central role in our balanced portfolio, giving us the opportunity to spend from it in order to invest in each of the other six capitals. So while increasing Financial Capital is critical for our later years, its use is always important for robust balances in our other life capitals.

Temporal Capital seems limitless when we are young and ever more precious as we age. We spend Temporal Capital on the maintenance of every other Life Capital. This is just as well, because Temporal Capital has a naturally sinking balance; we give up 24 hours of it every day. It is better to use it than to just let it go. We replenish Temporal Capital by spending some of it to increase other Life Capitals that increase longevity, which happens to be all of them.

Portfolios of Life Capitals

Although I've discussed each of the Seven Life Capitals separately, they are not individual assets to be considered in isolation. Yet neither should they be balanced at all times as fixed and equal investments in a Life Capital portfolio—1/7th Emotional Capital, 1/7th Physical Capital, etc.

Each of us creates our own Life Capital portfolio as a unique combination of these assets, according to strengths and limitations that we are born with or acquire, our individual interests, our preference for safe investments or intriguing investments with higher risk, and of course outside forces. In addition, the stages of life exert a biological and social influence over the capitals that we accrue and spend.

Your personal Life Capital portfolio is as unique as your financial portfolio. Probably no two individuals have exactly the same assets in either of these portfolios. Start now to assess your investment in each of the Seven Life Capitals and plan what you want your portfolio to look like in six months, one year, five years. Then take action on your plans, investing in and spending from your Life Capital Portfolio in ways that will enhance your present and your future.

The Seven Life Capitals is a concept for balancing our lives and fulfilling our dreams. We all have dreams that we've been saving for later. *Now* is the time, independent of your age, to take steps toward the realization of your dreams. The information and life lessons in this book can help you establish and manage your Life Capital portfolio. You can shape your investments and expenditures to reach for your personal star.

Epilogue: From Endings Come Beginnings

Writing my final words on this book is an ending of sorts, but the story of *Rosie's Daughters* doesn't end here. It gives rise to new beginnings. Originally I envisioned that the Seven Life Capitals chapter would serve as the ending for the book and the beginning of a new way for women to approach living mindful and balanced lives. What I didn't expect was for the creation of *Rosie's Daughters* to become such a powerful personal journey and source of new beginnings for both the women I interviewed and for me. It is my great hope that you, my readers, will come away from this book inspired and eager to seek new beginnings throughout your life.

The Stories Are Important

Perhaps Joan Didion said it best in the opening line of *White Album*: "We tell ourselves stories in order to live." Personal stories—the big life story as well as the small stories of well-remembered events—are at the core of our being. Consider your own oft-repeated stories: A funny time from your childhood. A touching memory about you and your mother. A special day with your children. A defining event in your career. You would not be "you" without them.

When I originally conducted interviews for *Rosie's Daughters*, I didn't fully appreciate the significance of these stories. I was thinking like a researcher, intent on collecting data and finding patterns that would explain my FW2 Generation. As the number of interviews grew, I realized the importance of the story for its own sake rather than only as a contributing factor to the larger set of scientific findings. Quantitative analysis may provide a structure upon which we can build but it is the qualitative that brings insight and, in the case of the FW2 Generation, brings it to life. In each story we find an individual; with a preponderance of stories we begin to see the patterns that define our generation.

This respect for the story, for each woman's individual story, led me to completely reorganize and rewrite this book. I may have started as a social scientist but I grew into as a memoirist. Although I had always viewed *Rosie's Daughters* as a collective memoir of a generation, it took one revelation and one discovery for my conversion to be complete. The women I interviewed planted the first seed although I had to hear their words several times before I was struck with the significance of what they were saying. They told me they had never stopped to reflect—they'd been too busy living. They said only at the conclusion of the interview did they see the ill-considered pattern repeated, or life's challenges well met, or goals too long deferred that should now be accomplished, or joys finally acknowledged. I was helping these women to *see* their own lives for the first time. Telling (or writing) one's life story is a transformative event. You will not be the same at the ending as you were at the beginning.

Second, as I researched the lives of famous FW2 women, I was struck by how many had written memoirs. Within a few months of this discovery, I had acquired more than 125 of their life stories. In reading these public accounts of lives, I saw that telling (or, in their case, writing) one's story can be more than a transformative event for the self—it can create the context for a transformative event *for others*. Women's memoirs reveal unexpected insights to readers. Jill Ker Conway, who has written three memoirs (thus far) about her eventful life, wrote that memoirs are "where we look when we try to understand our own lives."

Here's a small sampling of memoirs written by FW2 women. Their titles tell their attitudes:

- *Don't Look Back: We're Not Going that Way* by Marcia Wallace
- *There Are Worse Things I Could Do* by Adrienne Barbeau
- *A Lotus Growing in the Mud* by Goldie Hawn
- *A Woman's Place...: The Freshman Who Changed the Face of Congress* by Marjorie Margoles-Mezvinsky
- *Saturday's Child* by Robin Morgan
- *Business as Unusual* by Anita Roddick
- *Between Each Line of Pain and Glory* by Gladys Knight
- *In Our Time: Memoir of a Revolution* by Susan Brownmiller
- *Don't Pee on My Leg and Tell Me It's Raining* by Judge Judith Sheindlin
- *In My Place* by Charlayne Hunter-Gault
- *A Good Fight* by Sarah Brady
- *24 Years of House Work and the Place is Still a Mess* by Pat Schroeder

My Beginning as a Memoirist

In an unexpected turn of events, I embarked on a new journey. Using my experiences from interviewing more than 100 women and reading more than 100 women's memoirs, I decided to share my respect for and passion about life storytelling by teaching women's memoir writing workshops. I now regularly offer these classes through local colleges as well as privately. In working with the wonderful women in these workshops, I continue to be amazed at the power of the personal narrative both for the self and for others.

When we bravely and honestly discuss—in conversation, in our journal, or in a memoir—whatever happened, when we can look at the untidy parts and initiate the process that will enable us to move past them, then we may be able to see the redeeming whole. (My colleague Linda Joy Myers has recently updated her excellent book on this topic, *Becoming Whole: Writing Your Healing Story*.)

As far as I can tell, everyone has some dark nights of the soul; most of us can acknowledge these times and move on. Many women do turn lemons into lemonade. The relationship that got away, the job that worked out badly, the health scare or the continuing health crisis, the children who don't understand us or vice versa may be vignettes in our story but they do not need to define us. I think you'll find much more happiness than sadness in our stories.

I admire the emotional truth in women's stories. Educator and memoirist Jill Ker Conway said that men tell how they changed the world while women tell how the world changed them. The FW2 Generation of women bridges that contrast. They have written scores of memoirs about what happened when they strove harder than they ever thought possible to accomplish what others thought they couldn't. Cadences of kitchen table confidences can be heard in the wisdom and humor of their accounts.

I encourage you to join me in making life stories part of your new beginnings. My website, www.womensmemoirs.com, serves as a starting point for learning, collaboration, and ongoing discussion of the ancient but ever-contemporary art of storytelling. There you will also find reviews of women's memoirs as well as links to excellent books about memoir writing such as those by Susan Wittig Albert, Judith Barrington, Louise DeSalvo, Vivian Gornick, Maureen Murdock, and others.

Paths to Your Beginnings

By now, you know that Yogi-isms, the sayings of Yogi Berra, appeal to me. A favorite is: "When you come to a fork in the road, take it." I've already taken my next fork—a new beginning from *Rosie's Daughters*. I hope this book provides a fork in the road for you as well and that you'll take it.

- *If you are an FW2 woman, or of an older generation,* I hope you gain further insights into your life and a better understanding for the impact of the times on our generation and how our decisions helped to change the expectations and lives of those who followed. At this fork, perhaps you'll choose to actively manage your life portfolio, investing in and spending from your Seven Life Capitals in ways that let you enjoy life more. The lesson of the Seven Life Capitals is that you really are in charge of your present and your future. Perhaps you will write your life story for yourself, to share with your family, or even to publish.

- *If you are a Boomer,* you've seen opportunities expand almost exponentially during your lifetime. It's likely you've been caught in the midst of the two-shift lifestyle—one at work and one at home. Boomer women moved more quickly into the workforce than men moved into the homeforce. I hope you'll find insights from the Seven Life Capitals and create a portfolio that will lead to a more balanced life now and in the decades to come. The Boomer generation is legend with a story that is larger than life. Yet each Boomer has her own story. Are you keeping a journal? If not, perhaps you'll start one to record the events, insights, and moods of your life and to better understand your actions. Perhaps you'll consider writing vignettes as a way of capturing your life stories. Later these might become part of a personal website or blog or gathered more formally into a memoir.

- *If you are a GenXer,* it's likely that you've learned about your mother's generation from reading this book. As an FW2 woman, she had no blueprint for how to build her life in a changing world. From what I've heard in the course of many conversations, I am confident that your mother is all too aware of the many occasions she didn't meet her own high standards for being a mother. At the same time, she feels proud that you have more opportunities than she did. Each generation does the best it can, given changing expectations and external circumstances.

A Few More Words (of Hard-Earned Wisdom) from FW2 Women

As encouragement as you continue on your life path, the women I interviewed would like to share some words of wisdom. At the end of each interview, I asked, "Given what you have learned during the past decades, what advice can you give to younger women?" Their responses fall into seven imperatives—all of which should serve you well in your quest for your own new beginnings:

1) "Do It Now!"

The words vary from woman to woman, but their message is clear. Go for it. "Don't wait," says one woman. "You fit in what you want to do with your life now. You find a way to make it work." Another says, "Just go for it, and if you are lucky you *can* have it all, just not all at once."

To give direction to your assault on life, you need to plan. "Make a list of what you want to do in your life," counsels one woman, "and begin to do each item now. External events may make deferred goals unreachable at some later date. Don't wait." Diane Selewski has taken these words to heart. Diane did an incredible job of transcribing all my FW2 interviews. As such, she is also the first person to listen to all these women. Late in this process she emailed me to say she had just returned from REI where she bought her dream bike, a Novara. She had wanted to regularly bike the more than 100 miles of scenic trails around Madison but kept postponing the purchase. After hearing so many women *tell her* to "go do it," she followed their advice and was preparing to hit the trails.

2) "Take Charge of Your Life"

If you are going to follow the advice to Do it Now, you need to ensure that your decisions truly are your own. I am struck by the impassioned words of this FW2 woman: "You are the author of your own life. You may not know where you're going or how you're going to get there. But there are choices along the way that you make whether consciously or unconsciously. Even the decisions you *don't* make are choices. You are influenced, but at the end of the day you're the person who makes those decisions. You can't blame or give that power away. Don't be afraid to be a risk taker. Focus on what's important to you. Live out your dreams."

Here is another expression of taking charge that may inspire you: "This has been the best decade of my life. Think positive, and this could be the best part of your life. Do what *you* want to do. You've earned it." And equally strong advice came in these words, "Grab hold of your life. Be the master of your own ship."

If you are still holding back, consider these words, "Follow your dreams. Don't wait for life to happen to you. You're in control." Good advice for women who so frequently put everyone else's needs before their own. Life often seems out of our control, so an occasional reminder to be in charge is especially helpful.

If you accept that you need to be in control of your life, then your marching orders are to Claim Your Independence. "If you haven't gained any independence, then do so. Your husband may die, your children may move away. You need to have the confidence in yourself to carry on independently." Another woman is even more succinct: "You must be independent. You need to have your own life, your own money, your own career."

3) "Look On the Bright Side"

FW2 women most definitely are not Pollyannas, and the advice of one woman reminds us all, "Don't ever let the bastards get you down." Many of the FW2s I interviewed, however, urge women to enjoy life and find positive aspects to each day. Life, they say, is to be lived to its fullest; let their words be your inspiration:

"Count your blessings, and be optimistic in everything you do."

"Don't look back. Play each day for what it has to bring."

"Keep a bright, cheery outlook by seeing the glass as half full and not half empty."

Sharing your optimism can be contagious. One woman, after careful consideration, suggests, "Take time to smell the roses. Say something nice to someone each day. It is amazing how often this simple act isn't done."

If you haven't yet found the bright side of life, you may have to start your journey by first letting go of previous hurts, insults, and even injustices. Sometimes that is the only way to move forward.

4) "Take Care of Yourself"

A number of the women's comments remind us of the importance of staying well—not just hoping for the best but ensuring we are doing everything possible. "Be proactive concerning your health. Don't just sit back and be passive." The advice doesn't seem to be health for health's sake, but health because it allows for a fuller life. "Do everything you can to keep yourself healthy so you can enjoy life." Echoing the previous statements about independence, one woman told me, "Take care of yourself because if you don't no one else will."

Taking Care has two dimensions. As one FW2 woman reminds us: "Take care of yourself, not just physically, but emotionally as well." Another prescribes communication as part of the task of Taking Care: "Talk with your friends about health issues because everybody has the same concerns. It is good to get together, have a support group, and laugh about our changing bodies."

5) "Become Yourself"

Women are faced with many external demands. When young, they want to please parents and teachers. Later they want to please boyfriends, husbands, children, even co-workers and bosses. While trying to navigate in an overcrowded landscape of expectations, it is difficult to figure out who you are separate from the expectations and needs of others. Learning who you are and fully becoming that person is one of the joys of aging (and, dare I say, growing up). Embrace it.

When I asked one woman to use her experiences to give advice to younger women, she paused to think then responded softly, "I just had a visual answer. I may start crying. This brings up so many emotions. I see this flower, like a rose or a lotus, opening up. When you are younger, you're trying to control the flower and trying to keep it from opening up too far. As you age, you can just let go and let that flower blossom. Let it open up wide. You should embrace everything life has in every way that you can. With age, you should find you are at a place where you have the wisdom and the experience to let yourself be you. That's the greatest gift you can have. Be yourself. Now is the time to put yourself first. Let go of all those fears that are holding you back and fully blossom."

6) "Stay Mentally Alert"

It is impossible to follow through on the previous five imperatives without healthy cognitive abilities. One great fear of aging is an extreme change in our mental capacity such as Alzheimer's or dementia. Although medical research may bring a cure for these conditions in our lifetime, there are things you can do today. These include the same general advice for a healthy life—maintain an appropriate weight with a low-fat diet and food rich in omega-3s, exercise, control high blood pressure and cholesterol levels. Other keys to maintaining cognitive alertness include mental exercise and lifelong learning. The brain can be successfully stimulated through a variety of activities—playing a musical instrument, visiting museums, reading, writing (including memoirs), working on crossword puzzles are just a few. Research also shows that the brain needs the stimulation of *new* activities and *regular* challenges. "Variety is the spice of life" was one of my mother's sayings. Little did I know that this spice was a critical ingredient of the recipe for a long life with a sharp mind—something both my parents had until they died at the ages of 90 and 95. Some of their simple advice such as "learn something new each day" and "keep making new friends" suddenly has great value to me.

Most FW2 women are past the years of formal education, but they understand what everyone needs to know—learning can happen in many ways and needs to keep happening. Although I frequently heard "keep learning" from the women I interviewed, the words of one woman in particular bear quoting: "Learn constantly. Educate yourself because that keeps the neurons active. Equally important, learning keeps you open to new ideas." It is learning and new ideas that will keep you engaged in discovering and enjoying new beginnings.

7) "Savor Friendships"

Perhaps it isn't surprising that almost all the advice given by the FW2 women I interviewed focused on the self—do it now, take charge, look on the bright side, take care of yourself, become yourself, and stay mentally alert. Having devoted their lives to parents, boyfriends, husbands and children, they realize now how often they put themselves last. Their words encourage you to make your own needs at least as important as those of the people around you. At the same time, they see friendships as the critical link between the self and others. Friendships are important throughout our lives, and the longer we live the more we come to cherish the ways friends and family enrich our lives. There is a simple but elegant truth in the FW2 women's words of wisdom:

"Rejoice in the love of your family. Savor your friendships and protect them because they are very important."

"Go out and enjoy life and make new friends."

"Work at friendships and family."

Back to Endings and Beginnings

If at the ending of this book, you see that you've come to a fork in the road and decide to take it, you will find two maps. When you open the first, you'll find a well-worn printed page showing the routes others say you should take. The map is useful as a point of reference and suggestion. You can study the maps of others to learn something about the paths they followed, just be aware that their recommendations may take you to the destination *they* think best. To chart your own journey, you need to pick up the second map as well. You will open it to find a crisp, new, blank page. Feel free to draw new lines and create your own map. It's a more challenging, and potentially circuitous, road you travel, but the destination is by choice and the journey uniquely your own. If you choose the blank page, you may want to note your location from time to time so friends and family can stay connected and provide encouragement along your journey. This blank map is like the fresh pages in a journal that you will fill with the story of the life you create. And with each trail's end, I hope you find your fork and chart a new beginning.

Acknowledgments

.

Many women made *Rosie's Daughters* possible by sharing their stories with me. How I regret that I can't print your actual names, but you know who you are. I hope you'll show *Rosie's Daughters* to your friends and tell them, "I helped make this book."

My next appreciation is extended to Iaso Books of Two Bridges Press for their valuable support and enthusiasm for this book.

I want to thank my adult children, Ken, Edward, Andy, and Will who seemed to know just when to ask about the progress of *Rosie's Daughters* and when to keep quiet about this major undertaking. Their ideas and support are important to me. They have become people I am proud to know.

This book contains several autobiographical vignettes about life in my family of four during the postwar years, which gives me a rare opportunity to express my appreciation for my parents and sister. My father gave me the most important ingredient for the *Growing Up Successfully* recipe—unconditional love. My mother was a steel magnolia before that term was invented, and she taught me that I could be whatever I wanted to be—although we were both surprised that I believed her. My sister Ann encouraged my ventures from the days when I was the little sister who insisted on tagging along.

A growing number of women writers around the country are dedicated to telling the stories of women's lives, and I am lucky to live near many of them here in the Bay Area. I have benefited so much from the ideas of women like Martha Alderson, Betty Auchard, Lori Hope, Cathleen Miller, Linda Joy Myers, Beth Proudfoot, Carmen Richardson Rutlen, Cathleen Rountree, Teresa LeYung Ryan, and others. I am also fortunate to be active in our local writer's group where the support of women like Catherine Alexander, Maryann Bartram, Kristiane Maas, Erin Palmer, and Diana Paul has meant so much to me.

Wonderful friends graciously housed me during the interviewing phase of the book, provided details that enriched the book, and read draft chapters. Suzanne Pingree needs to be mentioned by name for going beyond the call of friendship in developing www.WomensMemoirs.com where reading and writing resources can be found. I hope you all know how much I appreciate your help.

Although the Internet is an incredible resource for a writer, some information just isn't there. At that point, I turned to a number of people who dug out key facts about women's education, employment, and other topics. My thanks go to Tom Snyder and Aurora D'Amico at the National Center for Education Statistics, Emy Sok at the Bureau of Labor Statistics, and Gloria Mundo and Karen Denise Thompson at the US Census Bureau—expert sources of needed data.

Kendra Bonnet's insightful questions and editing skills are evident throughout this book. Neither of us will forget that afternoon we dared to imagine bringing together stories, analyses, photographs, and timelines. This book is written in the first person singular, but Kendra knows how much of a "we" project it has been.

Rees Maxwell's aesthetic judgment and drive for perfection allowed him to design and lay out this complicated format from our book concept. Using very powerful but complex publishing software, he assembled and adapted every element on every page of this book. The artful whole speaks for itself. Words are inadequate to express my gratitude for his significant contribution.

And special thanks to my life partner, Bill Paisley, who urged me forward when I wanted to retreat, who reacted to most of the ideas that are in this book and many others that are not, who had the knack of finding the perfect information nugget just when I needed it, and who has loved me and nurtured our relationship for more than thirty years.

List of Photographs

The photographs in *Rosie's Daughters* illustrate the times, places and events that helped shape the lives of the FW2 Generation. Only photographs with public figures are captioned in the book. Following are the details of all photographs.

Prologue: A Tale of Generations

Chapter 1: Origins of the FW2 Generation

Chapter 2: The Education of FW2 Generation Women

Source:
[1] Personal files
[2] U.S. National Archives and Records Administration
[3] Kent State University Libraries and Media Services, Department of Special Collections and Archives
[4] Personal file of Ann Claypool

References, Quotes and Notes

Prologue: A Tale of Generations

p. 2   William Strauss and Neil Howe. *Generations: The History of America's Future, 1584 to 2069.* Harper Perennial, 1992, p. 294.

Chapter 1: Origins of the FW2 Generation

p. 13   Inez Sauer. Transcript of video presentation by Sheridan Harvey. www.loc.gov/rr/program/ journey/rosie-transcript.html.

p. 13   Alison Ely Campbell quoted in: Nancy Baker Wise and Christy Wise. *A Mouthful of Rivets: Women at Work in World War II.* San Francisco, Jossey-Bass Publishers, 1994, pp. 94-95.

p. 14   Sybil Lewis. Transcript of video presentation by Sheridan Harvey. www.loc.gov/rr/program/ journey/rosie-transcript.html.

p. 14   Inez Sauer. Transcript of video presentation by Sheridan Harvey. www.loc.gov/rr/program/ journey/rosie-transcript.html.

p. 15   Delana Jensen Close. www.nps.gov/pwro/collection/website/delana.htm.

p. 15   Tessie Hickam Wilson. www.nps.gov/pwro/collection/website/tessie.htm.

p. 16   Kay Bailey Hutchison. *American Heroines: The Spirited Women Who Shaped Our Country.* New York: William Morrow, an imprint of HarperCollins Publishers, Inc., 2004, pp. 360-361.

p. 19   Sherry Lansing quoted by: Sean Smith. "The Goodbye Girl." *Newsweek*, January 24, 2005, p. 61.

p. 21   Nancy Pelosi. Press Release of speech as newly elected Speaker of the House, January 4, 2007.

p. 25   Anna Eshoo quoted by: Jen Graves. "What Makes a Woman Successful?" www.superkids.com/ aweb/pages/features/girls/jgl.shtml.

Chapter 2: Education of FW2-Generation Women

p. 35   Bernadine Healy quoted by Kay Bailey Hutchison. *American Heroines: The Spirited Women Who Shaped Our Country.* New York: William Morrow, An Imprint of HarperCollins Publishers, Inc., 2004, p. 124.

p. 39   Sarah Weddington. *A Question of Choice.* New York: G.p. Purnam's Sons, 1992, p. 19.

p. 45   Data sources and notes for Bachelor's Degrees Conferred in 1964 and 2000: Percent Female within Fields of Study.

Notes: All majors with at least 1000 degrees awarded are included. In 1964, the field shown as English Language & Literature was known as Letters. In 1964, the field shown as Visual and Performing Arts was known as Fine and Applied Arts. In 1964, the field shown as Public Administration was known as was Public Affairs and Services.

Sources: 1964 data from US Department of Education, National Center for Education Statistics; 2000 data from Digest of Education Statistics, US Department of Education National Center for Education Statistics, Integrated Postsecondary Education Data System (IPEDS), "Completions" survey, Table 269.

Chapter 3: The FW2 Generation Marries

p. 61 Loni Anderson (with Larkin Warren). *My Life in High Heels*. NY: William Morrow and Company, Inc., 1995, pp. 14-15.

p. 62 David Halberstam. *The Fifties*. New York: Fawcett Columbine, 1993, p. 509.

p. 63 Joan Baez. *And a Voice to Sing With*. NY: Summit Books, A Division of Simon & Schuster, Inc., 1987, pp. 150-151.

p. 66 Cokie Roberts and Steve Roberts. *From This Day Forward*. NY: William Morrow and Company, Inc., 2000, pp. 17-18.

p. 67 Cokie Roberts and Steve Roberts. *From This Day Forward*. NY: William Morrow and Company, Inc., 2000, p. 18.

p. 68 Priscilla Presley. *Elvis and Me*. NY: G.p. Putnam's Sons, 1985, p. 224.

pp. 72-73 Stephanie Coontz. *Marriage, A History from Obedient to Intimacy, or How Love Conquered Marriage*. NY: Viking, 2005.

p. 73 Stephanie Coontz. [Marriage was a lot...] "Why marriage today takes more love, work – from both partners." *The Christian Science Monitor*, June 28, 2005.

p. 73 Stephanie Coontz. [As late as...] "The Heterosexual Revolution." *The New York Times*, July 5, 2005.

pp. 73-74 Cathleen Rountree. *The Heart of Marriage: Discovering the Secrets of Enduring Love*. San Francisco: HarperSanFrancisco, 1996, p. 25.

p. 76 Cathleen Rountree. *The Heart of Marriage: Discovering the Secrets of Enduring Love*. San Francisco: HarperSanFrancisco, 1996, p. 91.

p. 77 Cathleen Rountree. *The Heart of Marriage: Discovering the Secrets of Enduring Love*. San Francisco: HarperSanFrancisco, 1996, p. 164.

p. 77 Eric Berne. *Games People Play: The Psychology of Human Relationships*. NY: Ballantine Books, 1964.

p. 78 Robert Sternberg. *Love is a Story: A New Theory of Relationships*. New York/Oxford, Oxford University Press, 1998, p. 7.

p. 82 Loni Anderson (with Larkin Warren). *My Life in High Heels*. NY: William Morrow and Company, Inc., 1995, p. 28.

p. 82 Daniel Levinson. *The Seasons of a Woman's Life*. NY: Ballantine Books, 1997.

p. 83 Judge Judy Sheindlin. *Beauty Fades, Dumb Is Forever*. NY: Cliff Street Books, An imprint of HarperCollins Publishers, Inc., 1999, p. 177.

p. 85 Gloria Feldt quoted by: Michael Neill. "The voice of experience: onetime teen mother Gloria Feldt takes the helm at Planned Parenthood." People Weekly, June 24, 1996, v45, n25, p.67(2).

p. 92 Sally Jessy Raphael (with Pam Proctor). *Sally: Unconventional Success*. NY: Wiliam Morrow and Company, Inc., 1990, p. 19.

p. 94 Jane Adams. "Seeking Mr. Right – and Finding Something Better" in: *Are You Old Enough to Read This Book?: Reflections on Midlife*. Pleasantville, NY: Readers Digest, 1997, p. 121.

Chapter 4: The FW2 Generation Gives Birth

p. 102 Barbara Ehrenreich. "Stop Ironing the Diapers." *Brain, Child: The Magazine for Thinking Mothers*, Fall 2000, p. 34.

p. 103 Ellen Galinsky. *The Six Stages of Parenthood*. Boston, MA: Addison Wesley Publishing, 1987.

p. 103 Edith Grotberg. *Tapping Your Inner Strength: How to Find the Resilience to Deal with Anything*. Oakland, CA: New Harbinger Publications, 1999.

p. 105 Stephanie Coontz. *The Way We Never Were: American Families and the Nostalgia Trap*. NY: Basic Books, A Division of HarperCollins Publishers, Inc., 1992, p. 34.

p. 107 Abraham Maslow. "A Theory of Human Motivation." *Psychological Review*, 50, pp. 370-96.

p. 111 Faye Dunaway (with Betsy Sharkey). *Looking for Gatsby: My Life*. NY: Simon & Schuster, 1995, pp. 43-44.

p. 113 Margo Howard. *A Life in Letters: Ann Landers' Letters to Her Only Child*. NY: Warner Books, Inc., 2003, p. xii.

p. 116 Fanny Howe. *The Wedding Dress: Meditations on Word and Life*. Berkeley, CA: University of California Press, 2003, pp. xx-xxi.

p. 119 Gloria Feldt. *Behind Every Choice is a Story*. Denton, TX: University of North Texas Press, 2002, p. 101.

p. 120 Kate Michelman. *With Liberty and Justice for All: A Life Spent Protecting the Right to Choose*. NY: Hudson Street Press, Penguin Group, 2005, p. 2.

p. 121 Kate Michelman. *With Liberty and Justice for All: A Life Spent Protecting the Right to Choose*. NY: Hudson Street Press, Penguin Group, 2005, p. 3.

p. 121 Andrea Tone. "Contraceptive Consumers: Gender and the Political Economy of Birth Control in the 1930s." *Journal of Social History*, v. 29, 1996.

p. 122 Faye Wattleton. *Life on the Line*. NY: Ballantine Books, A Division of Random House, Inc., 1996, pp. 84-85.

p. 122 Kate Michelman. *With Liberty and Justice for All: A Life Spent Protecting the Right to Choose*. NY: Hudson Street Press, Penguin Group, 2005, p. 3.

p. 123 Gloria Feldt. *Behind Every Choice is a Story*. Denton, TX: University of North Texas Press, 2002, p. 97.

p. 124 Tess Gallagher quoted by: Melvin Sterne in an interview for *Carve Magazine*, February 23, 2001. www.carvezine.com.

p. 125 Adrienne Barbeau. *There are Worse Things I Could Do*. NY: Carroll & Graf, 2007, p. 124.

p. 127 Doris Kearns Goodwin. *Wait Till Next Year: A Memoir*. NY: Simon & Schuster, 1997, p. 255

p. 129 Gloria Feldt. *Behind Every Choice is a Story*. Denton, TX: University of North Texas Press, 2002, p. 114.

p. 133 Shere Hite. *The Hite Report on the Family*. NY: Grove Press, 1994. p. 371-372. Also found on: www.hite-research.com/artfamilyexplodingnuclearmyth.htm.

pp. 134-135 Erica Jong quoted by: Ariel Levy. *Female Chauvinist Pigs: Women and the Rise of Raunch Culture*. NY: Free Press: A Division of Simon & Schuster, Inc., 2005, p. 85.

Chapter 5: The FW2 Generation Goes to Work

p. 142 Lori Harp quoted by: Marguerite Zientara. *Women, Technology & Power: Ten Stars and the History They Made*. NY: AMACOM, Division of American Management Association, 1987, p. 29.

p. 143 Cokie Roberts quoted by: Kay Bailey Hutchison. *American Heroines: The Spirited Women Who Shaped Our Country*. New York: William Morrow, an imprint of HarperCollins Publishers, Inc., 2004, p. 297.

pp. 144-145 Peter Drucker. "How to Manage Your Time." *Harper's Magazine*, December, 1966.

p. 145 Billie Jean King quoted by: The Associated Press. "Wimbledon to Pay Women Equal Prize Money." The New York Times, February 22, 2007.

p. 146 Judith Richards Hope. *Pinstripes & Pearls: The Women of the Harvard Law Class of '64 Who Forged an Old-Girl Network and Paved the Way for Future Generations*. NY: A Lisa Drew Books, Scribner, 2003, p. 41.

p. 147 Sarah Weddington. *A Question of Choice*. NY: Grosset/Putnam Book published by G.P. Putnam's Sons, 1992, p. 19.

p. 148 Sandra Bem and Daryl Bem. "Does Sex-bias in Job Advertising 'Aid and Abet' Sex Discrimination?" *Journal of Applied Social Psychology*, 3(1), 6-18, 1973.

p. 149 Ann Piestrup quoted by: Marguerite Zientara. *Women, Technology & Power: Ten Stars and the History They Made.* NY: AMACOM, Division of American Management Association, 1987, p. 50.

p. 155 Alison Gordon. *Foul Ball! Five Years in the American League.* NY: Dodd, Mead & Company, Inc., 1984, p. 130.

p. 159 Mary Schroeder. Press Release, 11/20/2000.

pp. 159-160 Ann Branigar Hopkins. *So Ordered: Making Partner the Hard Way.* Amherst: University of Massachusetts Press, 1996.

p. 161 Jane Harman. www.janeharmancongress.com.

p. 162 Dorothy Cantor and Toni Bernay. *Women in Power: The Secrets of Leadership.* Boston: Houghton Mifflin Co., 1992, p. 187.

p. 164 Barbara Boxer [My husband thought...] quoted by Catherine Whitney. *Nine and Counting: The Women of the Senate.* NY: William Morrow, An Imprint of HarperCollins Publishers, 2000, p. 103.

p. 164 Barbara Boxer [If you were married...] quoted by Catherine Whitney. *Nine and Counting: The Women of the Senate.* NY: William Morrow, An Imprint of HarperCollins Publishers, 2000, p. 102.

p. 164 Barbara Boxer. [almost a masochistic experience...] *Politics and the New Revolution of Women in America.* Washington, DC: National Press Books, 1994, pp. 73-74.

p. 165 Kay Bailey Hutchison [I always thought...] quoted in "Senator Mom: Kay Bailey Hutchison." *Baptist Standard*, September 9, 2002. www.baptiststandard.com/2002/9-9/pages/hutchison.html.

p. 165 Kay Bailey Hutchison [I was one of only five women...] quoted by Catherine Whitney. *Nine and Counting: The Women of the Senate.* NY: William Morrow, An Imprint of HarperCollins Publishers, 2000, p. 21.

p. 167 Kay Bailey Hutchison [So when I'm asked...] quoted by Catherine Whitney. *Nine and Counting: The Women of the Senate.* NY: William Morrow, An Imprint of HarperCollins Publishers, 2000, p. 53.

p. 167 Kay Bailey Hutchison [One day, after yet another disappointing...] quoted by Catherine Whitney. *Nine and Counting: The Women of the Senate.* NY: William Morrow, An Imprint of HarperCollins Publishers, 2000, p. 22.

p. 167 Kay Bailey Hutchison [When Harris County Republican chairman...] quoted by Catherine Whitney. *Nine and Counting: The Women of the Senate.* NY: William Morrow, An Imprint of HarperCollins Publishers, 2000, p. 22.

p. 168 Kay Bailey Hutchison [When I entered the field...]. *American Heroines: The Spirited Women Who Shaped Our Country.* New York: William Morrow, An Imprint of HarperCollins Publishers, Inc., 2004, p. 292.

p. 169 Patricia Schroeder quoted by Catherine Whitney. *Nine and Counting: The Women of the Senate.* NY: William Morrow, An Imprint of HarperCollins Publishers, 2000, p. 87.

p. 171 Isabel Allende. Paula Goldman, Editor. Isabel Allende *Introduction. Imagining Ourselves: Global Voices from a New Generation of Women.* Novato, CA: New World Library, 2006, p. 16.

p. 173 Portia Isaacson Bass quoted by: Marguerite Zientara. *Women, Technology & Power: Ten Stars and the History They Made.* NY: AMACOM, Division of American Management Association, 1987, p. 40.

p. 178 Judge Judy Sheindlin. *Beauty Fades, Dumb Is Forever.* NY: Cliff Street Books, An imprint of HarperCollins Publishers, Inc., 1999, p. 97.

p. 178 Connie Douglas Reeves. www.waldemar.com. [original page with quote no longer online]

Chapter 6: The FW2 Generation Divorces

p. 180 Judge Judy Sheindlin. *Beauty Fades, Dumb Is Forever.* NY: Cliff Street Books, An imprint of HarperCollins Publishers, Inc., 1999, p. 186.

p. 181 Maureen Reagan. *First Father, First Daughter: A Memoir.* Boston, MA: Little, Brown and Company, 1989, pp. 145-146.

p. 181 Joseph Campbell. *The Hero with a Thousand Faces.* Princeton, NJ: Princeton University Press, 1972.

p. 181 Carol S. Pearson. *Awakening the Heroes Within: Twelve Archetypes to Help Us Find Ourselves and Transform Our World.* San Francisco: HarperSanFrancisco, 1991.

p. 181 Maureen Murdock. *The Heroine's Journey.* Boston: Shambhala Publications, Inc., 1990.

p. 186 Carol S. Pearson quoted by Michael Toms. "Archetypes and Everyday Heroes." Interview broadcast aired July 21, 1998 on New Dimensions World Broadcasting Network. Transcript of interview available at: www.chivalrytoday.com/essays/pearson/pearson-carol.html.

p. 187 Robin Morgan. *Saturday's Child: A Memoir.* NY: W.W. Morton & Company, 2001, pp. 366-367.

p. 190 Annette Funicello. *A Dream Is a Wish Your Heart Makes: My Story.* NY: Hyperion, 1994, p. 176.

p. 192 Joan Baez. *And a Voice to Sing With.* NY: Summit Books, A Division of Simon & Schuster, Inc., 1987, p. 160.

p. 196 Wilma Mankiller (with Michael Wallis). *Wilma Mankiller: A Chief and Her People.* NY: St. Martins Press, 1993, pp. 201-202.

p. 197 Wilma Mankiller (with Michael Wallis). *Wilma Mankiller: A Chief and Her People.* NY: St. Martins Press, 1993, p. 159.

p. 199 Susan Cheever in: Karen Propp and Jean Trounstine, eds. *Why I'm Still Married: Women Write Their Hearts Out on Love, Loss, Sex, and Who Does the Dishes.* NY: Hudson Street Press/Genguine Group, 2006, p. 114.

p. 201 Deborah Tannen. *You're Wearing That?* NY: Random House, 2006, p. 98.

p. 202 Nancy Atherton. *Aunt Dimity's Death.* NY: Doubleday, 1997, p. 5.

p. 201 Erica Jong in: Karen Propp and Jean Trounstine, eds. *Why I'm Still Married: Women Write Their Hearts Out on Love, Loss, Sex, and Who Does the Dishes.* NY: Hudson Street Press/Genguine Group, 2006, p. 76.

Chapter 7: Spiritual Lives of the FW2 Generation

p. 210 Jaune Quick-to-See in: Wilma Mankiller. *Every Day is a God Day: Reflections by Contemporary Indigenous Women.* Golden, CO: Fulcrum Publishing, 2004, p. 164.

p. 214 Diana Eck. *A New Religious America: How a "Christian Country" Has Become the World's Most Religiously Diverse Nation.* San Francisco: HarperSanFrancisco, 2002.

p. 215 Virginia Wade (with Mary Lou Mellace). *Courting Triumph.* NY: Mayflower Books, Inc., 1978, p. 190.

p. 216 Patti LaBelle (with Laura Randolph Lancaster). *Patti's Pearls: Lessons in Living Genuinely, Joyfully, Generously.* NY: Warner Books, Inc., pp. 51-52.

p. 218 Wade Clark Roof. *A Generation of Seekers.* San Francisco: HarperSanFrancisco, 1994, p. 30.

p. 218 Joanne Beckman. "Religion in Post-World War II America." National Humanities Center. www.nhc.rtp.nc.us/tserve/twenty/tkeyinfo/trelww2.htm.

pp. 218-219 White House Conference on Aging. "Subjective Measure of Spiritual Well-Being: Review of Religious Research." www.naaas.org/2005monograph3.pdf.

p. 219 Harvey Cox. "Old-time Religion." *The Boston Globe,* July 9, 2006.

p. 225 Wilma Mankiller (with Michael Wallis). *Wilma Mankiller: A Chief and Her People.* NY: St. Martins Press, 1993, p. xxi.

p. 227 Karen Armstrong. "The Art of Compassion." *AARP Magazine,* March-April, 2005.

p. 227 Bernadine Healy quoted by Kay Bailey Hutchison. *American Heroines: The Spirited Women Who Shaped Our Country.* New York: William Morrow, An Imprint of HarperCollins Publishers, Inc., 2004, p. 123.

p. 229 Alice Walker. *In Search of Our Mothers' Gardens.* NY: Harcourt Brace Jovanovich, Publishers, 1983, p. 265.

p. 232 [The spiritual component...] *Toward Healthy Aging: Human Needs and Nursing Response.* St. Louis, MO: C.V. Mosby, p. 992.

p. 232 [spirituality is the...] J.M. Thibault, J.W. Ellor, F.E. Netting. "A Conceptual Framework for assessing the spiritual functioning and fulfillment of older adults in long term care settings." *Journal of Religious Gerontology*, 1991, 7(4): 29-45.

Chapter 8: Seven Life Capitals

p. 236 Candace Pert. *Molecules of Emotion: The Science Behind Mind-Body Medicine.* NY: Simon & Schuster, 1997, p. 189.

p. 236 Linda Ellerbee. Alison Pollet, Ed. And Linda Ellerbee, Introduction. *When I Was a Girl.* NY: Pocket Books, A Division of Simon & Schuster, Inc., 2003, p. xv.

p. 237 Sarah Brady in: Nancy Neuman, Ed. *True to Ourselves: A Celebration of Women Making a Difference.* San Francisco, CA: Jossey-Bass Inc., Publishers, 1998, p. 115.

p. 239 Virginia Wade (with Mary Lou Mellace). *Courting Triumph.* NY: Mayflower Books, Inc., 1978, p. 75.

p. 240 Patti LaBelle (with Laura Randolph Lancaster). *Patti's Pearls: Lessons in Living Genuinely, Joyfully, Generously.* NY: Warner Books, Inc., p. 85.

p. 241 Ruth Simmons in: Nancy Neuman, Ed. *True to Ourselves: A Celebration of Women Making a Difference.* San Francisco, CA: Jossey-Bass Inc., Publishers, 1998, p. 23.

p. 242 Joyce Kennard quoted by Elizabeth Vrato in: *The Counselors: Conversations with 18 Courageous Women Who have Changed the World.* Philadelphia: Running Press, 2002, pp. 157-161.

p. 246 Annette Funicello (with Patricia Romanowski). *A Dream is a Wish Your Heart Makes: My Story.* NY: Hyperion, 1994, p. 220.

p. 246 Lyda Judson Hanifan. "The rural school community center." *Annals of the American Academy of Political and Social Science*, 1916, 67: pp. 130-138.

p. 246 Jane Jacobs. *The Death and Life of Great American Cities.* NY: Random House, 1961.

p. 246-247 Polly Baca in: Nancy Neuman, Ed. *True to Ourselves: A Celebration of Women Making a Difference.* San Francisco, CA: Jossey-Bass Inc., Publishers, 1998, p. 156.

p. 247 James Coleman. "Social Capital in the Creation of Human Capital." *American Journal of Sociology*, 94 Supplement, 1988, pp. S95-S120.

p. 247 Robert Putnam. *Bowling Alone: The Collapse and Revival of American Community.* NY: Simon & Schuster, 2000.

p. 251 Judge Judy Sheindlin. *Beauty Fades, Dumb Is Forever.* NY: Cliff Street Books, An imprint of HarperCollins Publishers, Inc., 1999, pp. 100 & 102-103.

p. 252 Linda Ellerbee quoted by: Rena Pederson (with Dr. Lee Smith). *What's Next? Women Redefining Their Dreams in the Prime of Life.* NY: Perigee Books, The Berkley Publishing Group, A Division of Penguin Putnam Inc., 2001, p. 197.

p. 253 Lewis Thomas. *Lives of a Cell: Notes of a Biology Watcher.* NY: Viking Press, 1974.

p. 253 Walter Bortz. *DARE To Be 100: 99 Steps to a Long, Healthy Life.* NY: Fireside, 1996.

p. 255 Martha Reeves quoted by: David Thigpen. "Her Second Act." *Time*, November 26, 2006. www.time.com/time/printout/0,8816,1562951,00.html.

Index

Printed in the United States
207472BV00003B/103-524/A